TERRORIST MINDS

COLUMBIA STUDIES IN TERRORISM
AND IRREGULAR WARFARE

COLUMBIA STUDIES IN TERRORISM
AND IRREGULAR WARFARE

Bruce Hoffman, Series Editor

This series seeks to fill a conspicuous gap in the burgeoning literature on terrorism, guerrilla warfare, and insurgency. The series adheres to the highest standards of scholarship and discourse and publishes books that elucidate the strategy, operations, means, motivations, and effects posed by terrorist, guerrilla, and insurgent organizations and movements. It thereby provides a solid and increasingly expanding foundation of knowledge on these subjects for students, established scholars, and informed reading audiences alike.

Harrison Akins, *The Terrorism Trap: The War on Terror Inside America's Partner States*

Rita Katz, *Saints and Soldiers: Inside Internet-Age Terrorism, From Syria to the Capitol Siege*

Tricia L. Bacon and Elizabeth Grimm, *Terror in Transition: Leadership and Succession in Terrorist Organizations*

Daveed Gartenstein-Ross and Thomas Joscelyn, *Enemies Near and Far: How Jihadist Groups Strategize, Plot, and Learn*

Boaz Ganor, *Israel's Counterterrorism Strategy: Origins to the Present*

Arie Perliger, *American Zealots: Inside Right-Wing Domestic Terrorism*

Erin M. Kearns and Joseph K. Young, *Tortured Logic: Why Some Americans Support the Use of Torture in Counterterrorism*

Lorenzo Vidino, *The Closed Circle: Joining and Leaving the Muslim Brotherhood in the West*

Aaron Y. Zelin, *Your Sons Are at Your Service: Tunisia's Missionaries of Jihad*

Mariya Y. Omelicheva and Lawrence P. Markowitz, *Webs of Corruption: Trafficking and Terrorism in Central Asia*

Bryan C. Price, *Targeting Top Terrorists: Understanding Leadership Removal in Counterterrorism Strategy*

Wendy Pearlman and Boaz Atzili, *Triadic Coercion: Israel's Targeting of States That Host Nonstate Actors*

Stephen Tankel, *With Us and Against Us: How America's Partners Help and Hinder the War on Terror*

Bruce Hoffman, *Inside Terrorism*, 3rd edition

For a complete list of books in the series, please see the Columbia University Press website.

JOHN HORGAN

TERRORIST MINDS

The Psychology of Violent Extremism

from Al-Qaeda to the Far Right

Columbia University Press / New York

Columbia University Press
Publishers Since 1893
New York   Chichester, West Sussex
cup.columbia.edu

Library of Congress Cataloging-in-Publication Data
Names: Horgan, John, 1974– author.
Title: Terrorist minds : the psychology of violent extremism from Al-Qaeda
to the far Right / John Horgan.
Description: New York : Columbia University Press, [2024] | Series:
Columbia studies in terrorism and irregular warfare | Includes index.
Identifiers: LCCN 2023035323 (print) | LCCN 2023035324 (ebook) |
ISBN 9780231198387 (hardback) | ISBN 9780231198394 (trade paperback) |
ISBN 9780231552608 (ebook)
Subjects: LCSH: Political psychology. | Terrorism—Psychological aspects. |
Radicalism.
Classification: LCC JA74.5 .H67 2024 (print) | LCC JA74.5 (ebook) |
DDC 303.6/25—dc23/eng/20230817
LC record available at https://lccn.loc.gov/2023035323
LC ebook record available at https://lccn.loc.gov/2023035324

Cover design: Noah Arlow

For you, Kris.

"The study of psychology is very dangerous and very important."

Osama Bin Laden

CONTENTS

PREFACE

Ulrike Meinhof was forty-one years old when she hanged herself in Germany's Stammheim Prison.[1] The former journalist, mother of twin daughters, and intellectual anchor of the Baader-Meinhof terrorist group used a towel to end her life on May 9, 1976. A year later, Meinhof's surviving comrades of what later became known as the Red Army Faction (RAF) followed her to the grave. Gudrun Ensslin, her boyfriend Andreas Baader, and coconspirator Jan-Carl Raspe killed themselves mere hours after a failed attempt to spring them from the same prison. Throughout the 1970s and 1980s, the RAF railed against capitalism in Europe and beyond, inspiring radicals, revolutionaries, and dreamers worldwide. By the time they fizzled out in the early 1990s, the left-wing group had cemented a legacy built on shootings, bombings, and bank robberies.[2]

In years since, speculation about the Stammheim suicides has only increased. Did Meinhof take her own life, or did prison officials murder her? Despite being kept in separate cells, Baader and his colleagues somehow coordinated their suicides. Like Meinhof, Ensslin hanged herself, but Baader and Raspe killed themselves using Heckler & Koch pistols smuggled into the prison. A fourth RAF member, also a prisoner at Stammheim, tried but failed to kill herself using a bread knife, further fueling suspicions that, at the very least, all the suicides were allowed to happen.[3] Despite the lingering questions, those events would be overshadowed by another controversy. Almost twenty-five years after the suicides, it emerged that German officials had secretly authorized the removal of the brains of Meinhof, Ensslin, Baader, and Raspe for scientific study. At the time of the terrorists' deaths, none of the respective families knew of this decision.[4] It was decades later that one of Meinhof's daughters, Bettina Röhl, discovered her mother's brain had been divided up between at least two German research institutions, the remains preserved in a jar of formaldehyde. Ensslin's, Baader's, and Raspe's brains were reported missing, with no documentation clarifying whether they were cremated or genuinely lost.[5] At least three of the brains were reported to have spent time at Tübingen's Institute for Clinical Brain Research, but when pressed by *Der Spiegel* magazine in 2002, Dr. Richard Meyermann, the institute's head, stated, "They are no longer there."[6]

Bernhard Bogerts, a professor at the University of Magdeburg, which once housed Meinhof's brain, revealed at a news conference what he and his team found: "The [brain] displays characteristics of neurological abnormalities." These abnormalities were traced back to surgery Meinhof underwent at twenty-eight to remove a benign brain tumor, which was reported to have been "pinched off" but not removed.[7] A neuropathologist involved in Meinhof's official autopsy reported "damage near the amygdala," mostly caused by the actual surgery rather than the tumor itself.[8] Meinhof's daughter alleged the damage might have meant that her mother was unfit to stand trial in the first place.[9] In a 2002 interview, Bettina Röhl stated, "A dead terrorist has a right to be treated fairly and the right to a decent burial."[10] A German state prosecutor in Stuttgart told the German newspaper *Bild*, "If Ulrike Meinhof did not give permission for her body to be used for scientific purposes, then the brain should have been destroyed after her autopsy."[11] Meinhof's brain was ordered cremated by the Stuttgart prosecutors' office and was returned to Röhl in an urn. Today, it lies buried next to Meinhof's grave on the southern outskirts of Berlin.

I used to tell my students that one of the reasons terrorist psychology is so challenging to study is because we can't peek inside the brains of those who conduct acts of terror. But in some cases we literally can. The average human brain weighs about three pounds and is easily dissectible. Would studying the brains of dead terrorists tell us something, *anything*, about why they became terrorists? Many years after the German controversy, Bogerts and colleagues published a scientific paper with this conclusion: "The radical political ideas [Meinhof] fought for can of course not be explained by the postsurgical limbic brain damage but are rather a result of the special political and social environment of her time. But the fact that she developed a personality change with increasing aggressiveness and violence has to be regarded as a result of the brain injury closely related to the amygdala."[12] While Meinhof's brain suggests some possible influence on her terrorist activity, it fails to really paint a complete picture.

So how do we understand what someone like Meinhof fought for, and why? This book seeks to provide answers. It explains how psychology helps us understand terrorist behavior and is the culmination of over two decades of studying terrorism and terrorists. It might be wise to temper expectations at the outset, so here comes the spoiler alert—if you stay until the end, you might ask yourself, *Twenty years and he still can't figure it out?* That's fair. Terrorism is a hard problem. It is hard to understand and hard to explain. The term is so politically charged that it's hard to even talk about it. There is no single issue that causes terrorism, and, as a result, there can be no single solution. It has an incredibly long history, one we frequently ignore. Many different academic disciplines approach terrorism, and so far, no single perspective has proven more useful than the others. And despite how dramatic the public face of terrorism can be, so much of what goes into it remains in the shadows. The people we call the terrorists, for the most part, think and toil and plot and scheme in a semiclandestine world to enact the most shocking and brutal violations against our communities. Professor Noémie Bouhana, of University College London, tweeted in 2019 that "chasing any form of knowledge without theory is like trying to solve a vast puzzle without a picture and starting from the middle."[13] Her analogy is a perfect fit for terrorism. Not only do we have no picture to guide us, but sometimes the pieces we have don't even fit together. And just when we think we've finished the puzzle, we realize there are pieces left over. Show it to anyone and their response is often that the picture doesn't look quite right. To put it mildly, as the terrorism expert Professor Alex Schmid lamented, "Our subject of investigation . . . is about as difficult to study as it can get in the social sciences."[14]

To try to make sense of it all, a lot of people study terrorists very closely. They range from investigators who hunt them to academics like me who try to understand their logic and behavior by studying what they do and how they do it. Over the years, more have been drawn to finding answers. Terrorism research—even psychological research on terrorism— has become so vast that no researcher could possibly distill it all. My goal instead is to trace the lines around the terrorists and tell you what we know so far about who they are, what they do, and why. I take some comfort from the words of Tracy Kidder and Richard Todd's *Good Prose*: "The honest nonfiction storyteller is a restrained illusionist."[15]

I present to you findings from a significant body of research by psychologists (and others), while also leaving out a far greater body of work, from diverse academic disciplines. I want to offer you an accurate story of where we've come from in trying to understand the terrorist from a psychological perspective. I know with certainty I will offend some researchers—by virtue of not what I say but rather what I don't say about their work. I gave up trying to cover everything a long time ago, so if you are one of those authors whose work I have not included, don't take it personally.

Studying terrorism requires asking not just the right questions but sometimes uncomfortable ones. Under the right circumstances, could anyone become a terrorist? Could *you*? Depending on the circumstances, this might seem like either a dangerous question or just a corny one. There's a risk that it might come across as concession—while not legitimizing what terrorists do, asking questions like this in a way acknowledges injustice, oppression, and discrimination as real forces shaping people's lives. If you or someone you love is targeted, tormented, threatened, harassed, beaten, or victimized, isn't the most understandable reaction to want to hit back? One of the biggest questions facing researchers is in figuring out not necessarily why someone would want to become involved in terrorism, but why it is that so *few* people do. In his essay on jihadism, the journalist Tanjil Rashid writes about influences that help shape terrorists: "The grand canvas frames whole communities as victims of imperialism, or marginalized by Islamophobia, or indoctrinated via Saudi petrodollars. But these forces embroil staggeringly more people than the few who are radicalized; so what makes these characters special?"[16] Rashid's point is central to this book. It is easy to point to grand ideals, principles, and sweeping ideological forces that constitute the local, regional, or global winds of change. Researchers will often call such influences the "structural conditions" that give rise to terrorism. It is a different thing entirely to understand why so few try to harness those winds for their own propulsion. Neither a penetrating account of the development of an ideology nor the most comprehensive statistical database of events can answer such questions. As the terrorism scholar Alexander Meleagrou-Hitchens noted in his authoritative study of Anwar al-Awlaki, number-crunching "can tell us only so much."[17]

I am a psychologist. I have interviewed terrorists around the world about why they do what they do. Psychologists study behavior—what people do and how they do it—and then we try to interpret *why* they do it. Because we are all to a greater or lesser extent social beings, psychologists typically study individual behavior in groups and organizations. A sociologist also studies behavior but might study changes in a community. An anthropologist, on the other hand, also studies behavior but focuses on bigger, broader issues related to race and culture. Terrorism may be a social process, and yet it is about people, first and foremost. In most cases, people *choose* to engage in terrorist activity, but they do this in part because they believe they are acting on behalf of a community that will embrace them for doing so. They feel they have a role to play in changing something much bigger than themselves, their immediate group, or the broader community from where they enjoy support. And, lest we forget, how can we understand what drives and sustains the individual terrorist without considering how state actors and agencies respond to terrorism, often only making the problem even worse in the process?

In his 2021 book, *Extremism: A Philosophical Analysis*, the scholar Quassim Cassam wrote that "psychological studies [on terrorism] are not necessarily a better guide to the extremist mindset" than works of fiction.[18] I strongly disagree with that. It is my view that psychology has much to offer for understanding terrorism. And while psychological research on terrorist behavior still has a long way to go in providing the kinds of answers we want, the rigor of psychology, its reliance on tried and tested methods, informed by rich theoretical insights, means we know a lot more about terrorist behavior now than ever before. So, this book not only covers what we know and don't know but also identifies what we might be able to know just a little further down the road. We will explore the profiles, backgrounds, motivations, and mindsets of those who would, in some circumstances, kill you or me in the name of some ideas with which we might not even be familiar.

Now I'll temper your expectations just a little more. Not only are there no easy answers or solutions to terrorism, but an additional challenge is not to become frustrated by the complexity of what we are trying to understand. This is easier said than done, I know. The first time I gave a talk at the Pentagon I was a young academic eager to impress attendees with what I thought I knew. Most of my small audience was either asleep (literally) or otherwise uninterested after about fifteen minutes. It was also my first lesson in just how polite the Department of Defense staff was. The person in charge of the event profusely thanked me for coming. At the end of my talk, when he was escorting me out of the building, he put his hand on my shoulder and said, "Let me give you a piece of advice. Make it simple. These guys need the bottom line up front." Telling an academic to make things simple is a surefire way to make them feel useless. "But it *is* complex," I answered. "Yes," he countered, "but you want them to *understand* it." I burned his words into my brain. You can be the judge of whether I learned that lesson. For a change, this book is not aimed at my fellow academics or terrorism experts. If you are among those groups, you will probably be better served by examining the original studies (mine included) that I cite throughout. This book is aimed squarely at readers who want to begin to learn about terrorists and their psychology.

The chapters that follow start by explaining what terrorism is—and by extension what it is not. They ask the question of *who* becomes involved in terrorism. We'll consider the social, demographic, and other features that enable us to ask about the "profile" of the terrorist; that will allow us to explore *why* terrorists do what they do. How do the thinking patterns associated with being involved in terrorism emerge, and how does terrorist activity change the behavior and minds of those who participate in it? This further knowledge will help us understand how recruits to terrorism learn to kill, as well as how they learn to justify to themselves and others what they do and why. We'll also consider issues that have garnered considerable attention from recent researchers—how people *disengage* from terrorism and whether they can be safely reintegrated back into the communities they once fought against. In chapter 6, I present a case for why we need to talk to terrorists. This is one of the central arguments of the book. For us to continue diving deeper into terrorist minds, we must commit to a far more comprehensive approach to understanding their involvement through their own eyes, which requires talking with (and listening to) the terrorists themselves.

In understanding the terrorist, I want to both complicate and simplify. Terrorism *is* complex. But simplifying that complexity is essential if we're going to try to offer solutions aimed at disrupting or even preventing terrorist attacks. I don't claim to be able to do that here, but at a minimum I hope to provide you a way to think about the complexity of what's involved, and in doing so, offer a blueprint to inform planning. Whether you are a counterterrorism practitioner, a policy maker, or someone just interested in terrorism, I hope that the arguments and findings presented here offer food for thought, whether they reinforce or challenge (or even contradict) what you already know.

TERRORIST MINDS

1

WHAT IS TERRORISM?

At 19,347 feet above sea level, the snow-capped summit of Mt. Kilimanjaro is the highest point in Africa. It isn't nearly the highest mountain in the world—the summit of Everest reaches nearly ten thousand feet higher—but because of Kilimanjaro's accessibility, many amateur adventurers (especially those who have yet to climb it) dismiss it as a mere "walk-up" mountain. And without fail, season after season, its trails are littered with shuffling hordes laboring under the intense headaches and nausea of altitude sickness, a consequence of ascending too quickly. For the twenty-four-year-old Danish hiker Louisa Jespersen, Kilimanjaro wasn't originally part of her 2018 African climbing plans. Her sights were set on Morocco's Mt. Toubkal. The summit, at over thirteen thousand feet, is prominent, with stunning vistas in all directions. Louisa spent months thinking about what the climb might look like. She posted on social media about her desire to go, imploring her outdoorsy friends to offer any tips and advice to help her succeed.[1] Louisa lived for the outdoors. She climbed throughout South America and dreamed of one day going on a polar expedition. Earlier in 2018, she applied to the outdoor company Fjällräven, hoping to be selected for its annual dogsledding expedition across the Arctic.[2]

At the time, Louisa was a student at the University of South-Eastern Norway, and it was there that she met Maren Ueland, a fellow outdoor enthusiast. Four years Louisa's senior, Maren grew up in Norway. The two were well met. Their Facebook and YouTube accounts chronicle multiple hikes, climbs, and treks across all seasons. In one picture, Maren's goofy smile atop a frigid summit betrays the kind of joy only other mountaineers can appreciate. It was hardly surprising that both were intent on becoming outdoor guides.[3]

On December 9, 2018, the pair landed in Marrakesh to begin their Toubkal adventure. A few miles outside the remote village of Imlil, they set up camp.[4] Eight days later, Maren and Louisa's bodies were found by two other hikers following the same trail the women had taken. They had been descending the mountain when they encountered what was described as men "searching for Westerners to kill."[5]

Journalists covering the subsequent murder investigation and trial documented a social network of nearly two dozen men indicted for having some role in their deaths. Three were directly responsible. Abdessamad Ejjoud, twenty-five years old, was identified as the ringleader. Along with Younes Ouaziyad, twenty-seven, Ejjoud stabbed the women to death in their tent while a third man, Rachid Afatti, thirty-three, recorded the attacks on his phone. After delivering twenty-three individual injuries to a blindfolded Louisa, Ejjoud and Ouaziyad beheaded her. They then beheaded Maren. In the video, one minute and sixteen seconds long, one of the men calls the women "enemies of Allah," justifying their deaths as "revenge for our brothers in Deir al-Zour,"[6] a reference to jihadists killed in Syria. Ejjoud had earlier been imprisoned after a failed attempt to travel to Syria to join the Islamic State. He was released in 2015. Now, sitting in front of another judge four years later, he admitted, "I decided to make jihad here,"[7] adding "I regret what happened and I am still trying to grasp it." The three were sentenced to death. A fourth, who left the scene prior to the murders, received a life sentence. One of the men's defense team announced plans to appeal the judgment.[8] The basis of the claim was that the men "came from poor backgrounds and were badly educated."[9]

The Islamic State movement ignored the men. That didn't stop the video recorded on Afatti's cell phone from being viewed on social media eight hundred thousand times in just one month. In addition to enthusiastic supporters of the Islamic State circulating evidence of the murders, extreme right-wing supporters eagerly shared the video as proof of Islam's "evils." Inevitably, the video found a ready audience: those unable to resist their morbid curiosity or displaying the usual impulsive behavior afforded by social media. Even in Denmark, many young children shared the video over several social media platforms.[10]

I didn't know Louisa or Maren. I've never met them or any of their friends or family. Like them, I love the mountains and spend as much time as I can outdoors. In the days and weeks after their murders, I read multiple media accounts, poring over one forensic-style reconstruction of the events in the *New York Times*. I tried to find out as much as I could about what had happened. I wondered why Louisa wanted to climb in the Atlas Mountains. Was it a picture in a climbing magazine? A random glance at a photo in somebody's Instagram feed? Two years after their deaths, I weighed the merits of writing about them. To dissect such a heinous act for the purpose of engaging readers seemed wrong. If I turned their deaths into an intellectual exercise, was that really any different than sharing video of their murders online? Writing about mass murderers, the psychiatrist James Knoll warned about those who engage in "motive mongering." These people are willing to speculate about killers, typically with obscene haste and precious little direct knowledge of the events in question. There is a real risk in scrutinizing terrorist behavior that, if not done right, reveals more about the person doing the scrutinizing than anything useful about the subject matter. I've read enough true crime books to be wary of such dangers. And yet, what kept the memory of these women in my mind wasn't just the manner of their death, or the gross injustice of it, but its pointlessness. If fantasies of getting noticed drove Louisa and Maren's killers to compete for attention from the Islamic State, they failed. Instead of being celebrated as righteous soldiers, they sat sobbing in a Moroccan courtroom, begging for mercy from a judge who would only sentence them to death.

At its most basic, terrorism is a gruesome violation. Its victims are mostly symbolic, rarely known in any personal sense to their killers. They happen to be at the wrong place at the wrong time and are killed in the name of some cause that they probably haven't even heard of. Their deaths are incidental, despite being celebrated by perpetrators and their supporters as righteous, justified, and even necessary. For terrorists, victims are disposable. They are bit players in other people's games, which in turn are part of a broader agenda that rarely produces desirable outcomes for any of its participants. Louisa and Maren went to the Atlas Mountains because they likely fell under the spell that only mountain adventure can cast. Instead, they died blindfolded at the hands of three men who didn't know them. In turn, what these men hoped to achieve by murdering the women, and documenting it, was to get noticed—to make an impression on a group of people they themselves didn't know either.[11]

TERRORISM AND TERRORISTS

Once upon a time, we used to think that terrorists were crazy. And we were wrong. We slowly came to see them as rational, highly motivated men and women whose beliefs allowed them to indulge in the most despicable acts of violence. Talk about rationality can be a hard pill to swallow when we consider what terrorists do. And yet these terrible behaviors are the product of a calculation, one that is shaped and informed by planning, justified by ideology, done in the name of defending (or seeking revenge for) a larger community, and sustained by the expectation of some reward or recognition. Terrorist violence is about killing and injuring, but it aims to accomplish more than that because it serves a broader agenda. It seeks to set in motion other events and often inspires more violence. The agenda might be to draw attention to a goal of political autonomy for an occupied nation. It might be done in the name of defending a community from an enemy seen to encroach on its freedoms. It might be about something even more specific, such as the liberation of animals or to protest abortion.

4

The strategy of terrorism can serve many different types of causes. Rationality is in the eye of the beholder, but terrorism is fed by the logical reasoning that an act of public violence is considered useful, *necessary* even, to push an agenda onto the consciousness of an otherwise ignorant public or apathetic government.

In late 2007, I sat in the London flat of a former terrorist who, over cold pizza, told me several hours after our "real" interview had ended that some twenty years after he decided to walk away from terrorism, he still never really understood why he got involved in the first place. I was stunned to hear that. If achieving such insight is tough for those who participate in terrorism, what hope do the rest of us have? Terrorism books certainly ask a lot of their readers. An honest student will either begin or conclude with a picture of just how complex terrorism is. But the subject can be complex to the point of frustration, and that's not necessarily a bad thing. Navigating that complexity is important because it can inoculate us from expecting easy answers and make us skeptical when politicians or pundits offer them. Asking readers to embrace that complexity as a step toward understanding might even backfire. The Holocaust survivor Primo Levi wrote that Nazi hatred "cannot be comprehended, or rather, shouldn't be comprehended, because to comprehend is almost to justify."[12]

One thing is certain. Regardless of how we feel about terrorism, we can't ignore it. A big part of how it captures our imagination is that every so often, it jolts us out of any complacency we have about it. Terrorist acts routinely bring shock and outrage to audiences that previously might have considered themselves numb (or at least adjusted) to its effects. Sometimes terrorists shock us by simply doing something they haven't done before. They do it by killing more people in a single attack than was previously imagined, as on September 11, 2001. They do it by changing the way in which they choose who lives and who dies, targeting and killing those considered invulnerable. In May 2020, gunmen thought to be affiliated with the Islamic State burst into a maternity ward in a Kabul hospital and killed sixteen mothers and two newborn babies. Such violence sickens us. And it should. The calculated decision to violently end someone's life is, on one level, a deeply unnatural act that defies any pretense of rationality or sanity.

Most of us are so far removed from terrorism that it can be a difficult task to ask someone to carefully ponder its psychological and strategic variables. Anyone familiar with any of the events I've mentioned so far will find it hard to think back on them with anything more than a feeling of despair and no small amount of anger. Why kill newborn babies? What beliefs could possibly support such an act? The injustice we feel is compounded by its sheer futility. Terrorist groups rarely achieve their broader objectives, yet that indisputable fact does not deter even the most poorly resourced of groups to attempt to exert undue influence by publicly taking the lives of whoever happens to be a convenient target. Often, it's simply the *belief* in their own righteousness that sustains terrorist groups even when faced with insurmountable odds and a far more powerful enemy.

Terrorism is a strategy whereby violent tactics serve a bigger objective than simply killing for its own sake. It is a strategy full of contradictions: terrorists seek freedom for some by taking it away from others. They use violence in the pursuit of their goals because they want to be seen and heard. But that same violence makes their intended audience less likely to want to listen because of what they've just done. In turn, terrorists respond with *more* violence. Complicating matters is that responses to terrorism all too often make the problem worse, not better. Heavy-handed government reactions the world over involve repression, torture, extrajudicial killings, kidnappings, and other gross violations of human rights, all conducted in the name of preserving the same kinds of freedoms and liberty that terrorist groups themselves say they fight for. The cycle accelerates until, ultimately, what first gave rise to terrorism is often forgotten in an ever-escalating spiral of reciprocity that sweeps up terrorists, state actors, and an anxious public caught between the two.

A common justification for terrorism is that it is defensive—a necessary, strategic option used by the weak when faced with offensive actions from (usually) a significantly larger foe. One of the many reasons terrorist groups find the strategy so attractive is that it packs an enormous psychological punch. The attacks of September 11, 2001, may have exceeded the expectations even of Al-Qaeda's leadership, but their aim was to harm and humiliate the United States—to remind them, in the harshest way possible, that they were not invulnerable to attack by a much smaller, hidden enemy. The response from the United States that followed, aided by an almost global coalition, saw invasions of Afghanistan and Iraq, hundreds of thousands of violent deaths in the ensuing political instability, and, twenty years later, a still-functioning Al-Qaeda network.

To a small, determined group of fanatical believers, the attractiveness of terrorist tactics is easy to understand. What might appear to be small, localized acts of violence, if planned and executed the right way, can have profoundly greater effects when delivered to a global audience. Such amplification has psychological benefits for the believer—it reinforces their commitment by providing instant gratification that the act was worth it. The strategic rewards, on the other hand, tend to be short-lived. Terrorism is so effective in the short term because of its psychological impact. The shock, horror, humiliation, and helplessness felt by the audience in the wake of terrorist violence can be profound. Terrorist attacks freeze us in our tracks, causing us to wonder if we, or someone we know, might be next. We find it impossible to look away from endless media coverage while experts ponder all the issues associated with those responsible. *Who are they? What do they want? What have they done before? Can they do it again? Should the public be afraid? What can we do about it?* It has been said many times that terrorism is theater, and theater has become an ever-more collective experience whose power feeds on audience participation.

TERRORISM TODAY

In recent years, the theater of terrorism has become more intimate. More than ever before, terrorists are known to us. We used to think that terrorist groups continuously worked to get our attention by pulling off complex operations. But sophisticated terrorist acts can be costly. They take time to plan, some degree of competency to execute, and no small amount of strategic acumen to exploit after the fact. The Provisional Irish Republican Army would routinely time some of its bombings so that the evening news would be dominated by the day's events. But that was then. The past thirty years have seen such fundamental changes in our interactions with technology that we are now virtual pseudoparticipants in terrorist violence. On October 27, 2018, this message was posted to the social network Gab: "Screw your optics. I'm going in." Moments later, Robert Bowers, forty-six years old, entered the Tree of Life synagogue in the Squirrel Hill neighborhood of Pittsburgh, Pennsylvania. Armed with an assault rifle, he shot and killed eleven people, injuring seven more. The attack was the deadliest on the Jewish community in the United States. Some saw the massacre as the culmination of heightened anti-Semitism in recent months—less than a year earlier, neo-Nazis and other far-right groups assembled in Charlottesville, Virginia, in a dramatic attempt to unite a resurgent, if fractured, American white nationalist movement. That event drew widespread condemnation, although anti-Semitic activity and hate crimes continued to rise.

Six months after Pittsburgh, another attack happened, this time in Christchurch, New Zealand. Brenton Tarrant, twenty-eight, murdered fifty-one men, women, and children inside two mosques during Friday prayer ceremonies. Tarrant, an avowed white supremacist, broadcast his attacks live via a Facebook account. And then, not quite six months later, a shooter in El Paso, Texas, killed twenty-three people in a local Walmart. Patrick Crusius, twenty-one, had earlier published an anti-immigrant manifesto on the notorious message board 8chan. Crusius claimed he was inspired by Tarrant's actions in New Zealand. Today's terrorists choose their victims not only based on nationality or religion but because of their ethnicity, gender, race, and sexual orientation. But terrorism has thrived in a world that seems to be getting smaller and smaller. We used to distinguish between domestic and international terrorism. Yet now, an attack in New Zealand is just as likely to inspire an attack in Texas; violence in California can spur on violence in Toronto. As far as influence and inspiration to act is concerned, the distances involved have shrunk to virtually nothing.

Technology has utterly transformed terrorism and amplifies its psychological impact in ways few of us could have imagined. The sense of immediacy and intimacy such attacks bring when live-streamed across social media platforms is hypnotic. The temptation is to go look, even though we know we shouldn't. We might try to convince ourselves that we look because we want to understand. Yet, even if in some cases this is true, such access doesn't necessarily bring with it an understanding of the attackers or their motivation. Even when attackers explain their actions in detail, observers can be forgiven for thinking *I don't get it.* On April 23, 2018, a small van mounted a sidewalk in downtown Toronto. The driver killed ten people on the spot, eight of them women. Sixteen more (mostly women, again) were injured, one of whom would die of her injuries three years after the attack. When he eventually surrendered, Alek Minassian, twenty-five, was taken into custody by the police. Minassian explained to the interviewing detective that he was an "incel," short for "involuntary celibate."[13] He explained, "It's basically a movement of angry incels such as myself who are unable to get laid." The cause of this involuntary celibacy, incels claim, lies at the feet of "the Staceys," the nickname incels give to women who deny them sex. The answer to this problem, some incels believe, is violence. Minassian explained, "I know of several other guys over the internet who feel the same way . . . [but they are] too cowardly to act on their anger. . . . It was time to take action and not just sit on the sidelines and fester in my own sadness. . . . I was thinking that I would inspire future masses to join me in my uprising as well." He proclaimed to the detective, "I feel like I accomplished my mission." Canadian authorities labeled Minassian's attack "isolated," calling him a "lone wolf." They also claimed there was no national security connection to the incident.

A closer look at Minassian's actions prior to the attack, however, hinted otherwise. He confirmed via a series of social media posts that he was inspired by Elliott Rodger, twenty-two, who lived in Isla Vista, California. Four years before, on May 23, 2014, Rodger went on a rampage near the University of California, Santa Barbara campus. After stabbing two roommates and their friend to death, he drove to a university sorority house, where he killed two women. Fleeing the scene, he indiscriminately shot at nearby pedestrians, killing one, and injuring pedestrians and cyclists with his vehicle. Rather than being captured, Rodger shot himself dead in his car. In a series of videos, including one he made a day before the attack, he promised a "day of retribution."[14] He explained, "For the past eight years of my life, since I hit puberty, I've been forced to endure an existence of loneliness, rejection and unfulfilled desires, all because girls have never been attracted to me. Girls gave their affection and sex and love to other men, never to me. . . . I'm 22 years old and still a virgin. . . . It has been very torturous." Rodger's tone then quickly changes:

> You girls have never been attracted to me. I don't know why you girls aren't attracted to me but I will punish you all for it. It's an injustice, a crime because I don't know what you don't see in me, I'm the perfect guy and yet you throw yourselves at these obnoxious men instead of me, the supreme gentleman. I will punish you all for it. . . . On the day of retribution, I am going to enter the hottest sorority house at UCSB and I will slaughter every single spoiled, stuck-up, blond slut I see inside there. All those girls I've desired so much. They have all rejected me and looked down on me as an inferior man if I ever made a sexual advance toward them, while they throw themselves at these obnoxious brutes. I'll take great pleasure in slaughtering all of you.[15]

In his 107,000-word manifesto, *My Twisted World: The Story of Elliot Rodger*, he writes, "I am the true victim in all of this. I am the good guy."[16]

When we think about terrorists, incels probably don't come to mind. They present themselves as lonely, depressed, helpless, and rejected. Many incels find themselves in a feedback loop of despair and self-loathing. They feel like they are failures and are ashamed as a result. Some learn to shift the cause of that perceived failure to women and ultimately come to dehumanize and victimize the same women they feel denied them sex in the first place. To many, their image is an unsympathetic one of lonely "losers" incapable of normal relationships, who retreat into the online world where at least some of them are free to indulge their revenge fantasies. The incel community is broader and more diverse than one might imagine, and very few incels will ever translate online misogyny into targeted or predatory violence in the real world. Yet the actions of Minassian, and Rodger before him, epitomize precisely what terrorism is—violence against civilians in the name of a broader ideological cause. Rodger and Minassian's targets were symbolic, incidental and personally unknown to them, but they were projections of everything they had come to hate. The goal of incel violence, at least according to Minassian, was to spark a rebellion, the details of which can easily be found in his and others' testimonies and manifestos. That the ideology may seem odd, however, and the goals unrealistic, have nothing to do with whether the act itself constituted terrorism.

Incel violence illustrates how, in the face of extensive, often tortuous self-explanation and justification, the act and its perpetrators seem to defy rational explanation, let alone classification as terrorism. The term *ideology* refers to a set of organized beliefs. It inspires, shapes, and gives urgency to the acts of others and plays a critical role in whether an act of violence might constitute terrorism. Crusius, who was in part inspired by the Christchurch attacker when he killed twenty-three people in El Paso, referred to the "Great Replacement," a white nationalist conspiracy theory argument originating in Europe that the mass migration of non-white people will inevitably threaten the social and cultural fabric of white existence, leading to what adherents think of as "white genocide." This ideology inspired one of the most notorious acts of terrorism in recent years. In 2011, the far-right extremist Norwegian Anders Breivik killed eight people in a van bomb attack in Oslo. A few hours later, he shot dead a further sixty-nine people on the island of Utøya, where a summer camp organized by the social democratic Workers' Youth League (part of Norway's Labor Party) was taking place.

WHAT CONSTITUTES TERRORISM?

We can't always identify acts of public violence as terrorism so quickly or easily. The aftermath of any act of an attack is a challenging time when people wait for answers to emerge. Immediate responses to mass shootings in the United States frequently implore people to "call it what it is: terrorism." Not using the word "terrorism" to describe a mass shooting might seem offensive to some, and it's often the case that otherwise well-meaning calls to label an attack that way are done to express solidarity with victims. An example of this confusion occurred in 2017. On the evening of October 1, Las Vegas welcomed over twenty thousand festivalgoers to an outdoor country music event, the Route 91 Harvest. Stephen Paddock, sixty-four years old, booked himself into a room at the Mandalay Bay overlooking the city. From adjoining rooms 32-134 and 32-135, Paddock fired over a thousand rounds of ammunition down into the screaming crowd of concertgoers. Of the twenty-four weapons he brought to his hotel room, his .38 Special was reserved for one purpose—Paddock would shoot himself when capture seemed imminent. The execution of his attack was aided by two small sur-veillance cameras he set up to alert him to approaching first responders. One camera taped to the door's peephole fed a live view of the corridor to a laptop computer inside the room. Paddock attached another camera to a hotel service cart placed just outside his room, which sent another live feed to a separate computer monitor he set up on his room's kitchen bar counter. Before taking his own life, it took Stephen Paddock eleven minutes to kill fifty-eight people. Almost *nine hundred* more people were injured either by his gunfire or in the ensuing panic. Two of the injured died in the fol-lowing days. Over four hundred concertgoers received gunshot wounds or other shrapnel injuries. Paddock also fired at fuel tanks at the nearby McCarran International Airport. Several shots missed, and those rounds that hit the containers failed to ignite the fuel. Forty-one minutes after Paddock stopped shooting, officers breached Paddock's room to find him dead on the floor.[17]

A ten-month investigation into Paddock's background, and his meticu-lous preparation and execution of the attack, produced a 187-page report by the Las Vegas Metropolitan Police Department's Force Investigation Team. Despite conducting interviews with Paddock's family, partner, ex-wife, doctor, acquaintances, and gambling contacts, no evidence was found to suggest he harbored ideological views.[18] In a public briefing, Clark County Sheriff Joe Lombardo went so far as to describe Paddock as "an unremark-able man." After pursuing 2,000 investigative leads, and reviewing 22,000 hours of video and 252,000 images, the report offered no insights into why

Paddock decided to conduct the attack. As part of the investigation, the Las Vegas office of the Federal Bureau of Investigation (FBI) made a formal request for postattack analysis from the FBI's Behavioral Analysis Unit (BAU) for any insights into what might have motivated Paddock. The BAU assembled a multidisciplinary team of psychologists, psychiatrists, and other researchers to review what was known about his behavior. The team constituted the BAU's Las Vegas Review Panel. Twelve months later, the panel issued its findings.[19] Their three-page report stood in stark contrast to the report issued by Vegas police. At the top of its list of ten key findings was the conclusion few wanted to hear—the panel found "no evidence that Paddock's attack was motivated by any ideological or political beliefs. . . . Paddock's attack was neither directed, inspired, nor enabled by ideologically-motivated persons or groups. Paddock was not seeking to further any religious, social, or political agenda through his actions."[20] The BAU concluded Paddock went to great lengths to "keep his thoughts private, and that extended to his final thinking about mass murder." They argued that Paddock intended to die by suicide, possibly fueled by what the panel assessed to be his steady "decline in physical and mental health" in combination with an "inability or unwillingness to perceive any alternatives to this ending." The panel concluded Paddock harbored a desire to not just die by suicide but in doing so "attain a certain degree of infamy." An analysis of Paddock's relationships revealed him to be someone who exhibited "minimal empathy" and a "history of exploiting others through manipulation and duplicity." Those interviewed as part of the police's enquiry into the shooting came to the same conclusion—Paddock "only cared about himself."[21]

The stark conclusions proved too frustrating for some. Despite the lack of any identifiable grievance or ideological dimension, Sheriff Lombardo said, "I would personally call it a terrorist attack. It had an influence on a certain demographic of people [and] intended to cause harm."[22] The judgment echoed popular reaction from the very first moments after the attack. On October 2, 2017, one day after the shooting, singer Lady Gaga posted this message on Twitter: "This is terrorism plain and simple." The pop star Ariana Grande, whose May 2017 concert in Manchester, England, was the site of a terrorist bombing, added, "look at this & call it what it is: terrorism." Whether they meant it literally isn't clear, but there was some substance to it. In 2019, following a wave of mass shootings across the United States, the common public refrain was again to "call it like it is"— terrorism. The similarities between mass shootings and terrorist attacks were undeniable. Mass shootings were acts of targeted violence. They were public. They captured the attention of audiences far and wide. And people certainly felt terrorized. Yet those mass shootings were not terrorist acts. And while Paddock was responsible for the largest mass shooting in U.S. history, his actions do not constitute terrorism.[23] In contrast to his devastating act of public violence, his motivation remains private. For an act to be considered terrorism, its message cannot be hidden.

You may disagree. Why *don't* we just call it terrorism? The reason is that knowing whether an attack was ideologically motivated has real-world implications. Consider the following. The Global Terrorism Index (GTI) is an annual report issued by the nonprofit group Institute for Economics and Peace. The data from which the index forms its conclusions is provided by the University of Maryland's START Center. START is the National Consortium for the Study of Terrorism and Responses to Terrorism, a center of excellence funded by the Department of Homeland Security. START is widely known and equally (and justifiably) widely respected. The 2018 GTI reported trends from the previous year.[24] One of the main conclusions of the report was a continued decline in terrorist events worldwide. In fact, it reported an almost 30 percent decrease in terrorism-related deaths between 2016 and 2017.[25] However, the report highlighted a different trend for terrorism in North America. The GTI reported that, for the United States, "total deaths rose from 64 to 86."[26] The reason? The researchers included the Las Vegas shooting in the terrorism database. Had the shooting not been included, the GTI would have reported a significant decline in terrorist events in the United States during that period. START researchers categorized the attack as conducted by "anti-government extremists."[27] This wording is counter to the fact that both the Las Vegas police report and the report produced by the FBI's review panel came to the same conclusions—Paddock acted alone, and there was no evidence of any ideological dimension to his actions. Likewise, he never left any kind of message imploring others to do the same. Nor did he claim to act, as Minassian did, because others lacked the will or the courage.

This issue is clearly not cut and dried. We sometimes focus on specific elements we assume are defining features of terrorism. On the surface, Paddock's actions *seem* like terrorism. He publicly killed many people and, in doing so, spread fear and terror. But terrorism involves more than that. It is a strategy open to all who are spellbound by its allure. Its illusion of effectiveness doesn't deter, either. Many debate whether terrorism "works," but whether it does or not rarely features in the decision to engage in it. The Islamic State movement is never going to achieve a global caliphate, nor are violent incels going to force women to reproduce with them. Does a mass shooting in which people are obviously terrified therefore constitute *terrorism*? If the media doesn't label an act that way, does it mean it's not terrorism? If a perpetrator commits murder, and clearly promotes ideological change, but is not actually charged with (or convicted of) a terrorist offense, are they a terrorist or not?

And aside from proper classification, there are the simpler issues of inconsistency and hypocrisy. In so many ways, terrorism is the ultimate trigger word. The very use of the term betrays, for some, a predetermined alignment with certain views. As an academic researcher, whenever I speak about nonstate actors who use terrorism, at least one person in the audience will ask, "But what about *state* terrorism?" Terrorism overall is perhaps more associated with the notion of "weak" actors using terror tactics to get noticed.[28] Its traditional and long-standing association is with nonstate actors attempting to overthrow or in some way destabilize a more powerful adversary, such as a ruling group or government. The reality of course is that state actors are just as likely to use terrorism to further their objectives. Talking about terrorism triggers righteous indignation and audience members will often assume that people who study terrorism are blind to the abuses of states and governments, often, ironically, in efforts to quell terrorism in the first place. Because terrorism is a special category of violence, the decision to *not* call an equally heinous act terrorism is less about not doing the right thing and instead about accurate and consistent classification.

For some, wanting to call the Las Vegas attack terrorism extended beyond the victims, signaling a long-overdue acknowledgment that terrorism is a hypocritically used label. Less than a month after the Las Vegas shooting, the researchers Matthew Dolliver and Erin Kearns surveyed over a thousand Americans to find out under what circumstances they are more likely to label an attack terrorism.[29] If the attacker is Muslim, the public tends to assume that violent attacks are terroristic in nature. The researchers concluded that media consumption is one of the most important variables affecting how people think about such attacks. In another study, Kearns and her colleagues found attacks involving Muslim perpetrators receive 357 percent more media coverage than other attacks.[30]

Another example of the inconsistency around terrorism lies in the discrepancies with which cases are treated legally. On July 17, 2015, Dylann Roof, twenty-one years old, entered a historically Black church in Charleston, South Carolina, opening fire and killing nine African Americans. Roof, an avowed white supremacist and neo-Nazi, embraced the idea of racial segregation. He complained to a friend that "blacks were taking over the world" and that "someone needed to do something about it for the white race."[31] Roof was not convicted of terrorism but instead on federal hate crimes. The public is understandably confused about why some offenders who have committed similar acts (in this case, targeted violence against a specific group to promote a hateful ideology) are charged, and ultimately convicted, under different statutes. There is no specifically designated federal statute for domestic terrorism in the United States, and one explanation that has been offered for this inconsistency has to do with whether the attacks are considered domestic or foreign.[32] Furthermore, journalists Ravi Satkalmi and John Miller explain, those convicted for offenses that are (or seem to be) connected to groups like Al-Qaeda or the Islamic State (i.e., foreign terrorist organizations) receive more "consistently severe penalties" compared to those offenders who kill for what are perceived to be "American issues."[33] Yet, despite the lack of a federal domestic statute, such distinctions increasingly feel unconvincing. White supremacy is a global problem and not just in an abstract sense. We've seen through the earlier examples just how globally interconnected such attacks and attackers now are.

Though the distinction between domestic and international terrorism was probably never quite as clear as we might think, today it has become meaningless, except perhaps in the context of a legal system where such distinctions may have differential consequences. Satkalmi and Miller illustrate this issue with the case of Devon Arthurs. Arthurs was a member of Atomwaffen Division, the international neo-Nazi group, before converting to Islam. Soon after, he sought the opportunity to embrace the Islamic State. The journalists noted, "The moment that Mr. Arthurs switched from Atomwaffen to the Islamic State, certain federal laws applied to him that didn't before."[34]

A report examining one hundred court cases of Internet-related terror offenses in the United Kingdom between 2015 and 2019 found that members of far-right extremist groups receive much lighter sentences relative to members of Islamist groups. Islamist-related offenders received an average sentence of seventy-three months compared to just twenty-four months for right-wing offenders. The authors propose that the disparity in sentencing exists partly because right-wing extremist groups are not classified as terrorist groups. Consequently, authorities in the UK mostly prosecute far-right groups under hate crime legislation.[35]

One implication of these distinctions is that it might convey to the public that some kinds of terrorism are considered more serious than others. Having a clear and consistent definition of terrorism is also important to be able to alert the public of the dangers of emerging threats. A 2012 study by the researcher Arie Perliger showed that many countries' counterterrorism policies are often shaped more by their *perception* of the threat rather than the volume of violence faced. From 2011 to 2016, terrorist attacks in the United States by extreme right-wing perpetrators outnumbered jihadist attacks three times over.[36] In early 2020, FBI Director Christopher Wray acknowledged that 2019 saw the most lethal activity from "domestic violent extremists" since the 1995 Oklahoma City bombing by the antigovernment extremists Timothy McVeigh and Terry Nichols. In testimony delivered to the U.S. House Judiciary Committee, Wray told members that the FBI had in early 2020 more than a thousand "active domestic terrorism investigations in all 50 states."[37] Simultaneously challenging the usefulness of the label "domestic extremism," Wray noted, "Such crimes are not limited to the United States, and with the aid of Internet like-minded hate groups can reach across borders."[38] The FBI's increasing caseload for domestic terrorism reflected the growth of hate groups, according to research conducted by the Southern Poverty Law Center, which reported a record high in 2019 of over a thousand active "hate groups," encompassing white supremacist groups, neo-Nazis, the Ku Klux Klan, and multiple black nationalist groups, among others.[39]

That there are many definitions of terrorism isn't in doubt.[40] And while it may be technically correct to say that there are actually hundreds, as the scholar Nicolò Scremin suggests, many are just slight variations of others.[41] Scremin argues that academic research would benefit from a uniform definition because it would enable researchers to collect data in a systematic and reliable way.[42] There is merit to this. The psychologist and researcher Wojciech Kaczkowski and colleagues from Georgia State University looked at some of the databases set up to measure the extent of terrorist attacks.[43] They found significant disparities. Between 2002 and 2016, they report that the U.S. government recorded almost two hundred terrorist incidents in Western Europe. The Global Terrorism Database at the University of Maryland, however, reports over a *thousand* terrorist incidents in that area for the same period.[44] The reason for the difference is that they vary in what they count. Each draws its data from different sources and has different criteria for what constitutes a terrorist incident. Kaczkowski and his team note that the U.S. State Department rarely includes activity from ethnonationalist terrorist groups such as the various IRA splinter groups in Northern Ireland, instead focusing more on the almost fifty jihadist groups named in its list of foreign terrorist organizations.[45]

Of course, having shared definitions, and reliable data, is important for other reasons, such as how different agencies coordinate their work, allocate resources, and prioritize action. The 2019 Department of Homeland Security (DHS) Strategic Framework for Countering Terrorism and Targeted Violence specifically, as the title suggests, addressed terrorism *and* targeted violence.[46] In the preface to that report, the then Secretary of Homeland Security, Kevin McAleenan, clarified DHS's intention to reflect not only that they are distinct yet related phenomena but because of their interaction, "necessitate a shared set of solutions" across preventative efforts and resource allocation.[47] Definitional debates on terrorism are far from trivial, and their contours echo debates about definitions more generally. As the philosopher Doug Walton explains in his analysis of what constitutes *persuasive* definitions, often the point of putting forward a definition isn't necessarily to explain something—rather it is to support an argument.[48] And if anything, the meaning of terrorism continues to expand. It remains a highly politicized term, one open to widespread abuse. On May 31, 2020, Donald Trump announced this via Twitter: "The United States of America will be designating ANTIFA as a Terrorist Organization."[49] Despite the fact that, as the terrorism researchers Jason Blazakis and Colin Clarke wrote, ANTIFA are "neither terrorists nor an organization," the White House appeared eager to link violence from protests in response to George Floyd's murder by police in Minneapolis, Minnesota, with "far-left extremist groups."[50]

When considering the intricacies of terrorism definitions and their consequences, I assure you that everything I have mentioned so far is merely the tip of a very large iceberg. But that's not to say that these problems cannot be tackled. It's that there is no clear solution, and any course of action comes with costs and benefits. Simply acknowledging what those are, and routinely doing so in analysis, may ultimately be more helpful. And to be fair, if we had an agreed-upon definition it doesn't necessarily mean we'd necessarily use it consistently. The supposed academic advantages of a universal definition are almost always overstated. In his classic essay 'On a Certain Blindness in Human Beings,' the philosopher and psychologist William James wrote, "Our judgements concerning the worth of things, big or little, depend on the *feelings* the things arouse in us."[51] This is key to acknowledging what *we* are willing and ready to consider terrorism, which is as much a type of psychological warfare as it is a strategy embraced by various actors, groups, and states. Most definitions cluster around several features, including that it is a form of political violence typically employed by nonstate actors directed against noncombatants. Some definitions emphasize the "political" nature of the violence. But as we have seen, groups who use violence against civilians don't seek to change politics in a conventional sense; instead, they push some social, religious, or other ideological agenda to the forefront. Progress isn't limited by having lots of definitions that differ a little here and there. On the contrary, such debates are helpful. They get us to appreciate how complex terrorism is and how inconsistent and hypocritical our responses to it often are. Embracing terrorism's complexity is a good recipe for some analytic modesty and equips us to better understand it.

CONCLUSION

Terrorism today is embraced by diverse actors and groups who espouse multiple, equally diverse ideologies (and sometimes more than one at the same time). From the extreme right to the extreme left, the religious and the secular, the progovernment and antigovernment to single issues such as animal rights and the environment, terrorism's diversity isn't just about ideology. An activity that was once an almost exclusively male domain is today a fertile ground for recruitment and frontline mobilization of women and children alike. Terrorism has become an equal opportunities employer, exploiting the appeal, accessibility, and convenience of social media to attract a wider pool of recruits than ever before. While Al-Qaeda and the Islamic State and its affiliates rose to prominence after 2001, a resurgent global wave of right-wing violent extremism currently threatens to become the new normal. For many, this recognition is too little too late. For others, it is an acknowledgement of just how rapidly white supremacist violence has leaped onto the global stage, again blurring distinctions between so-called domestic and international terrorism. In early January 2020, the FBI arrested several men suspected of being members of The Base, an international neo-Nazi hate group. One of those arrested was Patrik Mathews, described as a recruiter for the group. Mathews had earlier entered the United States from Canada illegally after earlier being kicked out of the Canadian Army because of his white supremacist views.[52] He used his military experience, which included "rudimentary explosives training" to train other members of The Base in their efforts to trigger a race war.[53] Trends come and go, to be sure, and some events merely represent the latest iteration of problems that have been bubbling up for decades. The May 2017 Unite the Right rally in Charlottesville, Virginia, proved to be a critical turning point in the United States.[54] Though racially motivated violence is as old as the United States itself, the Charlottesville event represented a concerted effort by a diverse group to organize and coalesce. Harnessing social media platforms and buoyed by the belief that they were becoming a force to be reckoned with in American social and political life, the rally proved successful in coordinating and mobilizing disparate groups to present a fresh, new (and much younger) face of white supremacy.

We have no small challenge ahead of us. How do we understand these developments, this diversity, this rapidly changing phenomenon, let alone those drawn to it, when we cannot always agree on what to call it? Given the negativity associated with the label of terrorism, it might be easier to hit the reset button and call it something a bit more neutral. *Political violence* and *violent extremism* are just two terms that seem more inclusive. In her analysis of serial homicide, mass shootings, school shootings, and lone actor terrorism, the forensic psychologist and professor Clare Allely uses the term "extreme violence."[55] In any event, a good definition of terrorism should mean we can, by sticking with whatever one we embrace, easily identify what is *not* terrorism. The question of what constitutes it is something that every student of terrorism must grapple with. It's accurate to say that there are hundreds of different definitions of terrorism, but that does not mean that we don't have a common understanding of what it is. Though these definitions differ in their precise wording, emphasis, and length, most definitions are similar—they acknowledge that terrorism involves the threat or use of violence against civilians (or noncombatants) in pursuit of some bigger, broader agenda. If we can continue to agree just on that (and remain consistent in how and when we apply that), then progress is made.

Perhaps the most important principle we can strive for in the short term is to encourage analysts and researchers to just explicitly state what their definition is. The reader can then decide what is missing and what, if anything, comes from that. The definition I offer here is that terrorism is the *targeted use, or threat of use, of public violence against civilians by nonstate actors in pursuit of some social, political, religious, or other ideological agenda.* That agenda may vary significantly from person to person or group to group. It may be overtly political, in terms of attempting to achieve independence from a state. It may be primarily religious, arguing for the return of Islamic law to rule a community, or as stated earlier, might pivot around a very specific single issue like abortion, animal rights, technology, or the environment. Those who commit acts of terrorism may belong to groups or may be lone individuals acting on behalf of groups to which they have no direct access. Ideology must be a major component of the perpetrator's motivation for it to be terrorism. Of course, what constitutes "major" is debatable, and that is not to say that personal fantasy and personal motivations don't feature in the psychology of the terrorist. They most certainly do, as we will see in later chapters. But the terrorist is governed or limited in some sense by a sense of logic and a set of rules that influence what, how, where, when, and why they do what they do. With that in mind, let's now turn our attention to the focus of this book—the terrorists themselves— and explore who precisely becomes involved in this activity.

2

WHO BECOMES A TERRORIST?

"The failure to explain is caused by a failure to describe."

BENOIT MANDELBROT[1]

Five decades of research tells us that terrorists are mostly young, adult men. Terrorist groups routinely enlist women, and children, too, but terrorism remains overwhelmingly an activity for adult men. Terrorism is not always open to all. Discovering who becomes a terrorist is not only an exercise in figuring out who wants to get involved in a terrorist group but also an exercise in discovering who is, at any time and place, allowed to join one.

This chapter focuses on this question: Who becomes a terrorist? We must identify as much as we can about our subjects before we can decipher what motivates them. We could answer the question in a few different ways. We can examine specific movements as a starting point. We might also look into why some people act alone while others engage with a group. Does that reflect a choice? Is it determined by opportunities (or lack thereof)? We could also pose questions in terms of ideology—for instance, are certain people more likely to join right-wing extremist groups than left-wing groups? It makes sense that some differences would be found here—we wouldn't ordinarily expect a neo-Nazi movement to be comprised of dozens of Muslim converts. From a wider perspective though, it stands to reason that at least *some* factors unite people who seek out and join certain groups as opposed to others. Our original question might be better phrased: Who joins this group, or who joins that group? Until, of course, we consider the Islamic State, a movement that seems to uproot many of our assumptions about the questions we should be asking, and appeared, for a time, to find ways to engage just about anybody who wanted to get involved. But there is more at stake here, and these questions quickly go beyond academic pondering.

Sometimes the question of who becomes a terrorist really depends on what we mean by the word. That's not quite the same issue as the definition problem. For instance, what if someone engages in terrorist acts but is charged and convicted of nonterrorist offenses? Would we still call them a terrorist? As we saw in chapter 1, Dylann Roof was not charged with terrorism offenses, yet few would not label him such. Despite that outcome, should offenders like Roof be included in databases of terrorist actors and be part of national security threat assessments? A related issue is whether the label *terrorist* really captures a specific class of offender at all—for example, is someone convicted of planting a bomb comparable to someone who sends money to a charity connected to a holy war overseas? Both acts are terrorism-related offenses and would likely be prosecuted as such, but if we were asked to say which person was actually a terrorist, would we say it was the bomber? As we discussed before, there are no easy or straightforward answers to any of these questions, and whatever we decide has consequences.

WHAT IS A TERRORIST?

In March 2020, as the gravity of the COVID-19 pandemic became apparent, a series of pranks intended to go viral in a different sense captured news headlines across the United States. In Missouri, a man was arrested after licking multiple sticks of deodorant in a store. He wanted to record a video mocking those afraid of the virus.[2] In Pennsylvania, a woman was arrested after deliberately coughing on food in a grocery store. Described as a "chronic problem in the community," her long-standing psychological problems did not protect her from being charged with "felony counts of terrorist threats, threats to use a 'biological agent' and criminal mischief."[3] Missouri's deodorant man was likewise charged with "making a terroristic threat." The moves followed a memo issued that month in which the deputy attorney general of the U.S. Department of Justice advised law enforcement personnel about the "purposeful exposure and infection of others with COVID-19." The memo explained, "Because coronavirus appears to meet the statutory definition of a 'biological agent' under 18 U.S.C. § 178(1), such acts potentially could implicate the Nation's terrorism-related statutes."[4]

To say these cases represented a "novel expansion" of antiterrorism statutes is an understatement.[5] The move was derided as a poor use of federal resources where local state laws could cover such offenses. In any event, such behavior is at odds with most ideas of what constitutes terrorism. But if our understanding of "terrorist," legally speaking, is someone charged with (and convicted of) a terrorism-related offense, these people would be considered terrorists. The accordion-like expansion and contraction of the label complicates what should seem straightforward, but a related challenge here is that, put simply, not all terrorists are created equal. Consider the case of Peyton Pruitt, an eighteen-year-old Alabama man. The FBI argued Pruitt provided "support for an act of terrorism," which involved sending bomb-making instructions to someone on the Internet he believed to be involved with the Islamic State. In her detailed portrait of Pruitt, the journalist Jessica Pishko describes how the young man had grown increasingly fascinated with the Islamic State and, through various online chatrooms, "communicated with more than one person who claimed to be interested in or affiliated with ISIS."[6] He was alleged to have expressed a desire to join a Tunisian university from where he would "cross the border into Libya and join a terrorist group."[7] Pruitt was determined to have cognitive functions "at the level of an 8-year-old-child," lacking "motor coordination and cannot button a shirt or put on a belt. . . . He speaks slowly, haltingly, and he has a tendency to rock his chair back and forth when he is anxious and to pace when he is excited."[8] Pishko explains how a developmental psychologist diagnosed Pruitt as having "cognitive deficits and attention-deficit disorder."[9] His defense team argued that he wasn't "competent enough to stand trial, never mind knowingly offer material support to people he believed were terrorists."[10] A forensic psychologist who assessed Pruitt concluded, "The defendant gives an account of the circumstances surrounding the offense that indicates that he was experiencing a mental defect . . . such that he was unable to appreciate the nature and quality of his actions or the wrongfulness of his acts."[11] Pishko reported that in October 2016 Pruitt was eventually released into his father's custody after the court found him "not guilty by reason of mental defect."[12] So should his case be included in analyses of who becomes a terrorist or instead be held up as an example of overzealous efforts to secure a terrorism conviction? At a minimum, and despite the outcome, it seems unwise to ignore the question of how a movement like the Islamic State appealed to a young, learning-disabled man from rural Alabama.

Other cases are more clear-cut. We would surely exclude from our analysis people forced to engage in terrorism against their will. These would include the Provisional IRA's "proxy bombers," men deemed to be collaborators and forced to drive truckloads of explosives into British Army checkpoints while their families were held at gunpoint.[13] We would also probably exclude the two women who, in 2017, approached a man in Malaysia's Kuala Lumpur airport, pushing a cloth containing liquefied VX onto his face. A few moments later, the man, revealed to be the estranged half-brother of the North Korean dictator Kim Jong Un, slumped over and died before he could be taken to hospital. The women claimed to the police they were duped into playing what they believed was part of a tele-vised prank and were not, in fact, state-sponsored assassins.[14] Elsewhere, the researchers Shafi Mostofa and Natalie Doyle analyzed profiles of Bangladeshi militants who joined Al-Qaeda and the Islamic State. They warned readers, however, that their subjects "can only be described as 'alleged' militants"[15] because the researchers collected information only on violent actors killed by Bangladeshi security forces. Those same forces are internationally regarded as committing multiple human rights violations in the name of security and counterterrorism.[16]

Finally, there is one big problem with terrorism research that many analysts quietly concede. If we only examine people who have become terrorists, and don't equally consider why so many comparable people in the same situations do *not* become terrorists, we can't be sure why those small few do (or even whether we have a reliable picture of who they are). Ideally, when we look at a group of people who become terrorists, we would also consider those in the same age group, from the same places, and exposed to the same conditions but who choose *not* to participate in terrorism—or perhaps they are just oblivious to it. By only considering those who ended up as terrorists, we overlook those who did not, rendering any conclusions speculative at best. Academics call this an example of "selecting on the dependent variable." It is a big problem for researchers attempting to understand people's motivation to take part in terrorism, but I offer this caution here before we consider the growing number of demographic studies on who becomes involved in terrorism. Fortunately, there are strategies for dealing with this limitation. But let's first look at what the studies reveal about who gets involved.

WHO BECOMES A TERRORIST?

Age

Demographic studies of terrorists abound. They offer data on age, gender, nationality, education level, marital status, and a bunch of other variables. The good news is that this kind of information tends to be concrete and resistant to the vagaries of interpretation (unlike, say, motivation). As I said earlier, we can confidently say that most terrorists are young, adult men. Countless studies support this. The Program on Extremism (PoE) at George Washington University examined seventy-one people charged with Islamic State–related activity in 2014 and 2015. They found almost

90 percent were men, with an average age of twenty-six.[17] The researchers concluded, "The profiles of individuals involved in ISIS-related activities in the United States differ widely in race, age, social class, education, and family background. Their motivations are equally diverse and defy easy analysis."[18] A 2018 update by POE, expanded to 170 people charged with IS-related offenses, suggested a slight increase in average age—to twenty-eight.[19] Their 2020 update (further expanded to 208 people) cemented the demographic—90 percent male and averaging twenty-eight years old.[20] Other studies largely corroborate the POE data. In his analysis of thirty-four reports and academic studies of Western men and women who became foreign fighters, sociologist Lorne Dawson found the average age of men was twenty-six, while the average age of women was twenty-one.[21]

Studies from around the world reveal similar dynamics. The psychologist John Morrison and I examined Irish Republican splinter group activity between 1997 and 2010.[22] We collected data on 641 people involved in both legal and illegal activity and found most were men in their thirties. A closer look revealed two distinct clusters, the pattern explained by an "older, experienced leadership . . . recruiting younger, inexperienced individuals"—those still part of these groups in their thirties had basically joined in their twenties.[23] In over six hundred terrorists active between the 1970s and 1990s, the Spanish terrorism expert Fernando Reinares found members of ETA, the Basque separatist movement, to be mostly young single men who joined in their late teens to early twenties.[24] The terrorism researchers Leonard Weinberg and William Eubank studied 572 Italian neofascists arrested for planning or committing violent acts between 1970 and 1984.[25] Ninety-three percent were men; most came from big cities. Over a third were twenty to twenty-four years old at the time of arrest, and more than 70 percent overall were twenty-nine or younger.[26] In Colombia, the researcher Mauricio Florez-Morris interviewed former members of several terrorist groups.[27] The average age of his interviewees when joining the group was nineteen to twenty. Elsewhere, the American-based (though international) neo-Nazi group Atomwaffen Division (AWD) recruited "mostly white males" aged sixteen to thirty.[28]

Studies of Islamist groups reveal similar trends. Nearly 90 percent of all jihadists arrested or killed in Spain between 2013 and 2018 were men, and most were eighteen to thirty-eight years old.[29] The researchers Robin Simcox and Emily Dyer analyzed records of 171 Al-Qaeda members in 2013 and found most were under 30 at the time of their offense.[30] The psychiatrist and terrorism scholar Marc Sageman's 2004 study of 172 jihadists found the average age for "joining the jihad" was twenty-five.[31] Of fifty-one attacks conducted from 2014 to 2017 by Islamic State followers in Europe and North America, attackers averaged twenty-seven years old, and all but two of the attackers were men.[32] Back in Spain again, Fernando Reinares's analysis of the jihadist network behind the 2004 Madrid train bombings revealed twenty-seven men distributed across four small clusters.[33] Most were aged twenty-three to thirty-three. Some were single while others were married; some had formal education and steady employment and others had neither.[34] And one comprehensive study of 120 lone actor terrorists (sometimes referred to as "lone wolves") based in European Union countries between 2000 and 2014 revealed an average age of 29.7 years old at the time of the attack or the arrest of the offender(s).[35] In 2016, researchers at West Point's Countering Terrorism Center analyzed Islamic State personnel records on over four thousand personnel. One of the researchers, Brian Dodwell, noted that recruits were, on average, "around 26, 27 years old but we're talking about everywhere from teenagers up until men in the[ir] 60s."[36]

Age at the time of . . . what, exactly?

There are dozens more such studies, far too many to even list here. With a few exceptions, which we'll discuss later, they all have the same findings—terrorism remains an overwhelmingly young man's preoccupation. But the more demographic studies one reads, the more an age-related question recurs: How can we know how old someone is when they get *involved* in terrorism? The task is deceptively difficult. Most of what we know here comes from data on captured, surrendered, or dead terrorists. But studies that report age often don't clarify what it refers to. It might be the age that was recorded when someone was arrested. It might be their age when they died in an attack, surrendered, or were charged with or convicted of an offense; in some cases it might even be years after apprehension, let alone initial involvement. To understand the difference between the time someone gets involved in a movement and the time they subsequently engage in terrorist activity, compared to the time at which they are arrested or otherwise stopped, we must look a lot closer.

Several years ago, the Irish researcher Paul Gill and I built a database of 1,240 Provisional IRA members active between 1970 and 1998.[37] The database contained information organized across thirty-nine variables, such as age at the time of joining the movement, age at the time of death, and type of activity the person was involved in. We identified data from several sources, including statements issued by the IRA, independent obituaries (from more than one source), and multiple newspaper archives. IRA publicity materials would routinely offer information on when members became involved, but in the case of the Irish Republican movement, this doesn't necessarily equate to involvement in *violence*, let alone terrorist activity. This proved to be a key issue in thinking about how long it can take between a recruit's initial involvement and their subsequent engagement in terrorist operations. We found that, on average, IRA members were twenty-five years old when they first became involved. Additionally, because we looked at this data across three decades, we found it illuminated something else—on average, the IRA age profile skewed a little older as the campaign progressed. Looking at a terrorist group over time is important for a fuller understanding of what demographic factors like age might mean. In the case of the IRA, for example, we were able to better understand the changing data when we also considered the bigger organizational and strategic changes affecting the IRA—in the early days of the IRA campaign, their recruitment was a lot looser and wider ranging. A negative effect of this, for the group, was that the movement was subject to infiltration by spies. In subsequent years, as it reorganized itself, tightening up structures, it began to recruit slightly older, more mature recruits. In contrast, Reinares's studies of ETA found the opposite. In the 1980s and 1990s, that movement "tended to accept whoever is available, regardless of their age."[38]

There are exceptions to every rule. In a study of violent anti-abortionists in the United States, the Christian extremist Army of God movement offered no discernible age pattern—members ranged anywhere from twenty to sixty.[39] The former CIA officer turned academic Ayla Schbley conducted 250 interviews with anti-abortionists over nine years, discovering that those activists who were senior citizens would spend their days "expressing their religious beliefs and freedom of speech by standing outside a known abortionist church or clinic with a sign or a banner."[40] In her interviews with female racists in the United States, the sociologist Kathleen Blee interviewed a woman in her eighties whose role for the skinhead movement involved editing a newsletter.[41] Of those anti-abortionists who engaged in *violence* (e.g., bombings or shootings), Schbley found it was mostly conducted by men aged twenty-one to forty-three.[42] Likewise, in a study of American Islamist terrorists, the Brandeis University professor Jytte Klausen and colleagues found that being younger seemed to be a risk factor for engagement in violent offenses but not for nonviolent activities.[43] These studies suggest that age (and in some cases, gender) doesn't restrict involvement but might actually predict role *type*.

That is not to say that older adults do not commit violence. Khalid Masood, a Muslim convert and Islamic State devotee, was fifty-two years old when he drove his car into pedestrians in London in 2017.[44] In East Africa, Al-Shabaab used a sixty-year old Somali-Norwegian man as its oldest suicide bomber to date.[45] A sixty-four-year-old grandmother attempted, via suicide bombing, to kill Israeli troops in Gaza in 2006.[46] From late 2016 to early 2017, the researcher Chelsea Daymon and others noticed that the Islamic State movement had begun to deploy older adults as suicide bombers.[47] By early 2017, at least twenty-seven older adults (aged sixty and older) were eulogized by the Islamic State in its propaganda materials. The eulogies revealed not only were those "elders with grey hair" revered for their sacrifice but suggested that the Islamic State used their images to shame younger men for their nonparticipation.[48] It's possible that the Islamic State saw older men as an additional, untapped source of recruits whom, if suitably prepared and precisely directed, could execute important operations that would simultaneously reap propaganda benefits. It may also have been that, at least in certain areas, the Islamic State just ran out of suicide bombers. In the months leading up to the movement using older men as bombers, it had suffered significant battle losses.[49]

The pendulum swings the other way, too, though children are still far more likely to be the *target* of terrorism than recruited into it. In a breathtaking attack, the Pakistan Taliban killed 132 schoolchildren in Peshawar in 2014, and said, "We targeted the school . . . because the [Pakistani] Army targets our families. We want them to feel our pain."[50] The Oxford Research Group found that by 2013, over eleven thousand children had been killed in the Syrian civil war. Aleppo alone saw over two thousand children die, nearly four hundred from sniper fire (a deliberate and precise act) by troops loyal to Bashar al-Assad. Between 2015 and 2019, over eleven thousand attacks were reported against schools in ninety-three countries.[51] However, several terrorist groups target children as recruits. A hallmark of effective terrorist movements is that they find ways to overcome age limitations, tailoring specific activities and roles to recruits. The IRA member Brendan Hughes acknowledged that adolescents would be considered potential future recruits by the movement but would first be engaged via "scouting work, for instance . . . on their way to school."[52] UNICEF found that, in 2014, over twenty-four thousand children were recruited by militant groups in South Sudan and the Central African Republic.[53] It is impossible to reliably estimate how many children have come to be involved with the Islamic State. Research on child socialization into the Islamic State suggests that in 2015 and 2016 alone, it appears to have trained and mobilized around two thousand child militants.[54] Still, such estimates are probably conservative. What we do know is that the Islamic State institutionalized a formal program of training, specialization, and deployment of its child militants, subsequently celebrating their achievements in multiple propaganda outlets. Many child soldiers in the Islamic State were filmed guarding, torturing, and executing prisoners or desecrating corpses. Between 2010 and 2014, a single NGO based in the country's Swat Valley successfully reintegrated over 150 children into local communities from Pakistan Taliban training camps. In a study of 135 male militants from Swat, the psychiatrist Dr. Feriha Peracha and her team found the boys ranged from twelve to eighteen years old (averaging 15.5).[55] About half the boys were forcibly abducted, while nearly the entire other half seemed to volunteer. The children were mostly poor, and two-thirds came from families with absent fathers, a factor the researchers believed resulted in a lack of protection from recruitment by local militants.[56] Most of the children were not involved in violent acts but were instead used as spies and lookouts or to perform domestic chores such as cleaning or cooking inside the training camps.[57]

Children increasingly feature in terrorism today—sometimes in unexpected ways. The Internet has facilitated what would have previously been unlikely if not impossible. The Feuerkrieg Division was described in 2020 by the Anti-Defamation League (ADL) as a "small, international neo-Nazi group that advocates for a race war."[58] ADL says the group draws inspiration from Hitler and Charles Manson and spreads "racist and vitriolic propaganda" online to accelerate what it hopes is the inevitable collapse of society. Feuerkrieg Division was linked to several terrorist plots in the United States, including plans to attack a Las Vegas synagogue and to detonate a car bomb outside the Cable News Network (CNN).[59] An investigation by Estonian authorities revealed the group's alleged founder was, in fact, a thirteen-year-old boy. He was subsequently revealed to have been in contact with another teenager, based in the United Kingdom, who was charged in 2021 with disseminating terrorist propaganda. The British child, in turn, was the youngest person in the UK ever charged with terrorist offenses.[60]

Gender

Acknowledging that terrorism is male dominated runs the risk of misunderstanding how and why women are represented (or not) in terror groups. The involvement of women in terrorism is in no way new despite often being presented in popular media as if it were. In fact, women's involvement in terrorism is far better researched than some think, but the findings are not always well integrated into the broader literature.[61] When women's involvement in terrorism is acknowledged, it is often done in a superficial and patronizing way. In their book *Homegrown: ISIS in America*, the George Washington University researchers Alexander Meleagrou-Hitchens, Seamus Hughes, and Bennett Clifford describe how the label "jihadi bride" quickly became ubiquitous for just about any foreign women who sought to join the Islamic State.[62] One of several consequences of this was, the authors say, the erasing of any sense of women's agency.

In an early study, Weinberg and Eubank found several differences distinguishing the early wave of Italian neofascists and left-wing terrorists.[63] Men comprised most of the membership in neofascist violent groups, while nearly a quarter of members in left-wing terrorist groups in Italy were women. The researchers argued that the difference cannot be explained without considering the process of recruitment. The male overrepresentation in neofascist groups, they suggested, stemmed from strong sibling relationships, with brothers recruiting brothers.[64]

Even in terror groups that have spawned famous female militants, the nature and extent of women's involvement is often shaped by the men. The sociologist Kathleen Blee studied right-wing racist groups in the United States, revealing what she called a deeply gendered phenomenon, with female members "lurking behind husbands and boyfriends."[65] The result was an underappreciation of women's attitudes and involvement in racist thinking and action, and this was reflected in equally gendered scholarship for many years.[66] Through the 1990s, however, Blee characterized then-modern racist groups (such as neo-Nazi, KKK, and Christian Identity) as comprising 25 percent women (they constitute nearly 50 percent of inductees in some groups).[67] Blee cites a KKK leader describing the rationale for targeting female recruits: "The men will follow the women. If a wife is against the husband's being involved, you can just about, you know, forget the husband hanging around for long. . . . The other way, if the wife is into it, she'll drag the husband along. I've seen that too many times to ignore it, so we don't hold women back from promotions or climbing the ladder."[68]

Fernando Reinares found women's involvement in ETA in many cases to function as preexisting social bonds with men already involved in the group.[69] The women may have already been ideologically sympathetic toward ETA, but their activity as militants was in large part a result of men vouching for them or otherwise bringing their girlfriends with them simply because they themselves were getting involved with the group.[70] Women who did join were, for the most part, subsequently barred from access to prestige roles such as violent actor or leader.[71] In Indonesia, the researcher Julie Chernov Hwang conducted over a hundred interviews with thirty-five jihadists from 2010 to 2016. She found all those involved in terrorist violence were male, noting that female members were relegated to childcare duties and finding ways to "supplement the family economy."[72] Blee's studies of American right-wing racist groups revealed similar dynamics. Women rarely held any significant leadership positions; some groups, Blee says, specifically designated women "an overtly separate, subordinate, and ancillary role within the movement as the helpmates of men and the nurturers of the next generation."[73]

Such gendered treatment of women by some groups does not diminish the operational effectiveness of female operatives.[74] The jihadism expert Aaron Zelin explains how Tunisian women played key roles in developing the Islamic State, helping to recruit others both at home and abroad.[75] And even in cases where women's agency in seeking out ways to be influential *is* clear, the extent of that influence is frequently stifled by men, even to the detriment of the movement. The UK female jihadist Safiyya Shaikh oversaw a Telegram channel, GreenBirds, featuring messages calling for supporters around the world to take up arms and for those in the UK to attack British targets. An undercover police investigation revealed that Shaikh was the channel's main administrator, managing twenty other administrators on both that channel and elsewhere. Male Islamic State supporters reacted negatively when they realized a woman was running the channel, one lamenting that fellow men should not "allow our precious pearls to run such delicate groups."[76]

Terrorist groups that accommodate gender diversity often do so for reasons that are as tactical as they are strategic. Comparing terror groups that seem to share ideology and goals illustrates this. For example, the researchers Jason Warner and Hilary Matfess studied 434 suicide bombers deployed by Nigeria's Boko Haram movement.[77] In contrast to most suicide bomber profiles, over half were women, and nearly a fifth children, some as young as seven.[78] In contrast, most of Somalia's al-Shabaab's suicide bombers were male—in their analysis of 216 suicide bombers deployed by the Somali terror group over an eleven-year period, Warner and fellow researcher Ellen Chapin found less than 5 percent of its bombers were female.[79] Child suicide bombers deployed by Boko Haram proved the most lethal, responsible for higher casualty rates compared to adults.[80] The researchers point to the group's logic for being "willing to subvert norms" around women and children in this way: "They are often viewed as being inherently innocent or non-threatening, thus arouse less suspicion than men."[81] To further test this notion, Boko Haram even deployed male suicide bombers dressed as women in 2015 and 2016.[82]

Education and Other Background Factors

A long-standing idea about terrorists is that they are mostly well-educated. One of the earliest serious attempts to develop a generic terrorist profile was published in 1977 by the researchers Charles Russell and Bowman Miller.[83] Their study revealed the terrorist to be "a single male, aged 22 to 24, with at least a partial university education, most often in the humanities."[84] These men came from "an affluent middle- or upper-class family that enjoys some social prestige."[85] Like many terrorist profiles, such observations make sense only for a particular time and place. For example, in the early to mid-1970s, young American students were frequently exposed to radical ideas. The Symbionese Liberation Army (SLA), a violent left-wing extremist group, is probably best known today for its association with Patty Hearst, the newspaper heiress kidnapped by the group before appearing to willingly participate in subsequent operations on its behalf. Fueled by outrage at the Vietnam War, the SLA comprised "a small clique of young, self-absorbed, guilt-ridden, emotionally and psychologically scarred white women."[86] It recruited new members from schools and universities, as well as from prisons.[87] Another well-known American terror group from the 1970s was the Weather Underground, a group with an all-white leadership comprised of many university graduates.[88]

Echoing Russell and Miller's 1977 study, the former FBI Special Agent Thomas Strentz argued that, at least in the 1960s and 1970s, most terrorist groups in the United States and abroad were "composed of males and females who were flexible, college-educated, well-trained, urban, multilingual, well-traveled, and reasonable sophisticated middle-class young people."[89] Strentz contrasted this terrorist profile with what he called the "Middle Eastern" terrorist profile in the 1980s, saying those who attacked Western interests were "more likely to be poorly educated, a member of a very large family, unskilled and unemployable, illiterate, rural, undisciplined, and an ill-trained male refugee. They are young, age 17 to 23."[90] Weinberg and Eubank found in their sample of 572 Italian neofascists, over 25 percent were drawn from high-prestige professions such as law, medicine, or architecture, while another quarter of the sample came from the Italian small business community.[91]

But what about modern cases? In his 2016 book, *The Way of the Strangers*, the journalist Graeme Wood argues that contemporary western jihadists "often fit a broad profile" characterizing them as "overwhelmingly left-brained, analytic types."[92] Wood cites a study showing "as many as 60 percent of Western jihadis have engineering backgrounds."[93] That study is one of the most well-known in terrorism research, and it's pretty much mandatory reading for most students of violent extremism. Conducted by the sociologists Diego Gambetta and Steffen Hertog, it was published in 2016.[94] They offered a simple and striking finding—there seemed to be a *lot* of engineers in jihadist terror groups. But why was that the case? The researchers suggested that social scientists tend to be associated with left-wing politics while engineers tend to be associated with right-wing groups, surmising that "certain degrees are a proxy for personality traits."[95] Hertog offered several possible explanations for the findings.[96] Perhaps engineers were selectively recruited for skills considered valuable to the terror group (like the ability to make bombs)? Or maybe their involvement was shaped by path dependency? In other words, one engineer recruits another engineer, who recruits another, and so on. Habit becomes history. This makes sense—multiple studies show recruitment to be a highly social process, heavily determined by who knows who as opposed to who knows what.

In a 2016 analysis of 373 terrorists charged, convicted, or killed in North America and Western Europe, the researchers Robert Leiken and Steven Brooke found that "contrary to conventional wisdom . . . [members] are not selected by virtue of proficiency in a required terrorism discipline (a forger, an explosives expert, a driver, etc.) but rather through ascriptive groupings such as family, nationality, region, or village and friendship circle."[97]

What else could explain the engineer findings? Was there some psychological vulnerability at play? The idea here is that certain personality traits (possibly) shared among engineers might predispose them to certain kinds of politics that, in turn, might make them susceptible to certain ideas or the allure of "certain types" of activities.[98] The researchers speculated that what they called the extremist mindset holds a certain appeal to engineers—the kind of person that would want to become an engineer might equally be attracted to terrorism. One of the essential qualities required for this outlook, the authors argue, is what they called a "need for cognitive closure," meaning a desire to remove ambiguity around situations or issues. The interpretation seems more than a little speculative, and we should also bear in mind that the notion of a mindset might also be what *results* from involvement and engagement in terrorist activity.[99] Nevertheless, the study offers some interesting hypotheses. Being so compelling, it attracted attention.[100] But some explanations seem more plausible than others. Upon closer inspection, the personality argument seems least credible—if engineers were drawn to terrorism because of a need for unambiguous, clearly planned behavior with little room for error, the day-to-day reality of terrorist groups would unquestionably give them pause. And if path dependency (that is, the idea that one engineer would be more likely to recruit another, and so on) theoretically explains the overrepresentation of engineers, reality might be very different. After all, once experiences of terrorist lives become known by one engineer, surely news of that reality would then spread to another engineer, and another, and so on. If that is how it all worked, it would probably reduce the involvement of subsequent engineers, if anything. Hertog himself considered another point. If engineers were found to belong to jihadist groups, it might reflect broader, and rapid, socioeconomic change in societies undergoing political transformation.[101]

At a 2009 book talk hosted by the Washington, DC, think tank the Carnegie Endowment for International Peace, Hertog conceded: "That's what we've often heard. . . . In those developing countries, everyone's studying engineering."[102] Hertog acknowledged that being an engineer in the Islamic world is tantamount to membership in an elite club, one that confers social status, and perhaps its members were more appealing to a terrorist organization or its recruiters. Perhaps, perhaps not. All were intriguing explanations nonetheless.

While Gambetta and Hertog offered stimulating findings, a more basic issue hinders generalization from their research. Yes, engineers were overrepresented in the sample. However, any claims of overrepresentation must overcome two major limitations. First, the number of people who become involved in terrorism is so small that any apparent effect would need to be detected in very large samples. Second, such effects tend to slowly diminish once smaller samples are considered against other, bigger samples that examine the same phenomenon. For instance, if we only consider the sheer scale of membership observed in the Islamic State, for instance, the presence of engineers is quickly dwarfed by that of nonengineers. In one study of a single Islamic State cohort,[103] nearly two-thirds of 784 Germans who joined the Islamic State comprised almost exclusively men "known to the police because of violence, property offences, or political criminal acts."[104]

We could dive even deeper into these issues, but let's pause here for a moment. Thinking more deeply about the Gambetta and Hertog study leads us to one inevitable conclusion—more fully understanding who becomes a terrorist is unlikely by just calling for more demographic studies per se. The deeper questions around what might explain such trends, and perhaps the question of mobilization to action, cannot be answered by considering recruit qualities alone. We must look more closely at terrorist organizations, and their recruiters, to identify what *they* look for in potential contributors and how (or if) they deliberately seek out desirable demographic, psychological, and other qualities in prospects. We know that some groups have done this. Largely overlooked in the terrorism literature is the Black Liberation Army (BLA). A short-lived group in the 1970s, the BLA sought Black nationalist revolution in the United States and was responsible for over twenty killings.[105] According to the terrorism expert William Rosenau, the BLA recruited heavily among common criminals, with the group's goal to "contain that energy, point it in the right direction and make them beautiful . . . revolutionaries."[106] It stands to reason, in groups where recruiters occupy formal roles and fulfil screening jobs, that a higher caliber of recruit might be selected on that basis alone. We must also accept that whatever those qualities, criteria, or traits are, they might themselves be subject to change depending on prevailing circumstances. Terrorist groups often target recruits out of necessity, or convenience, or both.

A ROLE FOR EVERYBODY

In so many ways, the Islamic State movement stands apart from previous terrorist movements, challenging us to think in new ways. One of the most immediate observations of the Islamic State was its diversity of membership. Graeme Wood wrote, "The breath of the appeal of the Islamic State was as shocking as its depth. Three generations of conservative Muslims from outside London, a skirt-chasing bachelor from South Australia, and tens of thousands of others had all drunk their inspiration from the same fountains."[107] That wide appeal reflected extensive outreach to diverse people and communities alike. In 2015, Islamic State media released a video specifically targeting English-speaking Westerners. "The Chosen Few of Different Lands" featured a young Canadian man, Andre Poulin, imploring fellow Canadians and others to come join the Islamic State project. Six years earlier, Poulin had converted to Islam. Speaking directly to the camera, he explains his point of view:

> I was like any other regular Canadian. I watched hockey. I went to the cottage in the summertime. I loved to fish. I wanted to go hunting. I liked outdoors; I liked sports; I had money; I had a family; I had good friends; I had colleagues. You know, I worked as a street janitor. I made over two thousand dollars a month at this job. . . . So, it's not like I was some social outcast, wasn't like I was some anarchist or somebody who just wants to destroy the world and kill everybody. No, I was a regular person.

Despite his best efforts, Canadian authorities described him as someone who spent years online learning how to build bombs.[108] But his recruitment message was as simple as it was clever:

> There's a role for everybody. Every person can contribute something to the Islamic State. . . . If you cannot fight, then you can give money. And if you cannot give money, then you can assist in technology. And if you can't assist in technology, you can use some other skills. You can even come here and help rebuild the place. If you have knowledge of how to build roads, or how to build houses, you can be used here, and you'll be very well taken care of here. You know, you can easily earn yourself a high station . . . for the next life, by sacrificing just a small bit of this wordly life.

This call, and others, did not go unanswered. Mobilization to the Islamic State was stunning in its scope. By 2017, over seven thousand Western foreign fighters joined the IS along with an additional thirty-five thousand foreign travelers from at least one hundred and twenty countries.[109] Admittedly, the Islamic State might well be an outlier in the sense that in scale alone, it is incomparable to most contemporary and historical terrorist groups. Throughout history, terrorists survive in part because they operate in the shadows; their semiclandestine nature helps prolong their life span while enhancing appeal. The Islamic State, in the words of Wood, captured and (at least for a time) held territory, openly documenting and advertising just about every facet of daily life in the so-called Caliphate with a "top-down structure to rule it [via a] bureaucracy . . . divided into civil and military arms, and its territory into provinces."[110] Many became fighters, others embraced administration and civil service, while online a "vast network of 'fanboys'" shared beheading videos and poked fun at their enemies.[111]

In rare circumstances, terrorist groups keep records of not only their practices and policies but also their own recruits. These materials show both the diversity of membership and the logic that underpins it. In what researchers from West Point's Combating Terrorism Center (CTC) described as the largest Islamic State document cache available to the public, 4,600 unique personnel records revealed a "remarkably diverse population . . . arriving with diverse skills and experiences."[112] The average age of prospective fighters was twenty-six to twenty-seven when those records were completed.[113] Nearly two-thirds reported they were single, and nearly a third were married. Most respondents also indicated having at least a high school education, with a quarter reporting university or other postsecondary education. In contrast to Gambetta and Hertog's engineer finding, CTC Director Brian Dodwell and his colleagues found that low-skilled jobs comprised the biggest category for occupational experience among Islamic State recruits.[114]

However people become terrorists, we can't limit our focus to the "supply side" (potential recruits) at the expense of weighing up the "demand side" (the process through which groups recruit some people and not others). When we studied patterns in Provisional IRA recruitment, my colleague Paul Gill and I offered a reminder that "far more young men, who experienced the same socialization in Northern Ireland, did not join."[115] As we concluded in that study that it didn't really matter in the Irish context if one *wanted* to join the group if there was no opportunity to do so.[116] For that movement, social and familial bonds were most often the essential lubricants for recruitment and involvement.

DIVERSITY AS THE NEW PROFILE?

The demographic data reported across all these studies (and several dozen more I have not even mentioned) are important. If accurate, and reliably determined, such data on age, gender, and background offer impermeable truths. But we must be cautious in our interpretation. In his analysis of Australian jihadists, the terrorism researcher Rodger Shanahan found that of the mostly male sample, nearly half were married.[117] This supported the idea, Shanahan explained, that having a family attachment wouldn't sufficiently dissuade a person from engaging in terrorist activity. That important point certainly has implications for thinking about how to prevent people from getting involved in terrorism. Shanahan says the average Australian jihadi "is or has been married," though this accounts for only around half of his sample, so it is just as valid to say that the average Australian jihadi is *not* married. Fully contextualizing such data, and considering all available interpretations, is critical for us to appreciate both the contribution and limitations of such findings. The diversity across terrorist groups might indicate that different ideologies attract different people, and that some ideologies may be capable of attracting diverse people within them. Several studies conducted in the 1980s revealed that left-wing terror groups typically attracted members who were "better educated and better-off" relative to those attracted to extreme right-wing movements.[118] Yet within an extreme right-wing community, *further* variety is detectible. In contrast to earlier studies, Kathleen Blee found that most of her interviewees in the United States extreme right scene were well educated, with "the majority [holding] middle-class jobs . . . as occupational therapists, nurses, teachers, and librarians."[119] However, she describes a third of her sample as "living in economically precarious conditions—holding jobs as waitresses, lay ministers in tiny, nonaffiliated churches, or teachers in marginal private schools."[120]

Diversity *across* terror groups might signal how recruitment often just reflects time and place—local context, basically. Diversity *within* groups may also exist for several reasons. We saw earlier how age and role can be closely related. Thomas Strentz's analyses of American domestic terrorists in the 1960s and 1970s revealed followers were aged twenty to twenty-five while leadership figures were twenty-five to forty.[121] Leaders, Strentz said, had higher verbal skills and exhibited what he called a "strong personality."[122] But he also pointed to another category of member—people who had engaged in "years of criminal activity," perhaps "recruited from prison" and for whom "politics are peripheral."[123] Strentz emphasized the need to consider such groups as very diverse. Members rarely shared the same motives.[124] As with the Islamic State, some violent extremist groups accommodate diversity, whether through distinct involvement opportunities or simply through broad appeal. Reflecting on her experiences studying America's white power movement, the University of Chicago historian Kathleen Belew observed, "The white power movement is, in many ways, an incredibly diverse array of activists. . . . Its supporters represent a cross-section of American life: rich and poor and middle class; religious leaders and felons; men and women and children; people in cities and suburbs and rural areas."[125] Strentz said of right-wing terrorism more broadly, "These groups generally surface in times of economic and social change. They provide quick fix solutions to complex problems for the easily manipulated. Their self-proclaimed messiah, who is usually very intelligent and well spoken, has the answer to their problems." The typical right-wing violent extremist, he believed, was "people who have a limited education . . . and have experienced a social or economic failure. Their age ranges from teenagers to senior citizens."[126]

Without the right context in which to decipher demographic data, to say such diversity "presents challenges" is an understatement.[127] What do these differences really mean? On the one hand, the answer is easy. Different groups offer different types of appeal, so they might attract different types of people or people with different expectations around what involvement entails. In his examination of Colombian paramilitary groups, the researcher Francisco Gutiérrez-Sanín considers whether group *tactics* might hold different attractions for members—he illustrates this by noting that "the FARC [Revolutionary Armed Forces of Colombia] is much more intent on fighting than the AUC [United Self-Defences of Colombia], kidnaps much more, and massacres less."[128] On the other hand, it's a matter of scope. Some groups offer a very narrow, tailored appeal, thereby limiting their recruit pool. Others, however, derive their appeal by recognizing the value in attracting a deliberately diverse pool. Thus, attempting to extract a generic profile as a guide to navigating future trends would appear pointless. At the most we could say that the terrorist is *likely* to be a young man in his twenties. That's about it, and this is a stunning reminder of how at least that part of researchers Charles Russell and Bowman Miller's 1977 terrorist profile remains the same. For everything else, time, place and multiple additional layers of context will matter. But there is just one more thing to consider here—embracing the fact that terrorism is diverse, attracting relatively diverse people, which may obscure the existence of more fine-grain trends both within and across groups. These trends are related not to *who* people are but rather *how* they do what they do.

DISAGGREGATING FROM DIVERSITY

The sheer volume of studies in terrorism research can be overwhelming, especially when trying to address the central question posed by this chapter. One way forward here is to see the value in disaggregation—breaking up a particular phenomenon into its various subcomponents.[129] Let's consider an example. Paul Gill and colleagues' work on lone actor terrorists revealed how diversity and the emergence of patterns aren't mutually exclusive.[130] Most of their sample, again, was male, but their analysis of 119 lone actors revealed three distinct subgroups—extreme right-wing terrorists, single-issue terrorists (e.g., one issue related to specific, focused concerns about the environment, animal rights, or abortion), and Al-Qaeda–related terrorists. When disaggregated by ideology, interesting differences emerged. Al-Qaeda lone actors were more likely to be students and less likely to have a criminal history, and they tended to be on average ten years younger than the other types. They were also more likely to be living away from home when they, via online exposure, began to develop extremist beliefs.[131] Single-issue terrorists were more likely to be involved in a personal relationship, have children, and engage in dry-run operations to practice their intended attacks. More than half of the single-issue terrorists displayed some evidence of a history of mental illness.[132]

The mental illness finding as applied to this sample was striking, and more researchers offered additional perspectives on this issue. The Dutch researchers Jeanine de Roy van Zuijdewijn and Edwin Bakker found that 35 percent of their 120 lone actor sample showed signs of some mental health disorder.[133] Recognizing a World Health Organization statistic that approximately a quarter of the adult population in the European Union and neighboring countries experienced "at least one" mental disorder in the previous year, they cautioned that finding this trend among lone actor terrorists didn't really indicate anything unusual—it would be what one would expect, given its prevalence in the general population.[134] They further acknowledge what is broadly supported by hundreds of psychological research studies. Because of the stigma associated with mental health and treatment-seeking in general, the prevalence of mental health problems in the general population is, if anything, likely to be higher.[135]

Let's reflect on these issues for a moment. Knowing that such differences exist in what might appear to be an already very narrow group (or type of group) is important. Researchers caution against viewing terrorists (even in specific *cells*) as too similar and remind us of the inherent diversity associated with terrorism and terrorists. Furthermore, validating such differences via systematic research could provide anchor points for informing investigative practice; in the longer run such information could even help develop prevention efforts. Intrigued by the possibilities from disaggregating terrorist samples in this way, from 2014 to 2015, my colleagues at the University of Massachusetts, Lowell, and I decided to take a closer look at precisely who was getting involved in jihadist terrorism in, and from, the United States. Armed with thirty-five student interns and a 121-variable codebook, we compiled court documents, open-source news reports, and thousands of other sources of publicly available information. We were left with 183 cases of people convicted in the United States between 1995 and 2012 for activities associated with Al-Qaeda or its affiliates worldwide. In 2016, our study was published in the *Journal of Forensic Sciences*.[136]

The sample was mostly male. No surprises there. Most were married with children and were American citizens. The activities for which they were indicted and convicted revealed some variation. Most were indicted on an average of fourteen counts and subsequently convicted on five. The charge most were convicted of related to providing material support to a terrorist organization. So, at least for our study, most of those convicted for terrorist offenses were not actually involved in committing (or attempting) violent acts. We found marital status a good predictor of whether someone operated as part of a cell as opposed to operating alone (i.e., as a lone actor). Lone actors were also more likely to have been inspired by an Al-Qaeda affiliate, as opposed to cell-affiliated actors who sought direct contact (or believed they were in contact with) Al-Qaeda itself.

The findings were tantalizing. They hinted at the need for much finer-grain analysis of not only who becomes a terrorist but also what specific kinds of activity those people became (or wished to become) involved in.

In subsequent work, again with my Lowell colleagues Neil Shortland and Suzzette Abbasciano, we took an even closer look at our jihadist cohort.[137] We wanted to see if, just like Gill's studies of lone actors, detectible variation existed within our own sample. We found evidence to suggest the existence of three main clusters of behaviors to which we assigned distinct labels—actors, supporters, and facilitators.[138]

- *Actors* directly engaged in (or attempted) a terrorist attack. They may have built, placed, or detonated bombs. They may have attempted to obtain specific guidance on how to do so. This subgroup is probably what most often springs to mind when we think about terrorists. However, they represented only around 9 percent of our sample.
- *Supporters* engaged in peripheral behaviors, mostly fraudulent or generally criminal in nature. These people were responsible for actions such as preparing or possessing false documents or handling money for illicit purposes connected to the broader movement. Supporters were the dominant category, representing nearly 33 percent of the entire sample.
- *Facilitators*, as the name suggests, supported the efforts of those seeking to engage in terrorist attacks. They provided resources such as funds, knowledge, and connections. They comprised almost 16 percent of the sample.

We also designated a fourth category, *hybrid*. This group was admittedly messier because we couldn't identify a person's focus or designate an obvious role type. But the data we collected allowed us to further distinguish four subtypes: *actor-supporter*, *supporter-facilitator*, *actor-facilitator*, and *actor-supporter-facilitator*. This last category was an unusual one in which nearly 2 percent of our sample featured people who essentially looked like genuine "do-it-yourself" terrorists—they were involved in just about everything.

Inevitably, such studies have limitations. What we offer is not intended to be a definitive classification type. We know how easy it is to get carried away with raw percentages and broad categories—that a third of our sample fall into the "supporter" category doesn't necessarily mean that this reliably represents what terrorist activity in the United States looks like.

It might suggest that people who fall into this category are most likely (for whatever reasons) to be arrested, and thus, appear more representative than they really are. Also, given how rare terrorism is in the first place, the kind of disaggregation that we and others did in these types of studies might put so much stress on models and data that we must be wary of relying too much on neat types or labels; we certainly cautioned against all that in our work.[139] But, and this is really the most important lesson from that study, thinking about terrorist activity in this way—building an understanding of it from the bottom up, as opposed to from the top down, allows us to appreciate not just the diversity of who becomes involved in terrorism but *what they do* as terrorists. Thinking about terrorist behavior in this way means that perhaps we'd be better off asking who makes the bombs, versus who's in charge of recruiting, or fighting, or hiding the network's money.

Caution notwithstanding, thinking about the diversity of terrorism in this way is increasingly evident in the research today. Robin Simcox and Emily Dyer identified five roles associated with Al-Qaeda members convicted in the United States—*active participants, aspirants, facilitators, trained aspirants*, and *ideologues*.[140] The terrorism expert Audrey Alexander found three main distinctions in her work on female American jihadists.[141] *Plotters* were those attempting to either concoct or execute actual attacks on U.S. soil; *supporters* procured material or disseminated propaganda; and *travelers* journeyed or attempted to journey abroad to be directly involved in the movement.[142] As we argued in our own study of 183 jihadists convicted in the United States, typologies are beneficial if they are supported by the data. The distinctions certainly lead us to ask better questions: Can we really believe that what might motivate one person to build and detonate a bomb in a public place is the same, or even similar, to what might motivate (or limit) someone else to send twenty dollars to a charity connected to a terrorist group? That may be an unfair question. Perhaps it's not so much a challenge of figuring out why the facilitator doesn't plant a bomb but instead what limits that person from doing other activity. The motivation to "do something" might still be the same. What's different from one offender to another might have to do with individual circumstances, perceived incentives, and opportunity. But make no mistake, thinking about and using broad categories like "terrorist," "religious terrorist," "right-wing terrorist," and "left-wing terrorist" is far less illuminating and useful than thinking about what specifically people *do* as part of their expression of commitment to a cause, ideology, or movement.[143] Just like the word "criminal," "terrorist" is a useful shorthand description, but its limitations quickly become evident. At a minimum, as we concluded in our typology study, while we might not yet be able to distinguish the terrorist from the rest of the population, research studies like these might at least help us differentiate different types of terrorists from each other.[144]

Finally, arguing that terrorists are mostly young men, while simultaneously arguing that terrorists are diverse, seems contradictory. The demographic studies described here support a long-established idea in terrorism research—that terrorists are, on some levels, widely dissimilar. But understanding why those dissimilarities exist, and why individual level profiles (even aggregated) may change over time, is important. What does this relative diversity mean? On the one hand it means we ought to resist any attempt by now at sweeping generalizations even within and across terrorist groups, group types, and cohorts. Importantly, it doesn't mean that there aren't patterns to be found. Newer research highlighting roles and types of involvement demonstrates that even *within* what one might assume is a narrow *type* of terrorist, i.e., lone actors or jihadist attackers from the United States, that there was still diversity across demographics, relationship status, education, mental health, and preattack behaviors. Disaggregation of even the smallest of samples, it would seem, can reveal much.

CONCLUSIONS

For decades, psychologists, psychiatrists, criminologists, and many others have struggled with the idea of a terrorist profile. As terrorism captured imaginations in the 1970s, attempts to produce a profile flourished. These studies were not perfect—none are, even though our data quality

has improved, and our methods more sophisticated. But what those studies gave us were valuable starting points for thinking about the terrorist in
more systematic ways. Any profile must meaningfully answer at least two
questions—*who* becomes involved and *why*? As this chapter has addressed,
figuring out the *who* is the first step to answering the *why*. Whether we
read terrorists' accounts of their own behavior, or we interview them to ask
our own questions about them, we can also do something far more basic.
We can find and collect and analyze data on gender, age, family background and composition (e.g., does the person have siblings, what is the
birth order, and were any of those siblings also involved?), education level,
employment history, and prior criminality. This information is, with a little
effort, retrievable, and more important, it is *knowable*. This kind of data is
generally less prone to the whims of subjective interpretation than such
issues as the role played by trauma, mental illness, meaning or perception,
and how those fuel motivations—those are the more challenging puzzles
that lie ahead in the next two chapters. Yet despite the increased accessibility to demographic data, deciphering what it means is not as easy as
it might first seem. Context is everything. In my experiences of sharing
research with law enforcement practitioners, I used to deliver one bottom-
line, up-front message about terrorist psychology: terrorism is diverse.
We see different people, from different backgrounds, getting involved in
terrorism for what (at least initially) seems like different reasons. To make
matters worse, we find that even within the smallest of terrorist groups,
let alone across different types of group. The conclusion? I used to say
that there is no terrorist profile. Except I can say now, with hindsight, that
wasn't entirely accurate. There *are* terrorist profiles, technically speaking.
They just aren't very stable, have zero predictive ability, and unquestionably
mislead more than they guide. Is that just splitting hairs? Maybe, but
specificity matters. Thomas Strentz describes how any terrorist profile
must be seen in a historical context: "Terrorism is different today that it
was yesterday, and it will, like every dynamic organization, change again
by tomorrow."[145] In 1991, reflecting on studies of terrorists, the Israeli
psychologist Ariel Merari advised that terrorism's diversity doesn't per-
mit generalization.[146] To paraphrase the neurologist and terrorism expert

Jeff Victoroff, the demographic pendulum swings back and forth.[147] How therefore can we be expected to arrive at a terrorist profile that doesn't encompass variety and diversity?

There are hundreds of studies of terrorist groups. There are hundreds of studies of individual terrorists. We could just collapse all these findings to produce an overall profile. That might appeal to law enforcement or anyone else looking for a bottom-line finding. But it might also give us something so simplistic and vague that it renders the very idea of a profile moot—not necessarily a bad thing, on the face of it. But an overall terrorist profile thus far would probably be something like "mostly young men who become involved in terrorism in different ways and probably through a combination of different reasons." It may be equally accurate and unhelpful.

We could also organize findings by ideology or group type. Perhaps that might allow us to see if there are any differences between, say, those who join nationalist or extreme right-wing terror groups and those who join ecoterrorist groups. But that too might mislead more than illuminate, especially if we don't appreciate how even within specific groups, certain demographics match distinct roles or functions. Furthermore, lest we forget, these might change over time, even within the same group. It might just be inadvisable to compare groups like this at all. How can we draw a line between the Provisional IRA of 1972 and the Provisional IRA of 1994, or the Al-Qaeda of 1999 and the Al-Qaeda of 2023? Or how can we meaningfully compare those jihadists who flocked to Afghanistan in the 1990s to those who moved to Islamic State territory in the 2010s? Or, to narrow the focus even further, can we meaningfully compare (or collapse) the differences between urban versus rural fighters in the same movement? Merari was deeply critical of Russell and Miller's terrorist profile study. While he acknowledges that the study tried to be comprehensive, Merari says that the terrorists that were part of the study were not representative of either their own groups or terrorism in general and the whole study suffered from inherent sampling bias.[148] He explains that, for the most part, those terrorists were either arrested or had their identity revealed.[149] His concerns are merited, and one unfortunate takeaway from his criticism is that even the most ambitious and well-intentioned studies may still sustain what he called "common misconceptions in the field."[150] And yet it is pre-cisely because of such limitations that it is too easy to overlook what these early studies do contribute. Often forgotten from Russell and Miller's pro-file study was a recognition of how trends change because of operational needs. The constantly shifting, ever-drifting demographic profile of what the terrorist looks like is as much a function of how groups and movements make available different roles for different people.

Answering the question of who becomes a terrorist is challenging even within a specific terrorist group. Not all groups last very long. Those that do endure tend to be pretty good about changing up their membership demographics if it's needed to survive. Trying to find common threads across dozens of different terror groups (indeed, different *kinds* of groups), each of which recruits from a particular pool, each at different phases of their own progression, seems pointless. Any outcome would be so riddled with contradictions that even the idea of comparing different terror groups seems futile.

One final challenge before we conclude this chapter has to do with an undeniable feature of most of the current research—we study only those who end up as terrorists. The temptation to find out what they have in common might reveal something important, but as we have seen, any alleged revelations can just as easily mislead. What finding such similari-ties does *not* do, however, is explain what distinguishes them from those who do not become terrorists. As researcher Bart Schuurman reminds us, becoming involved in terrorism is an "unlikely outcome of radicalization processes."[151] It is widely accepted that very few people who are radicalized will go on to engage in violent action. To be able to distinguish those who go on to become terrorists from those who do not, we would have to know about those people exposed to the presumed generating conditions associ-ated with terrorism who chose to not become involved. On the surface of things, that seems impossible; if you wanted to get involved in terrorist activity but after some deliberation decided against it, would you reveal yourself? What would others think about you if you emerged as "almost" a terrorist? Given this problem, one might wonder to what extent any of the findings from the research we've examined in this chapter are reliable.

That seems unfair, and at the very least, we must be mindful of the limits of interpretation for the data we do have.

A valuable perspective on this might come from data on those who appear to be on the pathway to violent extremism but are diverted. In the United Kingdom, the Prevent program is a multiagency initiative aimed at supporting those deemed at risk of becoming involved in violent extremism. The program is a sort of early intervention, off-ramp initiative to figure out if someone is vulnerable "and whether a tailored package of support is necessary and proportionate to address [those] vulnerabilities."[152] Over a twelve-month period between 2018 and 2019, nearly six thousand people were referred to Prevent. Most of those referrals saw further action through intervention, whether in an educational, health, family, or other setting. Of relevance here, however, is that nearly 90 percent of the referrals were men, and most were twenty or younger. This trend was observed across cases involving more than one type of ideology; referrals related to concerns about Islamism, right-wing extremism, and what was termed a "mixed, unstable or unclear ideology."[153] Some cases referred to the program might be subject to further referral—they were classified as "Channel cases." Those cases involve tailoring a specific intervention to specifically address vulnerabilities that seem connected to the prospect of violent extremism, such as exposure to a particular environment (including online), group, message, or influential figure. Men also comprised most cases that warranted such interventions. Of course, there is no way of knowing just how many of these referrals would, if uninterrupted, have resulted in terrorism cases. But drawing on such cases allows us a further point of comparison as we continue to build our understanding. And with that in mind, let us now turn our attention to the *why* question: What motivates the terrorist?

3

MOTIVATION

In August 2019, Patrick Crusius posted this statement to the 8chan message board:

> In general, I support the Christchurch shooter and his manifesto. This attack is a response to the Hispanic invasion of Texas. They are the instigators, not me. I am simply defending my country from cultural and ethnic replacement brought on by an invasion. Some people will think this statement is hypocritical because of the nearly complete ethnic and cultural destruction brought to the Native Americans by our European ancestors, but this just reinforces my point. The natives didn't take the invasion of Europeans seriously, and now what's left is just a shadow of what was. My motives for this attack are not at all personal.

He then proceeded to murder twenty-three people in a Walmart in El Paso, Texas. Why did he do it? Is there a simple answer, one we'd all agree on? Would it necessarily be the *right* one? Without reading his statement any further, we can see what matters to him—or at least what he wants us to believe matters to him. He allies himself with the Christchurch attacker Brenton Tarrant, identifies a local enemy, and presents a grievance against Hispanics. Crusius admits executing the attack but also says he's not to blame for it—he takes ownership while shunning culpability. He portrays his actions as both defensive and necessary. He also characterizes his actions as urgent. A failure to act, he contends, would be catastrophic. From his perspective, he had sufficient reasons to do what he did. From our perspective, can we reduce his motivation to one specific issue? Or even one dominant or overriding factor? Again, without reading further, would saying "racism" be enough? Probably not, since plenty of people hold racist views and don't engage in mass murder. Crusius appears to be influenced by ideology, presented here in the form of self-defense against an aggressor while presenting himself as acting on behalf of an aggrieved community. The context to what he highlights lies in what he calls an invasion—one he feels has already begun. Yet does drawing attention to Tarrant reinforce ideology as the overriding motivational factor or might it suggest that Crusius desires the personal gratification in being recognized as someone influenced by the New Zealand attacker? As well, we shouldn't assume these options are mutually exclusive. Terrorist violence today is routinely associated with a conflagration of cascading and intertwined motives that are as difficult to disentangle as the act itself is to comprehend.[1] Today's terrorists are just as likely to be ideologically promiscuous, grasping and groping at whatever ideas, from wherever they may find them, suit their own grievances. Our haste in applying specific labels to them, or their actions, often reveals more about our need for cognitive closure than it illuminates the attacker's motivation. Finally, like many terrorists, Crusius felt compelled to justify his actions. Why do that? To terrify the Hispanic community? To inspire others to commit similar acts of violence? To feel understood? Whatever the motivation to deliver the statement, the effect may have been all three.

DECIPHERING MOTIVATION

In a 116-page report about the involvement of American jihadists in Syria and Iraq, the George Washington University's Program on Extremism devoted less than a single page to their motivations.[2] To be fair to these meticulous researchers, we know more about what *doesn't* explain terrorist motivation than about what does. Many factors drive people to engage in terrorist activity. It's not that we don't know what they are; we just have trouble figuring out if, how, or when some of those factors matter more than others. Even more challenging, we don't know why it is that though so many people are exposed to the conditions we think make terrorism more likely, so few engage in it. What makes *them* different? Of course, their engagement with terrorism is what ultimately sets them apart, but still, why so *few*? In the 2008 introduction to Peter Matthiessen's 1978 travel memoir, *The Snow Leopard*, the novelist Pico Iyer reflects on why someone would willingly leave behind family in search of adventure in the Himalaya:

> Hostage to the needs of the expedition, and putting the requirements of the group before his own, the traveler has to stay away even longer than imagined. . . . Most travelers are guilty of a kind of infidelity when they leave their homes and loved ones, their other lives, in order to undertake a long and perilous journey—and almost all of them . . . choose to keep out from their records the less exalted, human trade-off. We like to present ourselves as conquering heroes, or lone wolves taking on the world in all its terror; we will use any literary device we can to keep out of the text the ones waiting for us at home, or the truth of what is always an uneasy compromise.[3]

To compare mountaineers to foreign terrorist fighters might seem trivial, yet the shared challenge of interpreting motivation is clear. For his part, Iyer concludes that any meaningful dissection can only portray the traveler "in a highly unflattering light."[4]

Now that we have a sense of who becomes involved in terrorism, our goal for this chapter is to try to understand why terrorists do what they do. So where do we begin? Perhaps we should consider what terrorists have to say about themselves and others. We can start by reading personal accounts, statements, or manifestos issued by terrorist actors. We can also, in limited circumstances, ask terrorists directly why they do what they do. Sometimes, we can do both. The kind of answer we get might be influenced by a few different things—whether the author is expressing their own personal perspective or a statement has been issued on behalf of a group; whether an author is still in the group or is disengaged; or whether they are contrite or remain defiant even after departing the fight. Even if we come face to face with a cooperative interviewee, a former terrorist who is willing to talk to us, should we assume they are telling the truth about what they did and why? And even if, and when, they sincerely believe they're telling the truth, can it ever be a reliable picture of what motivated them to get involved? Can we ever know if the cause was really *the cause*? More to the point, how can we advance without suffocating under yet another avalanche of questions?

Some structure might help. In 2005, I proposed a way to think about involvement in terrorism. It hinged on the idea that initially getting involved in terrorism is a separate issue from the process that shapes how terrorist acts are committed. This argument was based on a conceptual distinction first made by the psychologist and terrorism expert Max Taylor in the 1980s.[5] I developed this idea further in 2014 in what I called the IED model of terrorist behavior—involvement, engagement, and disengagement.[6] To distinguish these issues, let's consider them as follows:

- *Involvement* is about understanding the motivation for wanting to get involved and take action
- *Engagement* is about understanding what factors allow that action to happen
- *Disengagement* is about understanding the motivation for stopping

Understanding involvement is about deciphering motivation. The engagement phase requires us to consider mindset. We'll examine mindset in the next chapter, but for now we need a temporary placeholder. The psychologist Gerard Saucier and colleagues define what they call the "militant-extremist mind-set" as basically the thinking patterns that shape the behavior of violent extremists.[7] I will use mostly the same meaning here, with some caveats. I will argue that the terrorist mindset is just as likely to be an emergent quality of involvement in terrorism as much as it is a precursor or, in Saucier's words, a "dispositional component"; in addition, from my perspective, the terrorist mindset is as much the product of engagement in particular behaviors (i.e., *doing* things) that reinforce commitment, as opposed to just increased radicalization per se (i.e., just *thinking* about things).

But let's go back to the motivation question for now. The differences between involvement, engagement, and disengagement will become clearer and much more detailed as we go, but the main point here is that these phases should be considered potentially distinct. What motivates someone to become involved in the first place isn't necessarily going to tell us anything revealing about why a specific act of terrorism takes place, how someone learns to take a life, or why they commit the act. Likewise, none of those phases is necessarily going to help us understand what leads someone to stop their involvement or disengage. It might, in theory, but we ought to treat them as distinct phases of involvement. When I proposed this initial framework, I said at the time that we should say there were at *least* three phases. We could add a *deradicalization* phase, which means that just as people can develop a commitment to radical beliefs, they can also find ways to think differently and unlearn that commitment. But while every terrorist disengages at some point (which for some comes at the moment of death), not all terrorists necessarily deradicalize. In other words, just because someone stops doing things doesn't necessarily mean they've changed their mind about what they once did. Many people walk away from terrorism while remaining deeply committed to the radical views and ideals that drove them to their initial involvement in the first place (or that they acquired once involved). Though we use different terminology, the importance of such distinctions was recognized by the psychologist and renowned terrorism expert Randy Borum in a 2011 review of the literature. He acknowledged the "importance of distinguishing between ideological radicalization and terrorism involvement."[8] He stressed the need to understand *action pathways*—what he calls the "scripts" that allow terrorist behavior to unfold.[9] Again, we see the critical need to distinguish *involvement* from *engagement*—or radicalization and action.

RADICALIZATION

On the surface, the factors that motivate someone to violent extremism seem diverse. Thinking about their American Islamic State cohort, the scholar Alexander Meleagrou-Hitchens and his colleagues state, "It is a mistake to assume that all travelers were drawn to Syria for the same reasons."[10] The study's authors find weak (or no) correlations between jihadist travel and such factors as economic variables, lack of integration, or perceived "marginalization."[11] That diversity of motivation might reflect the variety of personnel—the Islamic State attracted from what the author Graeme Wood called the "psychopaths and adventure seekers" to the "*very* Islamic."[12] In theory at least, as the researchers Gavin Bailey and Phil Edwards suggest, it is "driven by a potentially infinite range of motives, encompassing all political outlooks, and made up by individuals, groups, societies and states."[13]

One basic way to think about motivation is that what drives a terrorist to action may be a combination of both public and private reasons. The public reasons are often the big-picture ones that are easily found in terrorist statements—they tell us about their grievances, their cause, and their ideology. We can learn their views on why they rationalize and justify to themselves and to us why they do what they do. Patrick Crusius, in his posted message, *wants* to tell us about his grievance, and he *wants* to be seen as inspired by Brenton Tarrant and his ideas; both attackers framed their respective actions within a broader ideological story—one where, again, they want us to believe they are acting in defense of a way of life that is under threat unless immediate action is taken. As briefly noted in the opening chapter, ideologies are basically organized belief systems that seek to guide behavior. They help people make sense of their actions and help them justify to themselves and others why they're doing what they're doing. Terrorists' own accounts of their involvement are often framed in terms of their moral outrage that, in the eyes of the believer, spurs on a need for action. Colleen LaRose, an American otherwise known as "Jihad Jane," offered the following:

> I was watching videos on YouTube. . . . The thing that had an effect on me was the brutality I was seeing against the Muslims. I would get upset. The blood and the bodies and the children. The day that I was watching the Zionists bombing the Palestinians, you could hear the children screaming and crying and all the women and the brothers. At the same time I was watching this on the internet, outside my window I could hear kids playing and laughing in the streets. And I was thinking to myself, Nobody knows what's going on.[14]

We find echoes of this theme throughout accounts worldwide. The social psychology professor Mauricio Florez-Morris interviewed many former violent extremists in Colombia.[15] When asked, "What were your motives for entering a guerrilla movement?" one interviewee said, "I had always been very sensitive to social issues. I was moved by the existence of street urchins, poverty and begging. I asked myself why these things were happening, why people were in this situation. And when I learned that I could do something about it, I did."[16] In Italy, the author Alison Jamieson spent years researching the Red Brigades, a far-left terror group.[17] She describes the typical Brigadist as "a person whose ideas are meticulously worked out through careful analysis and serious reflection, for whom everything is seen in terms of politics, someone who above all is 'well-prepared.'"

Accounts like these suggest initial involvement in terrorism resembles a carefully thought-out course of action. Reacting to a sense of unfairness, and yearning for a better life, are common themes throughout the history of revolutions.[18] These themes recur in accounts offered by people who engage in terrorism—*seeing* injustice, *feeling* outrage, and *wanting to do something* about it. Action is key—not wanting to just talk about doing something. A young Finnish convert to Islam who became a propaganda disseminator for the Islamic State explained it this way: "What drew me in was actually doing something, explaining stuff. You disseminate that propaganda, so it makes you feel part of something bigger."[19]

Exposure to the sources of injustice can happen in many ways. Ciaran Cassidy, a filmmaker whose documentary *The Echo Chamber: The Story of Jihad Jane* examined the history of the infamous convert, concluded that the role of religion was likely overstated at least in the case of his subject. Instead, Cassidy argues, the explanation has more to do with "people . . . spending eight or nine hours a day on computers."[20] The increasing role of the Internet in facilitating radicalization is now widely recognized. In a study of extremist offenders in the United Kingdom whose activities occurred between 2005 and 2017, the Internet played an increased role in the radicalization process over that time, reflecting, unsurprisingly, an increase in self-reported Internet use in general.[21] In fact, terrorism researchers rarely talk about the Internet in general; rather, they discuss how specific platforms appeal to, and are exploited by, extremists of all types. In late 2021, the researcher Ciarán O'Connor from the Institute for Strategic Dialogue released research that the social media platform TikTok was widely used to "promote white supremacist conspiracy theories, produce weapons manufacturing advice, glorify extremists, terrorists, fascists and dictators, direct targeted harassment against minorities and produce content that denies violent events like genocides ever happened."[22] Starting in 2014, the Islamic State recorded a series of sadistic and theatrical murders of prisoners under their control. They went from beheading individuals to beheading several people at the same time. They filmed their operatives throwing gay men off buildings to their deaths, and filmed children killing prisoners. Shortly after a Jordanian fighter pilot was captured inside Islamic State–held territory in January 2015, the movement asked its online followers to suggest ways in which he could be killed. Their effort to crowdsource ideas for the manner of his execution resulted in the pilot being burned to death.

Sometimes, people who become involved in terrorism find their way to it by initial exposure to terrorist propaganda. The Australian researcher

Rodger Shanahan found that his 179 Australian jihadists "consumed enormous amounts of social media featuring Australian and foreign preachers, general Islamic subjects and jihadist propaganda put out by Islamic State and other jihadist groups."[23] Knowing what recruits seek out and consume is important. Terrorism expert Donald Holbrook's research on material recovered in police investigations of Islamist terrorists stemmed from a desire to get researchers to refocus attention onto what prospective recruits want, and engage with, rather than assuming what we think they are motivated by from material produced by others. Holbrook's sample was also notable because it concerned people thought to be in the advanced stages of plotting or who had already conducted successful acts of terrorism. He found that those terrorists consumed a broad range of ideological material, with no groups or organizations particularly dominating the content. In particular, he found that the material consumed was more emotional in nature than strategic.[24] Strategic figures, often considered to be far more influential, were absent. Holbrook emphasizes that this doesn't mean they are irrelevant, but that the preferences of prospective recruits were different than those held by leadership figures, whose priorities often lay in developing strategy.[25]

Scholars of jihadi studies will argue incessantly about the finer points of obscure ideological differences between Islamic scholars. Worthy it may be, but these studies offer little about the *meaning* of such material for individual prospects or recruits. Understanding their preferences, and the unique appeal of certain ideological or historical figures, matters for our purposes in building an understanding of motivation. The Norwegian expert Thomas Hegghammer reflects on just how and why the jihadist ideologue (and mentor to Osama bin Laden) Abdallah Azzam (whose influence on Donald Holbrook's sample was evident) seemed to hold such wide popularity among jihadists worldwide. He argues that "the content of [Azzam's] message lent itself to being a common denominator across groups with different agendas. Azzam spoke about things that were relevant to many militant groups, such as the obligation to fight and the value of martyrdom, all the while staying vague on the practical application of these injunctions."[26] On Azzam's enduring impact and legacy, Hegghammer concludes,

"This combination of relevance and vagueness made Azzam appeal to many and offend few."[27]

Brenton Tarrant's attacks on the Christchurch mosques were influenced by the "Great Replacement" conspiracy theory, which urges believers to accept the notion that white people are on the verge of extinction. As the UK-based researchers Jacob Davey and Julia Ebner note, such beliefs are not new, but a resurgence in popularity in recent years has seen this fringe theory enter the mainstream consciousness. It has, in their words, provided "the ideological glue which ties together an increasingly cohesive, networked and transnational extreme-right."[28] Ideologies are designed, and refined, for widespread appeal. Yet far more is known about their content than how they exert influence. Despite the popularity of conspiracy theories, however, we are not all equally susceptible to them. And it's not so much a question of *who* is vulnerable to conspiracy theories or ideologies but *when* we are more likely to embrace them. So far, there isn't very clear research on the link between personality factors and susceptibility to conspiracy, but research points to personal distress as a major risk factor for when we are more likely to be open to such views.[29] That susceptibility is further compounded by anxiety, alienation, and reduced inquisitiveness—these can lead people to embrace "spurious but confidently held causal narratives that account for one's distress and resentment."[30]

But even exposure to ideologies, ideas, or beliefs is not sufficient to explain why people would engage in violent acts. If the reasons terrorists give for their motivations are accurate, exponentially more people would engage in violent extremist acts. The psychologists Clark McCauley and Sophia Moskalenko illustrate this by pointing out that while around 5 percent of Muslims surveyed in the United States and the United Kingdom justify the practice of suicide bombing aimed against civilians but "in defense of Islam," they note that "only hundreds of Muslims have been charged for planned or attempted violent action in either country."[31] Thus, they conclude, most Muslims with radical ideas will never commit violent acts.

So much for finding clear answers in the public reasons. Identifying private reasons may give us a more complete picture. But these reasons, by definition, tend to be a little more difficult to access, in part because terrorist actors rarely offer them. It's understandable that someone would want their actions to be considered in big-picture terms—*righteous anger, moral outrage at some injustice, responding to a sense of duty to fight for a noble cause.* It makes the terrorist feel significant, the struggle noble, and the sacrifice worthwhile. Private reasons include factors like wanting recognition or notoriety, wanting to belong to something, wanting to get away from something *else*, wanting to feel important, wanting a sense of purpose, and longing for the camaraderie, excitement, and the status that this newfound sense of mission involves. These qualities rarely bubble to the surface of accounts of involvement in terrorism. Does the experience of enjoying the journey in some way detract from its perceived nobility? Did Patrick Crusius *admire* Brenton Tarrant? Did Crusius want Tarrant to know the influence he had on him? Was Crusius's attack inspired by Tarrant's massacre, or did Tarrant's actions simply accelerate what Crusius had already planned? Crusius wants us to accept that his motivation is fueled by broader "political and economic reasons" that are "not at all personal." He presents his actions as a burden, a duty to be fulfilled despite the cost. We hear echoes of this in the author Graeme Wood's reflections on those who joined the Islamic State: "They believe that they are personally involved in struggles beyond their own lives, and that merely to be swept up in the drama, on the side of righteousness, is a privilege and a pleasure—especially when it is also a burden."[32]

RADICAL THOUGHT TO VIOLENT ACTION

How thought progresses to actual violence is unclear. It's easier to identify a long list of factors relevant to someone's biographical account than to figure out how any or all of them work for any one person, at any one point in time, during their labyrinthine journey into violent extremism. Randy Borum suggests that understanding why people get into terrorism will force us to see that "different pathways and mechanisms operate in different ways for different people at different points in time and perhaps in different contexts."[33] In other words, it's complicated. Certainly, highlighting one factor (e.g., ideology, the role of religion, grievance, or moral outrage) can give the impression that others don't matter as much or at all. There's such disagreement around how to even talk about this issue that fresh calls to "rethink" radicalization appear every few years before we've barely tested whether any particular model or theory might hold real-world promise.[34] Even the most specific and well-intentioned of words here can betray multiple meanings. When we read about people becoming involved in terrorism, we often hear the phrase "vulnerability," suggesting that a person can be receptive or susceptible to radicalization. But the criminologists Noémie Bouhana and Per-Olof Wikström explain that we can think about this in two distinct ways: susceptibility in terms of "moral and cognitive vulnerability," and exposure to "radicalizing settings."[35] In other words, it's not just *what* you might be susceptible to (and *why*), but *when* and *where* you may find yourself at risk.

In case you were wondering, there is no shortage of intriguing, intuitively attractive theories to help try to understand all this. To highlight all of them would be pointless or, at a minimum, a very different kind of book. To single out just one would be unfair. They are all, to greater or lesser degrees, helpful. I always tell my students that even the "not so good" theories are valuable if they lead us to ask better questions. Some theories are *very* elaborate, capturing the complexity of terrorism so well that they simultaneously scare away readers. Other theories are more parsimonious. They, however, run the risk of oversimplifying a process of whose precise contours and qualities we admittedly only have partial knowledge. Some theories are more like models or frameworks, while others are more like analogies and metaphors. Georgetown University's Fathali Moghaddam characterized radicalization as like walking up a staircase, each step moving the person closer to accepting and embracing terrorist acts.[36] McCauley and Moskalenko developed a similar model using a pyramid rather than a staircase.[37] They describe several core qualities for understanding how a person radicalizes. In subsequent work, they distinguished radicalization of *action* from radicalization of *belief*, and proposed a new, two-pyramid model.[38] As with trying to understand any human endeavor, different theories shed light on the subject or obscure more than they illuminate. A key takeaway here is acknowledging that, in Borum's words, "drawing upon existing social science theories might help researchers to ask better, more focused questions."[39] Let's bear that in mind when thinking about what different models of radicalization offer.

In a comprehensive review of the literature, the Italian author and terrorism researcher Alessandro Orsini recommended we view radicalization as a sort of *resocialization* process.[40] The idea here is that some people are, under certain conditions, highly motivated to seek out a particular type of group. So why would this happen? The social psychologist Michael Hogg provides an answer.[41] He says uncertainty about oneself motivates us to seek out groups that offer solace—in particular, groups that have a highly distinctive identity with explicit guidance on what to do and when. Uncertainty is an uncomfortable state, and so we do what we can to avoid feeling it. Critically, Hogg adds, not all groups are uniformly adept in decreasing uncertainty for their followers.[42] Those that are effective "are associated with distinctive, unambiguous, clearly defined, and tightly shared prototypes."[43] Because of this, he argues, when we experience uncertainty, we are drawn to things that increase our feeling of certainty.[44] Hogg's theory is supported via multiple studies. The dynamics on which his theory rests find strong validation in rigorously controlled experimental settings[45] as well as large-scale surveys.[46] Striving to reduce uncertainty isn't necessarily going to explain the emergence of terrorist acts, but it surely may go some way toward helping us understand why some people drift toward violent extremist ideologies and the groups that practice them.

Major reviews of radicalization research were conducted by both the neurologist Jeff Victoroff and Randy Borum, who have studied terrorist behavior for many years.[47] Victoroff concedes, however, that reliable psychological data points tend to be even more difficult to come by than the easier-to-find (and validate) socioeconomic data.[48] Consequently, he says, we're left with little more than vague impressions of who terrorists are and what might be motivating them. Ironically, he says, this is at least in part because the better psychological studies that exist "present a major challenge to some psychology theories of terrorism simply by recognizing heterogeneous psychological categories among terrorists."[49] In other words, we don't have a clear sense of terrorist lives because most theories of terrorist behavior do not appreciate the complexity, which is to say the *reality*, of terrorist lives.

Victoroff's review has become required reading for terrorism researchers. He systematically reviewed a wide range of psychological and sociological theories, across both individual and group levels, teasing out their respective applicability to understanding the terrorists. All of them, he argued, offer some intuitive validity. They encourage us to appreciate some specific aspect of terrorist behavior. Yet, paradoxically, each theory is easily challenged by pointing to a different element or quality of how terrorist lives function. For example, theories about terrorists as psychopaths might on first impression make sense—after all, terrorists frequently engage in brutal physical violence without expressing remorse for their actions. The French jihadist Amedy Coulibaly killed four Jewish hostages in a Paris supermarket in 2015. He had earlier been the subject of a psychological assessment that described "immature and psychopathic personality traits."[50] We can always find such impressions from individual cases—they seem to offer intuitive sense despite the danger of isolating specific features as indicative of something broader. Psychopathic tendencies would seem to be a useful prerequisite for life as a terrorist. At the same time, to be an effective terrorist, and an inspiration to others, is to have the capacity to sacrifice oneself for a cause, or one's comrades—qualities very much at odds with psychopathic behavior.

The challenges of reliably uncovering the radicalization process are many but can perhaps best be summed up with reference to two technical concepts—*equifinality* and *multifinality*. Two child development researchers, Candice Feiring and Michael Lewis, in 1987, defined these ideas.[51] Equifinality means that a particular result, or outcome, can be arrived at from an array of differential potential pathways, whereas multifinality means that "similar initial conditions" might culminate in a diverse array of outcomes.[52] Randy Borum, as well as Emily Corner and colleagues, bring these ideas to the study of terrorism.[53] To illustrate, engagement in terrorism can be reached from many different pathways (i.e., equifinality), while exposure to the same structural conditions that we believe make terrorism more likely can in fact lead to very different outcomes (i.e., multifinality)— usually with only very few engaging in acts of terrorism.

METHODOLOGY

It is easy to get so bogged down in the complexity of these issues that we lose sight of how to arrive at anything concrete. So, let's reconsider some of the key questions for a moment. Thinking about terrorist motivation, one challenge is to figure out what terrorists have in common. A different challenge is to figure out whether those characteristics or common themes or pathways to involvement distinguish terrorists from nonterrorists. The broad consensus is that little distinguishes terrorists from nonterrorists. But, strictly speaking, that remains a hypothesis. To substantiate any claims to the contrary, and move beyond mere impressionistic findings, we would need to investigate these issues across big samples using control groups. Although not impossible, it requires special access to people and records, a point we'll return to in more detail in a later chapter. So far, few researchers have been able to accomplish this.

In a study of terrorists in Northern Ireland, the psychiatrists H. A. Lyons and Helen Harbison examined cases of 106 people charged with murder between 1974 and 1984.[54] Forty-seven killed on behalf of a terrorist group, and fifty-nine killed for nonideological reasons.[55] The main difference between the two samples was one of stability. They found the average terrorist to be not only well-adjusted but far less likely than ordinary murderers to be under the influence of alcohol or drugs and to have virtually no evidence of mental or psychological disorders. The opposite was true of ordinary murderers. Most of the time, the terrorist murderers didn't know their victims, while the nonterrorist murderers often did. There were other differences. Within the political murderers, the researchers identified a special subgroup. These people, they noted, were not established members of the terrorist group but were "operating on the fringe . . . [and] were devoid of discipline. They killed in a most sadistic way while heavily intoxicated. This small group was by no means typical of the rest."[56] That group also contained three people who used a knife to commit their murders, a weapon that, in the context of political murder, was a highly unusual method.[57] Shootings and bomb attacks were far more common in Provisional IRA political killings.

As in all research samples, there was bias. The subjects were, of course, caught, so they were probably more broadly unrepresentative of both terrorists and nonterrorist murderers. But the researchers also point out that their subjects came to their attention only because they were referred for psychiatric assessment; those not referred to them for assessment were probably more stable. An especially valuable feature of the Lyons and Harbison study was that they only included the offenders who explicitly engaged in violent acts as opposed to those found guilty of, for example, driving the getaway car.[58]

Using a valid comparison group is key. If properly employed, studies may be able to identify possibly key distinguishing features of terrorist offenders. Such features, if they exist, may hold clues to what might differentiate the terrorist offender from others. Studies may also potentially be able to tell us whether certain personality types are attracted to certain types of terrorism or if psychological disorder plays some or any role in these processes. The criminologist and terrorism researcher Joshua Freilich and colleagues studied homicidal lone actors acting on behalf of extreme right-wing groups.[59] They compared those unaffiliated actors to members of extreme right-wing groups who also committed murders. The researchers found that "far-right loners were more likely than group-affiliated extremist perpetrators to have had a history of mental illness."[60] This valuable study illustrated how only through rigorous research methods can such differences be verified and validated.

Emily Corner and colleagues conducted a systematic review of the literature on the links between psychopathy, personality disorders, and terrorism, concluding that extremely little research supports the view that psychopathy fuels terrorism.[61] In another systematic review published at the same time, the terrorism expert Paul Gill and colleagues found that studies with access to law enforcement files or other sensitive data typically present greater evidence for mental disorder diagnoses than studies relying solely on open-source information.[62] The key differentiating factor, they argue, is that mental health problems in violent extremists are more easily detectable when "research teams are in proximity to their subjects, using standardized measures and/or have access to privileged closed-sources."[63]

As always, though, rigorous methods require meaningful questions. The Canadian sociologist Lorne Dawson cautioned that for us to know more about this relationship "more systematic, methodologically exacting, and enterprising comparative research is required."[64] And as Emory University's Shauna Bowes stated, "Personality tests are not very good measures of things we don't understand very well."[65] We see the same principle throughout terrorism studies with poor questions constantly threatening to seduce us down dead ends. For example, consider the question from Marc Sageman, a psychiatrist: "What leads a person to turn to political violence?" Alex Schmid, a terrorism expert, alleges that "in its general formulation . . . [it] is as unanswerable as the question 'What leads a person to turn to crime?'" Schmid continues, "There are many types of crime (e.g., crimes of need, crimes of greed, crimes of passion, etc.) and for some forms of crime criminologists are closer to an answer than for others."[66] The sociologist Kathleen Blee described in her interviews with American right-wing racists that "typical interviews and questionnaires yield information in such a way that makes it impossible to disentangle cause and effect."[67] She offers the following example: "Women racial activists often identify their boyfriends or husbands as being part of the racial movement, reinforcing the perception that women are recruited into racist groups as the girlfriends or wives of male activists. But it is equally plausible that intimate relationships between women and men racist activists are formed within the racist movement; that is, that women form ties to those who have beliefs and ideas similar to their own."[68]

RECRUITERS

As we saw in the previous chapter, roles matter. For our work in this chapter, they matter in terms of how expectations about a particular role might motivate one recruit and not another. They also matter because they turn our focus to what function the movement or key personnel—recruiters—play in the channeling of mere radicalization (i.e., attitudes, thoughts, and beliefs) into engagement (i.e., action). It is well established now that the Islamic State movement sought input from recruits on their preferences across *at least* three distinct roles—fighter, suicide bomber, or suicide "fighter" (in this high-risk activity, there was no expectation of return, as opposed to the more traditional action of simply walking or driving a device toward a target and detonating it from a safe distance).[69] The existence of this system is not to say the recruit necessarily gets to have that role, or that even when they choose the role, it is of their own volition. There is evidence from former Islamic State fighters that despite indicating their preferences, the decisions of their superiors ultimately determined what role was to be fulfilled.[70] But the point here is that, inevitably, if we want a fuller picture of how people come to be involved in terrorism, we have to look beyond just *them*. We must consider the process and mechanisms through which recruits are enabled. Some of this has to do with achieving a fuller picture of how ideology shapes behavior, and some of it will entail looking at the role played by others in helping new recruits make sense of what they are about to embark upon. Doing this sheds light on critical organizational functions within terrorist movements—especially the neglected role of individual recruiters. For our immediate purposes here, though, it will help distinguish radicalization from mobilization, the idea of becoming involved opposed to actually engaging in terrorist acts. Or, even more simply, in the words of the Canadian Security Intelligence Service, how people go from "talkers" to "walkers."[71]

Nate Rosenblatt studied Islamic State recruitment hubs in Tunisia for his doctorate.[72] He found that a major pathway into the movement was via interpersonal networks that drew in groups of friends and family members. Such networks both attracted and retained recruits "until they were fully indoctrinated."[73] Those recruiters had a specific job: they "deliberately re-shaped [the recruit's] personal network to surround him with like-minded members of the group, reinforcing their beliefs and practices to such an extent that their radicalization seemed normal."[74] In fact, so effective were such efforts, Rosenblatt found, that most of the approximately three thousand Tunisian foreign fighters in question were recruited by no more than about thirty recruiters.[75] In this sense, what we might consider vulnerability to recruitment is for some about being in the right place at the right time (from a recruiter's perspective) as it is about susceptibility to moral change (the distinction made by the criminologists Noémie Bouhana and Per-Olof Wikström) and the broader process of radicalization.[76]

The strategies employed by recruiters are often highly focused, deliberate, and very patient. A Dutch intelligence report from 2002 describes how local efforts by recruiters attempted to mobilize young men into jihadist groups through similar localized, bottom-up strategies: "The recruitment process is a long process, that starts with making and intensifying the contact, in which the relation starts to look more and more like a recruiter-recruit relationship."[77] In Tunisia, Islamic State recruiters followed a strategy that proved effective time and time again. As Nate Rosenblatt explains, "A recruiter would pick a target, collect information about that person, approach them at a particularly vulnerable moment in that person's life. Once they initiated contact, they would adapt their pitch to perfectly fit the target's concerns, making an appeal that, for some, felt almost impossible to resist."[78] Here, as well as in the Netherlands, such recruitment opportunities, these specific moments, were often so banal as to simply reflect times when young men were bored: "They had nowhere to go and nothing else to do but to listen to these recruiters. Weekdays in local cafes are filled with young men with few job prospects."[79]

Mauricio Florez-Morris's interviewees suggest similar dynamics at play in Colombia. According to one recruit, "I did not know that I was being recruited by the M-19 but I knew that I was with a group of people very motivated to do things."[80] Blee's research illustrates how studying recruitment reveals the existence of multiple pathways even within the same cohort. Of the thirty-four violent female racist respondents in her study, thirteen "were recruited . . . by friends or acquaintances (such as fellow "bikers"); another 10 were convinced to join by parents, siblings, cousins, or children. Three were recruited through a husband or boyfriend. Only 8 (less than one-quarter) sought out contact with the racist movement themselves, on the basis of prior ideological conviction."[81]

Gender has long been a key issue in recruitment, though as is clear from the previous chapter, the "public view on the agency of women has been neglected or marginalized."[82] Accounts of motivation vary not just because of this inherent neglect but can vary by gender because of recruiter techniques. The British psychologists Karen Jacques and Paul Taylor compared biographical accounts of thirty male suicide attackers and thirty female suicide attackers in Palestinian groups.[83] Their analysis revealed male accounts to be characterized by ideological themes, whereas female accounts were characterized in more personal terms, involving a desire for personal revenge. Female suicide attackers were more likely than men to be recruited through exploitation and peer influence. By illustrating these patterns, Jacques and Taylor not only showed how motivation can be constructed in different ways but also why the idea of women as subservient pawns for male actors is both simplistic and misleading. They conclude, "It suggests either that different forms of recruitment evoke particular motivations in those who are exposed to them, or that extremist groups are sensitive to the motivational vulnerabilities of those that they attempt to recruit, and that they adapt their recruitment accordingly."[84]

Little is known so far about the qualities sought in potential recruits, but there is evidence to suggest that recruiters intuitively know what makes a good recruit. The terrorism expert Ayla Schbley recalls the case of Abul Nasser Issa, a Hamas recruiter, featured in an MSNBC documentary on suicide bombers. Interviewed in prison, Issa was asked, "How do you know who is qualified to become a shaheed [a Muslim martyr, or more specifically in this context, a suicide bomber]?" He responded, "A shaheed has to have the motivation to become a martyr, to have faith. It is an ideological, religious, and also patriotic motivation, because this kind of a job requires a strong will and persistence."[85] Schbley also says Hezbollah had specific committees that even included psychologists who would review each individual applicant as part of the selection process.[86] In Northern Ireland, a senior terrorist commander offered me much the same perspective on how he selected people for jobs: "I can tell, you can just sense it. . . . You can see it in a guy's eyes. You can see it in their heart, you can feel it in them."[87] Thomas Hegghammer found that recruiters for Al-Qaeda in Saudi Arabia became attuned to certain predictors of success in recruits—piety alone was insufficient because it was a quality shared by many religious Saudis and could be faked.[88] Instead, the recruiters defaulted to whether the prospect had any prior experience of traveling abroad in the name of jihad.

Offering advice to Americans on how to "Start and Run a Militia," the website *Militia News* cautions, "Recruit good people. No one wants to hang around people who are egotistical, self-centered, dishonest, immature, lazy, or inconsiderate. If you or someone in your group has one or more of these traits, you must fix the problem, or else membership will decline."[89] The influence of a recruiter shouldn't lead us to assume recruits are duped or brainwashed. It can be tempting to believe that recruiters hold the power to sell seductive narratives to naive followers. In many cases, the effectiveness of the recruiter is to simply facilitate motivation by providing an opportunity, a critical connection, information about how to safely cover one's travel tracks, or just the right nudge at the right time. Despite what research they may do in advance, or what training materials or propaganda they consume, recruits will have their own ideas about what involvement may entail. Though all will acknowledge some level of risk, some may be more willing to entertain the prospect of an early death than others. Speaking about Islamic State recruits, the researcher Tyler Evans and colleagues conclude, "Still, a chance to live out this fantasy for a short time might nonetheless have seemed irresistible—particularly for Western recruits looking to escape the weight of perceived subordination and marginalization in their home country."[90] And we should not overlook the fact that sometimes recruits find the benefits of involvement to be far more rewarding than anticipated. On a certain level, involvement in terrorism is, as Victoroff says, "indisputably thrilling."[91] Sometimes the fantasy and the reality match. On joining the Afghan Taliban, the American John Walker Lindh admitted, "It is exactly as I thought it would be."[92] Speaking of his time in Palestine's Zionist anti-British extremist group, the Stern Gang, Yitzhak Shamir famously recalled, "That period in the underground was the best part of my life."[93] When the Islamic State propagandist Yahya Abu Hassan (otherwise known as John Georgelas) sent his family away so he could "pursue his dreams unencumbered by a wife and children," he was said to feel "liberated"—it was the "best day of his life."[94] Anna Morgan-Lloyd, who took part in the January 6, 2021, attack on the U.S. Capitol Building, told a friend who joined her at the event, "That was the most exciting day of my life."[95] The Proud Boys leader Ethan Nordean expressed a similar sentiment: "Violence isn't great . . . but justified violence is amazing."[96]

DOES MOTIVATION MATTER?

In his masterful review of the psychological literature on terrorists, Victoroff acknowledges that terrorists may be "psychologically extremely heterogeneous. Whatever his stated goals and group of identity, every terrorist, like every person, is motivated by his own complex of psychosocial experiences and traits."[97] He suggests that four traits may characterize the terrorist:

- High affective valence [whether something is perceived as good or bad] regarding an ideological issue
- A personal stake—such as strongly perceived oppression, humiliation, or persecution; an extraordinary need for identity, glory, or vengeance; or a drive for expression of intrinsic aggressivity—that distinguishes him or her from the vast majority of those who fulfill characteristic a [i.e., high affective valence]
- Low cognitive flexibility, low tolerance for ambiguity, and elevated tendency toward attribution error [a bias in thinking that, for example, might explain one's own behavior in one way but others' behavior in very different ways]
- A capacity to suppress both instinctive and learned moral constraints against harming innocents, whether due to intrinsic or acquired factors, individual or group forces—probably influenced by [the first three factors][98]

Victoroff considers all these issues avenues for future research. For his part, Randy Borum, after synthesizing several theoretical frameworks in the context of available data on terrorism, argues that most models of violent extremism address three factors:

- Developing antipathy toward a target group
- Creating justifications and mandates for violent action
- Eliminating social and psychological barriers that might inhibit violent action[99]

Identifying these factors is important. That we have difficulty establishing how they relate to one another is a different challenge. Victoroff chooses his words carefully, and he's right to do so. Saying that these traits "characterize" the terrorist doesn't quite distinguish whether these qualities of potential recruits are preexisting or are instead the product of learned experiences. Here's what it means for understanding motivation for now: Incomplete knowledge means we are unlikely to have satisfactory answers to hand, and that is likely the case for the foreseeable future. Alternatively, even if we had better data, would it automatically mean we could better interpret the fuzzy processes associated with motivation? Maybe. We just can't hide behind the "more research is needed" defense for every question here.

And yet even for the most dedicated student of terrorism, it is always a challenge to offer what the researcher considers a comprehensive review on topics addressing motivation. The most earnest reviews are still subject to what Corner and her colleagues acknowledge as bias and incompleteness.[100] Perhaps we might be better served by considering different questions, ones we can address while continuing along on our longer research journey. And yet, that might be seen as just another cop-out. We can't keep saying that everything is complex and expect others to uncritically accept this reality. On one level, motivation of course matters—identifying the various push and pull factors that drive radicalization, and radicalization to action, is important. Identifying these factors sensitizes us to the role of grievance. It makes us pay attention to how those grievances emerge and how they are sustained. Understanding why and how certain groups appeal to prospective recruits has implications for preventative interventions;

there is knowledge to be gained here which could be used to curb that appeal and warn the public about the strategies used by groups to radicalize and recruit. So, in a very basic sense, knowing about motivation matters. Bjørn Ihler, the Norwegian peace activist who survived the 2011 mass shooting by Anders Brievik, reflected on this, saying: "Although it is inherently irrational and impossible to make sense of something so senseless it still matters to know why the perpetrator did what they did and justified it to themselves even if I know it makes no actual sense to most others."[101] These factors are important in a policy context regarding the setting of strategic objectives and resource allocation. They also matter in an investigative context for such issues as disrupting networks, designing and conducting interrogations, and attempting to undermine or curb the appeal of involvement in the first place. For instance, Blee's sociological research on violent right-wing racists found some interesting differences between male and female group members. In contrast to the "swagger" found in male accounts, women describe participation "as a burden, an onerous responsibility, an unwanted obligation."[102] Some members said that such a burden was the reason they would *not* encourage others to join (a stark contrast to the accounts presented in earlier chapters by some jihadists).[103] Knowing about such issues and the ways in which they play out in radicalization and recruitment can, as just described, have profound implications for dampening enthusiasm for those motivated to join in the first place. Perhaps, we can at least agree that deciphering motivation is at least for now a matter of interpretation. We might benefit from Stephen King's advice to not waste time "trying to read between the lines, and don't look for a throughline. There are *no* lines—only snapshots, most out of focus."[104] After fifty years of psychological research on terrorism, even the most sophisticated research permits us only a partial understanding of terrorist motivation. Generic descriptors of motivation (e.g., to characterize an act as ideologically motivated), ironically, may serve us better than more sophisticated or elaborate portrayals that may have little relevance or utility to anyone.

But there is a more radical course of action available. We could abandon or at least reallocate efforts away from motivation. This might seem a spurious if not irresponsible argument, so to encourage you to consider it,

I'll raise an uncomfortable truth here. Even if we gained widespread consensus as to what could be said to motivate any particular terrorist (even high-profile cases where lots of information is available to us), knowing their motivation isn't the same as being able to predict who becomes involved (or rather, why only very few do). The things that terrorists say motivate them, and the judgements we as observers make about what appears to motivate them, are issues not exclusive to them, which is precisely why a preoccupation with the so-called structural factors that give rise to terrorism doesn't reveal anything useful for the kinds of issues under exploration here. Moral outrage at injustice, oppression, and foreign policies is a widely held and perfectly rational response to the unfairness of the world. In this sense, radicalization is in fact a normal, healthy, and morally just response to injustice and inequality. And it is nothing less than a rational and worthy impulse to want to do something it, to feel the need to act rather than just talk about a solution. Yet learning such thoughts, and feeling those emotions, is a far cry from taking up arms to defend a victimized community, let alone killing strangers in the name of such defense. Predicting who specifically becomes involved in terrorism is an impossible task. We cannot do it. Perhaps we ought to say it cannot be done. As academics, we might internally argue about the finer distinctions between, say, fuller or partial explanations for things, but for real-world purposes, we might be better served by acknowledging our limitations rather than continuing to skirt around the search for answers that may never come.

Furthermore, understanding motivation may ultimately mean having an explanation with which we feel temporarily comfortable as opposed to gaining any insight based on evidence. But even all this *still* does not mean that understanding terrorist motivation is pointless. It matters only if we ask better, more precise questions. Trying to predict who becomes involved may be impossible, but asking how people become involved, what the different pathways to involvement look like, how recruiters operate, how terrorists perform acts, how they experience it—these kinds of questions, if properly answered, lead to actionable knowledge. In the longer run, this kind of knowledge can reliably inform counterterrorism policy and practice.[105] More pointedly, the forensic psychiatrists James Knoll and

Ronald Pies argue that determining motive only tends to be more important in very specific contexts. Critical of responses to mass shooters, they condemn what they call the "ritualized hunt for . . . motive":

"[It is] usually an exercise in fruitless speculation and wasted resources. When pursued by the media, this quest almost always lacks the necessary data to reach a sound determination. Moreover, these exercises rarely yield any useful or actionable information that would help reduce the likelihood of future mass shootings. Almost invariably, we learn little more than what we have known for many years—that mass shooters are typically (though not always) angry, aggrieved, emotionally unstable, or socially isolated males who are seeking retribution or revenge for perceived mistreatment, rejection, or humiliation."[106]

Presented like this, the mass shooter profile resembles the terrorist profile—seemingly detailed and unifying yet never sufficiently specific to be of use in distinguishing the offender from the general population. "Motive," for Knoll and Pies, matters more in the context of criminal law. A better focus, they suggest, is to pay attention to warning signs and figure out ways to facilitate the reporting of those signs to the proper authorities.[107] The authors draw on FBI reports on mass shooters recommending a focus on identifying observable, pre-attack behaviors such as threats being made. Such knowledge, if suitably imparted, could both inform the public and increase the risk of such behavior being subsequently reported to authorities. There may be some merit to this. The U.S. Secret Service National Threat Assessment Center (NTAC) analyzed forty-one cases of school violence occurring between 2008 and 2017.[108] No overall student attacker profile was found, nor was there any meaningful profile to suggest that particular schools would be attacked. However, not unlike Paul Gill's research on lone actor terrorists discussed in the previous chapter, they found that by focusing on pre-attack behaviors, certain patterns emerged with implications for detection and prevention. School attackers held grievances against classmates or school staff, had ready access to firearms from their own homes, and had histories of psychological or behavioral problems.

The attackers also had histories of disciplinary action taken against them in school and were generally fixated on violence and violent actors without any suitable explanation.[109] NTAC reported that every single attacker showed some signs of worrisome behavior and that most of them leaked some intention of their attacks prior to actually conducting them.[110] Knowing about such behaviors means we can inform and educate people to better detect them in normal, everyday settings. The role of bystanders, as the psychologists Randy Borum and Terri Patterson emphasize, offers one meaningful way to ultimately prevent attacks.[111] And just like Gill's striking findings, the PhD student Ayca Altay and her colleagues at Rutgers University found that, in their review of lone actor terrorist cases, "most attackers leak intent at a time when preparations come to a close."[112]

CONCLUSION

The inability to produce a clear terrorist profile should not be seen as a failure of research. It is, in essence, the outcome of it. Likewise, the inability to reach consensus on the precise recipe for motivation doesn't mean motivation is unimportant or that efforts to better understand it are unimportant. But the search for terrorist motivation is dictated by the same logic governing the search for a terrorist profile; even if we get what we think we need (e.g., better data), there will still be limits to what we can do—that is, unless and until we ask far more specific and focused questions. It is only then that we can move closer to the realm of prevention and interdiction than by keeping our discussions at the broader, and admittedly more vague, level of motivation. I am not suggesting we abandon the search for terrorist motivations; rather, I want us to be far more precise in what we think we are doing and what it means.

For years, researchers have sought to distinguish different types of terrorism by producing typologies. This helps clarify what different types of groups want—in short, to understand their motivation. The FBI, for example, considers domestic terrorism cases to encompass antiabortion violence, environmental violence, racially and ethnically motivated violence, and "anarchism and anti-government extremism."[113] Understanding people with reference to such typologies might tell us something about the group's objectives but won't tell us much at all about individual motivation. Saying that a terrorist group is "jihadist" reveals little about why young men flocked to Syria or Afghanistan; "to do jihad" doesn't explain anything. It's plausible to assume that the individual traveler embraces at least some of the values of a particular group, that they *want* to see Sharia law implemented, for example, but it may tell us very little if anything about why someone wants to leave their home and join a group they may ultimately know little about. Typologies can be disappointing at an individual level and are not necessarily very illuminating. We must consider how terrorist actors construct a view of their own motivation—how they account for their actions and the strategies they use to normalize and rationalize to themselves and others why they do what they do or did.

So why do they do it? The answer's complicated. But it's important to know why—knowing and accepting that will help us decide what direction we wish to pursue in search of solutions. The strange thing about terrorist motivation is that, on the one hand, it's not very mysterious. Terrorist actors are certainly not shy about telling us why they do what they do. We can validate, corroborate, and triangulate all the different reasons people give about why they become involved in terrorism. The process involves a combination of factors, some big, some small—people see injustice in their communities, in other communities, in their own lives, and in the lives of the oppressed, the disenfranchised, and those without a voice. Faced with injustice, we either act upon it or we do not. Those who become involved in terrorism feel compelled to not just talk but to act. They come to view violence as a legitimate response against the oppressor. They find that others share those views (or others help them rationalize those views). For some recruits, their first exposure to potential involvement in terrorism is through exposure to an ideology that allows them to not just make sense of the world around them but to make them feel that their emotions, their outrage, and their sense of righteous anger at the grave injustices they witness allow them to take one step further. For others, it's only after they take steps toward involvement, or are recruited, that ideology emerges as an added feature—it is the glue that binds them to the group, their mission and newfound purpose. And then there are the many private reasons that most are reluctant to share. Recruits may justify their involvement with reference to serving a cause that is bigger than themselves, attending to a duty they now feel the weight of pride in aspiring to. Fundamentally, recruits seek out involvement because they believe a better life awaits them. They believe they will achieve far more in this new role than they would without it, and there they will find other like-minded individuals with whom to share this fantasy.

In his masterful analysis of Tunisian foreign fighters, the jihadism expert Aaron Zelin cautioned that "any commentator who boils jihadist mobilization down to one particular cause should not be taken seriously."[114] Despite the multitude of factors at play, radicalization and mobilization to action are parts of an intensely personal journey. We make a big deal about how public some of the broader influences seem to be because we too have knowledge of the events and emotions that drive such factors—in many cases, we may think and feel the same way with respect to the grievances at hand. But recruitment can be deeply personal, and some terrorist groups are very good at recruitment because they recognize the value of tailor-made efforts. A mistake we make in studies of radicalization is obsessing over the qualities of recruits rather than considering the processes by which they sought involvement or the routes through which they were recruited. Where recruiters operate, they tend to have a big toolbox at their disposal. They'll use everything from the allure of adventure to the glory of sacrifice to personal redemption. Every recruiter faces the same challenge: to mobilize their target into action. And they will use whatever it takes to make that happen if it involves convincing recruits that they have a personal stake in bringing about the change they desire.

As we've seen in this and the previous chapter, Islamic State recruits alone were very diverse. Some were religious and others were not. Some traveled to Syria and Iraq in search of action. Others went for a quiet life of retreat and solace. Recruits were both male and female. Most were young, impressionable, and hungry for excitement of one kind or another. They were typically in their early twenties (though some were as old as thirty-four at the time of their arrest). They came from varied backgrounds. Many felt out of place at home. They were at a stage in their lives where they were trying to find their place in the world. They identified as people struggling with conflict—for example, trying to reconcile dual identities as Muslims and Westerners. In many cases, we don't know if that's how they really felt or that's how they learned to think from exposure to the Islamic State movement and its propaganda.

What do recruiters look for? Piety? Evidence of a willingness to sacrifice oneself for the good of the cause? People with a particular set of skills? It's unlikely that recruits are simply taken on because of an expression of beliefs. Extremist organizations are paranoid places for good reason. They are careful about admitting spies and they become increasingly jaded over time and simply don't have the time for those who may, despite good intentions, turn out to be, well, just not very good. And just like most groups, they have their own share of petty rivalries, jealousies, insecurities, and mistrust. Any recruit can learn to talk the talk, but whether that corresponds to subsequent performance is, without adequate training, anyone's guess. Author and former FBI Special Agent Thomas Strentz examined numerous high-profile terrorist attacks (and attempted attacks) throughout the 1980s, especially in airport settings. He was surprised by what appeared to be a lack of preparation: "It is my impression that in each of these incidents, the commanders sent out what they thought was a suicidal team. Yet, under the stress of their self-induced brush with death, the veneer of training, discipline, and dedication vanished."[115] Not nearly enough is known about the nature, extent, and effectiveness of terrorist recruiters. As such, our knowledge is limited about how these issues really work. Data from seized Islamic State personnel records certainly suggested that the movement used those records to scout for talent—basically identifying recruits with certain skills that could be matched with tasks.[116] As always, however, different cohorts may yield different results. In his examination of UK cases, the researcher Donald Holbrook found that people who collected extremist material as part of their growing commitment to terrorist activity "seemed to enter the attack planning phase without seeking out dedicated content on bomb-making, firearms, or other recipes or guidelines relevant to participation in terrorism."[117]

We saw from chapter 1 that terrorism distinguishes itself from other forms of violence because it has an ideological dimension. But that doesn't mean that what we might call personal motivations are irrelevant. It's simply a reminder that there is more to it. We often overemphasize the ideology and think it reveals something about motivation. Sometimes it does, but more often it doesn't. It simply obscures those factors that really drive involvement. Terrorist actors rationalize, sanitize, and legitimize what they do in several ways. Their violence is, in their view, necessary—the only way to bring about the change they desire. It is defensive—they feel that they serve a greater good. It is urgent—they believe that by failing to act, and act now, that the enemy may become so powerful as to be unbeatable. The big question around radicalization has been whether (and how, and when, and where) radical thoughts lead to radical action. We must at a minimum distinguish radicalization from mobilization—changes in inner thinking versus changes in outward action—because most people who embrace radical views will never, ever engage in terrorism.

When we consider terrorist motivation and how ideologies are used to justify despicable acts of violence, it is easy to imagine brainwashed soldiers ready to take up arms in the name of some cause to which they have become increasingly committed. But the sources of what leads someone down this pathway aren't always found in obscure ideological tracts. Sometimes they are found by simply watching the evening news. Research on radicalization, despite its limitations, has confirmed the existence of these common themes. That same research has yet to confirm precisely how those factors relate to one another to produce terrorists. The identification of common themes does not easily translate into what we might consider *risk factors*—which is to say, just because we know what the ingredients are, it doesn't mean we know what the result might be. Identifying common themes among terrorists does not allow us to predict, with any confidence, who is more likely to become involved in terrorism. The science is simply not there. For now, at least, understanding terrorist motivation remains fundamentally an issue of interpretation.

4

MINDSET

"There should be essentially no difference between . . . [Islamists] and sim-ilarly extreme Christian zealots."

AYLA SCHBLEY

A s 2020 ended, weary and divided Americans faced a deeply con-tentious presidential election while COVID-19 continued to wreak havoc. Many wondered why so many others still refused to wear masks in public. Answers were couched in terms of political affiliation, tribalism, Internet-fueled conspiracy theories, indifference to the bereaved, and sheer apathy to the ongoing serious threats to public safety. Why did so many people seem to not care about the mounting death toll? The psychologist Paul Slovic offered an elegant if disturbing answer: "The more who die, sometimes the less we care."[1] The explanation, he says, has to do with the impersonal nature of death and how far we are from the reality of what it brings.

One of terrorism's many contradictions is that it has both deeply per-sonal and impersonal qualities. Dramatic, often hyperbolic, media coverage of a terrorist event can heighten our sense of personal vulnerability to what is an incredibly unlikely occurrence. An act of terrorism, however, can seem like a deeply impersonal violation for its perpetrators and their supporters. In a French courtroom in September 2021, Salah Abdeslam sat on trial for his role in the 2015 Paris attacks in which jihadists killed 130 people. Abdeslam characterized his attack thusly: "We fought France, we attacked France, we targeted the civilian population. It was nothing personal against them."[2] The researcher Julia Ebner wrote that many online extremists viewed Brenton Tarrant's attack in New Zealand in such a detached way as to make it sound like a kind of game.[3] The first online comment under Tarrant's livestreamed attack read "Get the high score." More broadly, the "gamification" both of terrorist attacks, and those responsible for them, has become a firm trend in twenty-first-century terrorism. In his case study of Patrick Crusius, the researcher Graham Macklin explains, "The personal status derived from placing on the 'leader board' within this online milieu appears to have fostered an element of competition among certain users; each successive act of violence fueling a cumulative carnival of cruelty in which heinous acts of violence are repeatedly glorified, their perpetrators lionized, and their victims further dehumanized."[4]

For her part, Ebner wondered if Tarrant's online audience were genuinely incapable of accepting what had happened. Did they really understand what he had done? The online reaction to Tarrant was reminiscent of the reaction to Dzhokhar Tsarnaev, the Boston bomber; after his arrest, he amassed "hordes of breathless fangirls," several of whom launched public campaigns to support him. One woman said, "He's someone that you can easily relate to. . . . When you see other psycho killers on the TV, they look like psycho killers, but [Dzhokhar] doesn't look like that."[5] Two years after the bombing, the Facebook group "Dzhokhar Tsarnaev is Innocent" had over fourteen thousand members.[6] "Too pretty to be guilty" became a popular catchphrase among his legions of followers.[7]

So, what does it mean to be able to grasp the reality of such acts? Does acknowledging the scale of death from COVID-19 equate to thinking more deeply about those affected by it? Would that, in turn, increase empathy, and translate to wearing a mask in public? What would this mean for terrorism? Does grasping the reality of terrorist violence mean not engaging in it or not supporting the act in the first place? That logic seems circular; surely if we sympathize with terrorist victims, we would hardly at the same time support those who practice such violence—or would we? In the previous two chapters we have considered who becomes involved in terrorism and why. But even a detailed consideration of terrorist motivation cannot explain how or why one person can willingly kill another. The act of killing, or even doing the work needed to develop a readiness to kill, seems to require a different type of explanation. We saw in the previous chapter that there are several good reasons to distinguish what the psychologist Max Taylor calls the broader *involvement* factors from the narrower factors that shape *engagement* in terrorist acts.[8] The things that might help us solve terrorism's collective action puzzle (that is, why so few who feel inclined to act actually do so) may not necessarily tell us much about how people prepare themselves (or are prepared by others) to kill and kill again. To put this into starker terms, it's one thing to feel outraged, to want to help, and to be seduced by fantasies of heroic actions in combat. It is another thing entirely to bring oneself to kill someone with a gun, a knife, a saw, or a bomb. No amount of theorizing on radicalization brings us closer to understanding the reality of how a person learns to take another person's life. This chapter seeks to help us do just that. Only by understanding the terrorist mindset—the thinking patterns associated with engagement in terrorist behavior—can we understand how participants commit acts of violent extremism.

DEHUMANIZATION

Let's start by considering a point raised by Macklin about the El Paso shooter—we can examine the process of dehumanization. The common thinking here is that terrorists learn to dehumanize their victims, which makes the act of killing easier to anticipate, execute, and justify after the fact. Terrorist propaganda and training manuals offer plenty of guidance for prospective recruits on how they should think about the enemy. Sometimes this is evident from the repetitive use of simple labels like "enemy" or "apostates."⁹ The Islamic State movement routinely carried features in its English language and Arabic publications demonizing its opponents, detailing war crimes by state actors, and celebrating the graphic executions of captured foes. This kind of material serves many functions, one of which is to entice prospective recruits from its readership. But this sword is double-edged. On the one hand, such material might appeal to a wide community of potential recruits contemplating involvement of some kind, whether near or far. On the other, it might speak more directly to a narrower group of people who might be drawn to terrorism specifically because they want to kill people. Do terrorist groups reach out to people likely to be turned on by the prospect of killing? Or is there something else going on here? No matter how different audience members might perceive the message, an important guiding principle for the movement is a consideration of *how* the act is portrayed. Terrorist groups often characterize killing in terms of hardship and sacrifice required on the part of the recruit. This signals to prospects that the business of killing is indeed ugly and, in doing so, reassures them that they are not sadists. They can instead take comfort in knowing that the "sacrifice" they make in being willing to kill others will be recognized as a sign of their commitment. Some movements make the cost of engagement explicit. The Al-Qaeda training manual stressed that members must "be willing to do the work" while warning prospective recruits of the need to mentally endure "psychological traumas such as those involving bloodshed, arrest, [and] imprisonment."¹⁰ But we must remember that it is precisely this challenge, this test, that appeals to prospective recruits.

Propaganda is one thing; reality is another. Reading terrorist manuals or manifestos, especially in isolation, might feel like little more than an abstract fantasy or, for some, a private hobby. What's more, the gruesome, often elaborate ways in which the Islamic State dispatch their victims might suggest their executioners had little problem adapting to the demands of the task. That suggests they either had a steady supply of bloodthirsty members or something else was at play that might help understand how terrorists learn the act of killing. In a 1977 analysis of terrorist psychology, the psychiatrist H. H. A. Cooper argued that terrorists have to work hard, psychologically speaking, to realize their full potential.[11] He added, "Serious terrorism . . . is not an occupation for the amateur."[12] Outside the right context, what might seem like praise for recruits preparing to do a hard job masks a clue into how terrorists have to work at what they do to be able to do it. We shouldn't necessarily see these as mutually exclusive, but they nudge us to consider the ways in which terrorists rationalize and justify to themselves (and us) why they do what they do.

Let's explore this further with an example. In or around April 2015, several close-up photographs circulated on Islamic State propaganda channels, and they inevitably caught the attention of Western news media. The photographs were taken in the then-IS-controlled area of Homs, Syria. One of the images showed two blindfolded men, captives of IS, being led toward their execution. A crowd had gathered to witness what was going to be a public stoning of the men, accused by IS of being gay. The movement had previously thrown gay men off the top of buildings as punishment. Now, four IS members were going to beat these men to death with rocks.[13] On the one hand, the photographs resembled countless other "about to die" images circulated by fans of IS to the world.[14] They even appeared to show the prisoners in a calm state, leading some to wonder if their captors had given them a sedative to help them face what was to come. But something else was captured in these photos. One accompanying IS member rested his hand and arm on a victim's shoulder as they walked to the execution site. Before throwing their victims to the ground, the men carrying out the sentence were photographed hugging them. Along with the embrace, the victims were told that their sins were forgiven.[15]

Was that all a sadistic game, just instilling false hope? Were the captors trying to make the prisoners feel like their deaths were dignified? One interpretation by observers was that IS supporters used the images as evidence that the group was compassionate. By hugging the victims, it proved they were not merely callous killers but cared deeply about their victims in their final moments. Given the act that followed, and IS behavior more generally, that seems hard to accept. Taken on face value, such behavior seems at odds with what is commonly thought of as dehumanization. In a formal sense, dehumanization is a process whereby the perpetrators display no concern for the welfare of their victims.[16] In the past, dehumanization was explained by suggesting that the perpetrator's "moral restraints" are reduced, and this allows them to engage in violence. By this logic, perpetrators must put in the mental work to transform victims into people who are of absolutely no consequence to them.[17] This seems intuitive. We can imagine how people can strip away others' humanity, often as a means of justifying a particular attitude or behavior directed at them. According to the researchers Nour Kteily and Emile Bruneau, if members of one group feel dehumanized by another group, they can start to respond aggressively.[18] Additionally, the less we know about other people, the easier it is to dehumanize them (the point Paul Slovic was making). The most effective way to reduce dehumanization, is, quite simply, becoming familiar with people who are different.[19] Where dehumanization leads is well documented. It is one of the main explanations offered for mass atrocities and collective violence more broadly.[20]

But the genocide scholar and psychologist Johannes Lang urges us to consider a different perspective. He says that the way in which we have usually understood dehumanization might distort our understanding of collective violence altogether. According to Lang, "a process of moral justification redefines the perpetrators' perception of the violence itself. Often such justifications rely on allegations about the targeted group's character and intentions that do not make sense in terms of dehumanization."[21] Put another way, popular ideas about dehumanization, Lang concludes, are misleading. The function of violence is for the perpetrator to have power over the target of the violence.[22] What does this mean for our example here? If we take accounts of these IS executions at face value, the behavior of the perpetrators doesn't suggest a denial of humanity, rather an assertion of it. The executioners appear to both willingly bring would-be victims to their imminent death while simultaneously exhibiting genuine compassion for them in their final moments. Far from denying their victims' humanity, the guards openly acknowledge it. Such acts are not like the traditional terrorist car bomb where the perpetrators may not even see the damage wrought by their actions. IS executions like those mentioned here, in contrast, are far from impersonal—they are intimate. It is that human quality, Lang suggests, that gives the violence its meaning.[23]

There are other possible interpretations of these acts. It is conceivable that treating victims this way is less about compassion and more about handling them as "stage props in the performance."[24] We certainly know enough about IS execution choreography to know that as a movement it cares deeply about staging, editing, and cinematography. Being seen to do a good job before a critical audience matters to them. However, such concerns are not restricted to terrorism. Until Britain abolished capital punishment by hanging in 1965, Albert Pierrepoint executed several hundred condemned prisoners. Pierrepoint was said to have carefully studied the "size and build of his doomed client through a peephole the night before, so as to determine the length of rope required for the most compassionate completion of the task. . . . Too short, and the client might strangle."[25] Was such preparation a sign of compassion for those about to die? Or was Pierrepoint preoccupied with making sure the job was done right?

We can extend this line of questioning even further. A common assumption in the terrorism literature is that terrorists don't feel guilty for what they do to their victims.[26] The logic seems unassailable—after all, why would terrorists do what they do if they felt guilty about it? But they *do* feel guilty for what they do. We routinely see this theme in terrorist memoirs, such as those written by Sean O'Callaghan, whose 1999 book, *The Informer*, chronicles his time in the Provisional Irish Republican Army and his decision to turn against his former movement.[27] The key issue relates to what they do to feel *less* guilty about it. In his research on dehumanization, Lang says that explanations have shifted emphasis to how perpetrators strengthen their own rationale for doing what they do.[28] Understanding how the perpetrators perceive the violence itself, and what steps they take to gradually build internal resolve, Lang emphasizes, offers a different (and potentially more accurate) way of understanding the act of killing. On the psychology of SS officers in Nazi concentration camps, Lang concludes that this resolve suggests a far more disturbing reality than dehumanization theories imply—he says that mass murder may indeed come to feel routine and normal for them, but it is because of the habituation and desensitization done by the perpetrators as opposed to them necessarily setting out to dehumanize their victims.[29] Lang illustrates this idea with an account of Franz Stangl, the commandant of Nazi death camps at Sobibor and Treblinka. When probed by his biographer about whether he recognized any humanity in his victims, Stangl hinted at what he did to reduce discomfort. In stark contrast to the IS guards, Stangl said, "I avoided at any price talking to those who were about to die: I couldn't stand it."[30]

Trying to understand such acts in terms of innate qualities of the people who commit them, the psychologist Herbert Kelman argued, won't provide reliable answers. In his own analysis of the psychology of mass violence, Kelman considered whether those Nazis who participated in massacres could be considered "sadistically inclined." He finds this explanation less than convincing, acknowledging, "To be sure, some of the commanders and guards of concentration camps could clearly be described as sadists, but what has to be explained is the existence of concentration camps in which these individuals could give play to their sadistic fantasies."[31]

There is always a danger of overemphasizing the psychology of the perpetrators. One obvious feature of IS executions, and their progressively elaborate choreography, was that IS was able to easily engage in such acts in the open air, safe knowing that they could freely perform such actions. The situation afforded greater opportunities for the perpetrator, and likely further reinforced the victims' sense of helplessness. This quality was evident in accounts from Nazi concentration camps. As Lang documents, "Terrified and confused, those about to die obeyed instructions more quickly; their very compliance in turn inspired feelings of disgust in the guards, making it easier for them to kill their victims."[32] We should not uncritically attribute these qualities to all perpetrators. But we should also not assume that the existence of extreme violence alone implies the terrorist must remove any sense of humanity from their victims. A key feature of being in control of the situation and environment, whether we are talking about Nazi concentration camps, the actions of Albert Pierrepoint, or the Islamic State, relates to the idea of "routinization," which, Kelman explains, serves two critical functions. It reduces the need for the person to make decisions and "makes it easier to avoid the implications of the action since the actor focuses on the details of his job rather than on its meaning."[33] How does such desensitization develop? It is hard to imagine this coming from exposure to and consumption of ideological content alone, no matter how persuasive and alluring that might be. The answer here is that we must consider not just what people learn but how people learn to do things as part of a terrorist movement. We must look at the role of *practice* in shaping what Taylor once called the "spiraling of commitment" observed in terrorist groups throughout time.[34]

PRACTICE, PRACTICE, PRACTICE

People who become involved in terrorism must quickly contend with multiple cascading realities. For those who travel to join a movement, the consequences of one's actions are stark. The recruit must cope with possible separation from family, the demands of training, and being instructed to do something they didn't necessarily go there to do. New recruits cope in different ways. Some immerse themselves in the ideology; others immerse themselves in alcohol or narcotics where available. I learned in Pakistan of multiple examples of children and young adolescents recruited into the Pakistan Taliban who were given marijuana to calm their nerves before an operation. In cases where the person knows they will engage in extreme barbarity, it's not uncommon to take alcohol or drugs both prior to and after the event. We've seen this in terrorist groups, and we've seen it in organized crime activity. But to dismiss killing as something done under the influence of chemicals is to overlook the process and neglect the more disturbing reality of how this happens. Imploring researchers to get closer to the environments where violence happens, the American journalist Theo Padnos says that reality has a way of getting us to quickly toss such theories aside: "A day or so inside [Syria] would have shown . . . that on neither side of the war do combatants require drugs, or, for that matter, money in order to kill one another."[35] In their study of terrorist prisoners in Northern Ireland, the psychiatrists H.A. Lyons and Helen Harbinson found that about 10 percent of the sample were intoxicated at the time of committing a murder, compared to over half of the nonterrorist criminals.[36] In their research on the Islamic State, the journalists Michael Weiss and Hassan Hassan explored the relevance of *The Management of Savagery*, a 2004 book of immense strategic significance to jihadists worldwide. They describe how its author, Abu Bakr Naji, cautions readers that it is one thing to discern meaning about religious matters from reading a text but another entirely to learn through participation. Weiss and Hassan explain, "Naji at one point lectures the reader, arguing that the way jihad is taught 'on paper' makes it harder for young mujahidin to understand the true meaning of the concept." They cite directly from the book: "One who has previously engaged in jihad knows that it is naught but violence, crudeness, terrorism, frightening [others], and massacring. I am talking about jihad and fighting, not about Islam and one should not confuse them."[37]

For the terrorist, a feature of the attraction to involvement is the emphasis on action—doing something, not just talking about it. Acting out is what distinguishes the terrorist from the mere radical. The credibility enjoyed by terrorist groups comes in part from their willingness to engage in visible acts, with visible consequences. From the perspective of the believer, the emphasis on *doing* is often just a matter of practice. The phrase "community of practice" might seem the stuff of obscure academic jargon, but it holds the key to understanding just how terrorists come to learn to do what they do and, in the process, acquire (or fine-tune) their mindset. The term doesn't originate in anything terrorism-related; it just describes any groups of people who "share a concern or passion for something they do and learn how to do it better as they interact regularly."[38] Examples might be "a band of artists seeking new forms of expression, a group of engineers working on similar problems, a clique of pupils defining their identity in the school, a network of surgeons exploring novel techniques."[39] The vital feature here is that the learning is done through collaboration; it is a social activity that goes beyond the formal, structured ways through which people usually learn things: old-fashioned, one-way instruction and traditional education.

The Norwegian anthropologist Karsten Hundeide[40] took these ideas even further by suggesting early community of practice models lacked a sense of the qualities involved in becoming a deeply committed "insider." Drawing on examples of militarized children (or child soldiers), Hundeide offered a way of understanding both the progression of novices into experts, as well as the psychological qualities that accompany (and culminate in) that progression—in other words, how the associated mindset, or thinking pattern, develops. He identifies several features. The first, those initial steps taken by novices, involves regular positive contact with others. The prospective recruit takes a few steps in the right direction and is rewarded with support and affection. Any further steps taken toward the group are shaped by positive reinforcement—the recruit is made to feel like they belong, that they are significant, and that they are valued, even loved. As both the means of signaling a willingness to learn and simultaneously the result of encouragement from peers, the recruit must walk the walk and talk the talk. The recruit must constantly signal that they are part of the group by adopting certain style and identity markers that signify this progression and mark their allegiance to the group. This might be expressed through changes in dress style, such as adopting a uniform, and learning to use language in specific ways. They acquire "vocabularies of violence" as well as "vocabularies of motive" as they move from peripheral figures to centrally engaged in the group.[41] The author Seyward Darby's interview with a former white supremacist illustrates this shift. Reflecting on her interviewee, Darby notes, "She didn't necessarily like using racist language, but she did it anyway because she wanted to fit in. The N-word," she said, "was everybody's third word."[42]

A key part of exposure to this new language is what Hundeide calls redefining the past. This helps solidify the recruit's efforts to learn new values shared by the group. In militant groups, this entails learning in explicit terms who the enemy is and why. As Kelman explained in his 1973 thesis on violence without moral restraint, "When a group of people is defined entirely in terms of a category to which they belong, and when this category is excluded from the human family, then the moral restraints against killing them are more readily overcome."[43]

Redefining the past can involve embracing conspiracy theories. The psychologist Anni Sternisko and colleagues point out that some people are drawn to conspiracy theories because of their content, while others find solace in their qualities.[44] To illustrate their point, the content of a particular conspiracy theory (e.g., the "big lie" that Democrats stole the 2020 presidential election from Donald Trump) might resonate with a particular in-group (Trump supporters) because it allows that community to hold continuing positive views about its own power, relevance, and strength while simultaneously accommodating negative views about an opposing group (in this case, Democrats). Alternatively, Sternisko and colleagues suggest that we gravitate toward conspiracy theories because when we feel uncertain about the world and our place in it, they help us feel safer, more in control, and more able to make sense of the world around us.[45]

People who strongly believe in conspiracy theories tend to have hostile intentions toward out-groups.[46] The social psychologist Michael Hogg talks about *category prototypes*, attributes that basically highlight and reinforce the similarities of people within a particular category, as well as the "differences between people in different categories." These prototypes, Hogg suggests, advocate how members of a category ought to behave. Put more simply, "we agree that 'we' are like this and 'they' are like that."[47] No matter the motivational pathway to conspiracy theories, the consequences are similar: "pointing to forces beyond our control, articulating an enemy to hate, sharply dividing the group from the non-group and, sometimes, legitimizing violence."[48] The authors Jamie Bartlett and Carl Miller point out, of course, that not all conspiracy theories are violent, and even those that are cannot in themselves lead people to violent acts. Their harm, however, can extend beyond the individual. They can foster mistrust between groups and the government and make the job of terrorist recruiters that much easier.[49]

For the terrorist recruit to nourish their growing commitment they must do more than just mimic the words and styles exhibited by more seasoned members. For commitment to deepen, they must prove themselves—sacrifice and hardship are essential, credible markers of this progression. Sometimes it might involve isolation from friends and family, the cutting of all previous ties. Such a move also constitutes a major demonstration of loyalty, signaling to the group that novices are serious about their commitment. Loyalty continues to be expressed and observed not just through major steps like that but in what Hundeide calls the daily collective practices, the rituals, the simple "on-the-job" tasks that eventually become routine. Internal discipline structures the progression into this new life, and this may culminate, for some, in a major test of loyalty by committing an extreme act—for example, executing an enemy prisoner. The culmination of this gradual progression of commitment is newfound status and respect. In many cases, Hundeide says, charismatic authority figures play a major role in guiding prospective recruits through each stage, moving them gradually from the periphery to the core.

The process of becoming a committed insider is essentially a model of highly collaborative social learning through a community of practice. The reason why communities of practice concepts are relevant to understanding the terrorist can be summed up by the terrorism and organized crime expert Michael Kenney, who in 2007 wrote that it is "not enough simply to claim, as many do, that . . . terrorists learn."[50] If we do that, he says, we just gloss over the process through which changes in behavior happen. The terrorist mindset doesn't just appear out of nowhere. The challenge, he says, is to closely examine the "informal apprenticeships, on-the-job training . . . and combat."[51] Kenney described how members of Britain's al Muhajiroun extremist group would expose new members to their "norms and practices through repeated interactions with more experienced activists."[52] In that network, a recruit would effectively learn by modeling the behavior of a more seasoned companion. Gavin McInnes, founder of the Proud Boys movement, explained in a 2017 interview how involvement in the group was (at least initially) based on a tiered system. Members learned how to progress through various levels; one involved a bizarre initiation process whereby new members were beaten until they were able to name "five breakfast cereals." Attaining a higher level required the member to "get arrested or in a serious violent fight for the cause."[53]

In a 2016 research paper led by me and Max Taylor, we applied Hundeide's model to how the Islamic State socialized thousands of young children from passive, peripheral bystanders into fully-fledged, deeply committed militarized actors. We proposed our own six-stage model to try to capture the experiences of those children.

1. *Seduction*—children were gradually led by curiosity and the allure of outreach activities by IS; children would routinely be present at public events run by IS members during which they might be "rewarded" with menial tasks like holding up a flag or being given prime viewing spots at executions or videos of executions.

2. *Schooling*—IS assumed de facto control of local schools, so children began to have more direct exposure both to the group's propaganda and educational curricula, as well as exposure to recruiters keen to detect children with aptitude for certain roles or levels of involvement.

3. *Selection*—IS would select some children for the "privilege" of attending special camps where they would be trained in various military techniques; children would be mostly isolated from their families at this point.

4. *Subjugation*—children were subjected to harsh discipline as part of their progressive military training, including more and more brutal resocialization to mold mental toughness and punish weakness or dissension.

5. *Specialization*—children exhibiting aptitude for certain tasks (such as recruiting other children or fighting) would receive additional, dedicated training for that role.

6. *Stationing*—children graduated as fully-fledged members to be deployed in their respective roles, along with other children or adult fighters. Often this would go hand in hand with committing an extreme act, such as torturing, raping, or killing a prisoner, sometimes while being recorded as part of a propaganda video.[54]

In contrast to their adult counterparts, children's progressive involvement and deepening commitment to IS was a far more systematic and engineered experience. Of course, action can emerge in different contexts, and sometimes, the recruit cannot necessarily benefit from such structures. In 2017, three British jihadists drove a vehicle into London Bridge, where they killed two pedestrians. The attackers then stabbed to death several more bystanders. One of the attackers, Khuram Butt, was found to have consumed an extensive amount of extremist material online, which ranged from images of violence to the sermons of radical religious figures.[55] In the United Kingdom, the Chief Coroner's report conceded it was "debatable what could be deduced from the material about his mindset and intentions."[56] The Chief Coroner concluded with a recommendation to the Secretary of State for the UK's Home Department that "serious consideration" ought to be given to criminalizing "the most serious material glorifying or encouraging terrorism."[57]

When we considered motivation in the previous chapter, we saw that accounts of involvement reveal certain qualities shared among terrorists. Acknowledging and seeing injustice against an oppressed in-group fuels moral outrage. This intensely emotional reaction in turn fuels a desire to act, to respond with violence that is considered a perfectly just, and defensive, reaction. The terrorist is aware that involvement brings profound risk, possibly a chance of death, but there are also rewards to be had. Identifying the factors that drive radicalization also leads us to acknowledge that it's one thing to hold radical views and another entirely to be mobilized into action. Why so few do this is unknown, but we know that some seek out opportunities to engage, while others happen to be at the right place at the right time and find opportunities. Developing a terrorist mindset, however, is simply the culmination of work—it takes effort, and requires actually doing things, not just thinking about them. For some, it is the product of a community of practice.

We can draw on insights from other areas to help further understand this. The psychologist Randy Borum argues that research from the sociology and psychology of religious conversion might be useful to understand the recruit's progression.[58] He highlighted Lewis Ray Rambo's seven-stage model of conversion, citing Rambo's emphasis on how "relationships, rituals, rhetoric, and roles interact and reinforce one another."[59] The psychologist and Colombian terrorism expert Mauricio Florez-Morris identified several more factors that appealed to potential recruits. Some were features of the group itself, such as the movement's stated values, ethics, and principles. Florez-Morris describes how recruits saw perceived benefits to deepening involvement. Exposure to prestigious role models helped new recruits associate certain traits or qualities with membership. Those qualities included having a serious demeanor, being physically fit, and conducting oneself in an empathetic manner.[60] Members also recognized the value and appeal of "brotherhood, self-sacrifice for the common good, and concern for social problems."[61] These same dynamics were evident in members of the American movement The Base. In August 2019, several members participated in a weekend meeting in Silver Creek, Georgia. They engaged in shared activities that included training in firearms as well as rope work, training in rudimentary first aid, and even, for reasons still unclear, a "pagan ritual that included a goat sacrifice."[62]

THE HIGH COST OF LOW-INTENSITY WARFARE

Just like in so many terrorist groups, Mauricio Florez-Morris's interviews with former Colombian guerrillas revealed that involvement was a gradual process. New recruits had to prove themselves with smaller, basic tasks before graduating to more important ones. These initial activities would include such things as stealing goods to help the cause, distributing propaganda, or painting graffiti. Those wanting to become suicide bombers for Somalia's al-Shabaab not only had to undergo substantial coaching and preparation but also had to then join a waiting list.[63] Isolating the prospective recruit from family to foster mental toughness was a practice not limited to the Islamic State. Colombian movements would either instruct members to present themselves for duty elsewhere or get recruits to believe that their families would be placed at risk if the recruit didn't leave home.[64] Florez-Morris found that Colombian recruiters would routinely test incoming prospects. He describes this in detail:

> After the person was invited to join, she or he was given several tests, such as meeting unknown people in strange places, usually at early hours in the morning to avoid family control. A typical situation would be

meeting someone under a bridge to receive an unknown package, often a hand grenade. At the moment of delivery, an unknown subject, who was really another member of the group, would unexpectedly appear on the scene. The recruit had to react quickly in order to hide the weapon and avoid arousing suspicion. A guerrilla member closely monitored the recruit's reaction for signs of ability to handle these types of situations.[65]

Terrorist groups must, by definition, operate in the shadows. Their illegality binds them to a semiclandestine existence. For decades, researchers have acknowledged how terrorist organizations must adapt to cope with the impact of such realities. Making leadership decisions based on available intelligence, raising money, harvesting other resources, and protecting against infiltration all pose significant challenges, which are made more difficult when simultaneously attempting to exude confidence to prospective recruits about the benefits of involvement. Place matters immensely. Terrorist movements epitomize the notion of an extreme environment, whether a clandestine organization like the IRA operating in the urban shadows of Belfast or the large-scale "pious society" of the Islamic State complete with multiple levels of civilian governance structures.[66] The British researchers Nathan Smith and Emma Barrett have for years explored the psychology of extreme environments, and in a 2019 research paper they highlighted how counterterrorism professionals must frequently work in highly dangerous situations. Smith and Barrett point out that the type of operation undertaken brings with it distinctive challenges. For example, intelligence operations may require personnel to "sustain themselves in a low-resource habitat with few comforts, be confined with limited personal space, and/or be exposed to physical stressors such as extremes of temperature and high altitude."[67] Surveillance activity involves a lot of just hanging around and watching someone or something, all very boring work for the most part.[68] In his review of the literature for the *Journal of Forensic Psychiatry and Psychology*, the researcher Daniel Koehler concurs that terrorist membership can be a highly stressful undertaking with an almost inevitable chance of deadly confrontation.[69] Protecting oneself against trauma (whether physical or psychological) can be critical for the novice terrorist.

We know how terrorist movements use propaganda through social media, films, online magazines, and so on. But the individual terrorist must also engage in what the British conflict expert Maurice Tugwell called "guilt transfer"—a technique whereby the perpetrator deflects attention toward the enemy's actions, and in turn, helps justify the perpetrator's own actions.[70] This deflection, Tugwell says, allows the terrorist to turn a "psychological liability into an asset."[71] Similarly, Professor Paul Wilkinson, one of the founding figures of terrorism studies, once said of terrorists that they "speak a different language."[72] How someone rationalizes and normalizes abhorrent acts can be explained through the process of neutralization. A common process among people who violate laws, neutralization involves adopting a specific thought pattern to enable oneself to feel more comfortable with an act that is about to happen.[73] In their seminal early work, the American criminologists Gresham Sykes and David Matza described five techniques used:

- Denial of responsibility (i.e., I was left with no choice but to do what I did)
- Denial of injury (i.e., what I did didn't cause the harm you said it caused)
- Denial of victim (i.e., whatever harm I did cause was deserved by the victim)
- Condemnation of condemners (i.e., you are only trying to deflect blame for your own actions)
- Appeal to higher loyalties (i.e., I did this for the greater good)[74]

Some of these qualities are evident in terrorism, and other concepts overlap with those presented in work on neutralization techniques.[75]

COPING AND PERFORMANCE

Smith and Barrett argue that research on performance in a broad range of extreme settings (e.g., mountains, space, or deserts) can inform such issues as stress and coping, adaptation, emotion regulation, and decision-making in counterterrorism contexts. Could the kind of research they developed help others understand how terrorist actors cope with the demands of their activity? Patrick Crusius, in his manifesto released just minutes before he started shooting in El Paso, provides us with some insight into his decision-making activity: "I didn't spend much time at all preparing for this attack. Maybe a month, probably less. I have to do this before I lose my nerve." Others appear to cope especially well. The journalist and author Joby Warrick memorably illustrated how Jordanian doctor Humam al-Balawi managed to become a triple agent.[76] Under the pretense of cooperating with American officials, Balawi successfully concealed a suicide bomb before detonating it inside the perimeter of a CIA facility in Afghanistan in 2009, killing himself and nine others.

It's important for us to think carefully about these types of issues. Might Crusius's minimal preparation reflect a priority for action as opposed to just remaining committed to talking and thinking about his grievances? Or does the simple fact that the attack happened constitute enough evidence to suggest his grievance was indeed deeply held? Moreover, thinking more about how recruits cope with the psychological demands of involvement and engagement forces us to consider not only personal disposition but also environments. The ability of Islamic State personnel to move freely around captured territory contrasts starkly with the ways in which the domestic violent extremist must conceal his or her intentions from the prying eyes of friends, family members, or law enforcement. In the past, both the IRA's Green Book (their famous manual issued to recruits) and the Al-Qaeda training manual contained detailed information about how respective operatives ought to conduct themselves. The latter acknowledged that different roles bring with them different types of pressures, with the commander having "special importance" because of the "large amount of information that he possesses," and "the difficulty . . . in replacing the commander."[77] The manual warned that "recruiting agents is the most dangerous task that an enlisted brother can perform" because of the high risk of capture or death.[78]

So how do members of these groups cope with such pressures? Several years ago, I traveled with my colleague Mary Beth Altier to meet a woman who had been involved in several violent right-wing groups in the

United States. "Sarah" (not her real name) was a one-time skinhead whose involvement with violent extremism was turbulent and often chaotic. Her internal day-to-day battles were about keeping at bay the creeping disillusionment she felt about being involved with people she was privately growing to despise. The 1995 Oklahoma City bombing, Sarah alleges, set in motion her eventual journey out of that world. She recalled seeing images of bodies being pulled from the rubble of the Alfred P. Murrah Federal Building and asked herself, "What are you doing?" But fearing that her fellow skinheads would detect her growing disillusionment, she decided she needed to quickly demonstrate renewed commitment. Sarah told us, "I literally made a point to go out and recruit more people and, you know, to be more hardcore and start more fights . . . because I felt 'Now I have to re-prove myself because they knew that I faltered.'"[79]

To this day, I use Sarah's account when I teach about the reality of life in violent extremism because it illustrates an apparent contradiction. From the outside, Sarah's decision to pick more fights, and increase her efforts to recruit others, might signal a deeper dedication and an escalation of commitment. Observers might assume she was hungry to chase down leadership opportunities in the group. Privately, however, she fought a constant battle to ward off her growing disenchantment. The only way to cope with the prospect of being found out, she concluded, was to double down on her efforts, which dug her into an ever-deepening hole. Sarah's experiences here are a classic example of self-concealment, which means actively keeping information from others because we perceive it to be "negative or distressing."[80]

The psychological cost of keeping secrets has been researched in multiple settings—from adolescents keeping secrets from their parents and people concealing their sexuality to a history of mental illness, how spies work to avoid self-exposure, and even how some cancer patients conceal that they still smoke.[81] Psychological research suggests that keeping information or identities secret comes at a cost. It can lead to deficits in cognitive ability, interpersonal restraint, and physical stamina.[82] Smith and Barrett note that undercover police officers and covert human intelligence sources operate sometimes under concealed identities and that a sense of being "cut off" can lead to feeling isolated and rejected.[83] They refer to Aimen Dean, an MI6 informant, who recalled, "The work has literally made me sick. I have no social life, no friends or colleagues. The rest of the world thinks I'm a jihadi."[84]

But the cathartic benefits of *revealing* secrets are also well documented.[85] It thus stands to reason that there must be a sound internal rationale for someone to conceal secrets. The Al-Qaeda training manual specifically advises members who train new recruits on the practice of concealment.[86] Given the kinds of pressures described by Sarah and others who lived that life, why are people drawn to it at all? Recruits' idealized fantasies are often at stark odds with the realities of the movement, and these realities are becoming increasingly well known. Aaron Zelin's case study of Tunisian foreign fighters describes the disappointment experienced by female recruits. He cites one example of a woman who lamented being placed in "a dormitory where a supervisor . . . mistreated her and her children . . . by denying them diapers and medicine."[87] Zelin cautions against the uncritical acceptance of claims of disillusionment since they are often self-serving and may be used to portray a process of exploitation, but there is no doubt that such challenges quickly test the most committed of followers.

Another perspective on this is that, for some of the most ardent of believers, sometimes the suffering *is* the point. The kinds of challenges and hardships faced by prospective recruits might just be the very challenges that inspire and attract some of them in the first place. Rinaldo Nazzaro, leader of the neo-Nazi terror group The Base, said, "I quit my job preemptively. Learned to live on much less money. Moved to Russia where the cost of living is cheaper. . . . I think each person's circumstances need a slightly tailored plan. But generally, the idea is to drop out as much as possible. That requires financial sacrifices, sometimes significant ones."[88] The history of terrorism is full of such examples. Let us recall the words of William Butler Yeats's poem about the early martyrs of the Irish Republican movement, "Easter 1916": "And what if the excess of love burdened them til they died?" The Armenian-American scholar Khachig Tölölyan tells us that Yeats's poem "inscribes [the martyrs] in a past and future narrative, valid wherever green is worn, where, the poem implies, the sacrifice and resurrection of

Christ which we celebrate at Easter are known as narratives of salvation."[89] The rare opportunity to sacrifice oneself for something greater is precisely what constitutes the appeal.

At a minimum, being mentally tough would seem to be a desirable pre-requisite for involvement in terrorism. Mental toughness can help people navigate traumatic events and aid decision-making relevant to that type of environment (in the context of sports like mountain climbing, "whether to continue or abandon a summit attempt in crisis situations.")[90] The sport and exercise psychologist Patricia Jackman and colleagues note that mental toughness can, on the other hand, lead to those same people being too focused on the end goals.[91] Obsession can result in unsafe, compromised situations in the blind pursuit of an objective. In the climbing world, this is known as summit fever. In Jackman's studies, mountaineers noted that the challenges associated with those risks were simply part of the benefits they reaped from participating. They enjoyed it.[92] More experienced climb-ers, however, worked hard to *reduce* risk and took effective precautions accordingly.[93] Would certain traits predict compatibility with engagement in terrorism? Perhaps. Just like mountaineers, however, and following the distinction made in mountaineering studies by Jackman and her team, we must weigh up both the personality characteristics of those who engage in terrorism and people's psychological experiences of terrorism.[94]

MENTAL ILLNESS

Questions around mental health and terrorism have long been evident in the research literature, and we have addressed their relationship in the pre-vious two chapters. In the literature, most of these issues have surrounded the question of whether involvement in terrorism can be explained using mental illness as the reason. It cannot. In his review of dozens of stud-ies of Western foreign fighters who went to Syria and Iraq, the sociologist Lorne Dawson found the data on mental health to be "highly inconsis-tent and inadequate."[95] Unfortunately, however, discussions about terrorism and mental illness are frequently so simplistic that some researchers see the role of mental illness as "completely downplayed," if not completely discounted.[96] And yet, mental illness is relevant. As Max Taylor has long argued, it can be an outcome of participation in terrorism and is also an issue that frequently arises in legal settings. Arguments about mental illness often constitute the basis of defense strategies for people accused of terrorist crimes. In 2017, Sarah Halimi, a sixty-five-year-old Jewish woman, died after being thrown out the window of her Paris apartment.[97] A retired doctor and mother of three, she was killed by her neighbour Kobili Traoré, who yelled "Allahu Akbar" during the attack. Prosecutors alleged that Traoré was motivated by anti-Semitism. The highest court in France ruled him unfit to stand trial because of his heavy cannabis consumption that resulted in a "state of acute mental delirium."[98]

One of the most notorious cases involving terrorism and mental illness is that of the so-called Unabomber. Over three decades, the former academic Ted Kaczynski single-handedly waged a domestic terror campaign in the United States. He targeted those he considered instrumental in promoting technological advancement. In early 1995, Kaczynski sent a letter to the *New York Times* in which he promised to end his attacks should the paper publish his manifesto warning of the dangers of industrialization. Six months later, both the *Times* and the *Washington Post* published it.[99] Kaczynski was eventually caught, and his lawyers' defense was that he suffered from paranoid schizophrenia. Establishing this would, they hoped, reduce his culpability by calling into question the nature of his intent in committing premeditated acts.[100] Kaczynski, bristling at the prospect of being seen as mentally ill, subsequently attempted to represent himself, only to be eventually convinced by his lawyers to "allow them to use mental illness as a mitigating factor in the event of a sentencing phase."[101] Despite continued protestations to the court that he was not mentally ill, he was diagnosed by a psychiatrist as paranoid schizophrenic. Facing a breakdown in proceedings, Kaczynski finally accepted a plea deal to spend the rest of his life in prison.

The forensic psychiatrist Sally Johnson examined Kaczynski over four days. She argued that he harbored two delusional beliefs. The first was that we are as a society "controlled by modern technology"; the second was that "his inability to establish a relationship with a female was directly the result of extreme psychological verbal abuse by his parents."[102] Johnson explains, "It does appear that Mr. Kaczynski's investment and convictions about the outcome of modern technology and the alleged abuse by his family are consistent with fixed belief in that he does not challenge them in response to new information. Both of these systems could be viewed as meeting the criteria of nonbizarre delusional beliefs."[103] By *delusion* she means "a false belief based on incorrect inference about external reality that is firmly sustained despite what all most everyone else believes and despite what constitutes inconvertible and obvious proof or evidence to the contrary. Delusional thinking occurs on a continuum and it is sometimes difficult to differentiate between over valued ideas or preoccupations and delusional thinking."[104] Reinforcing Johnson's diagnosis was the observation that Kaczynski's commitment to his ideas was nontrivial, lasting decades. The true causes of his behavior remain a matter of interpretation, as well as how those obsessions influenced his violent acts. The legal scholar Adam Magid noted that was no shortage of theories about the Unabomber, including some offered by Kaczynski himself.[105] Magid asserts that Kaczynski may frankly have been little more than "a sad, unhappy man who was never able to fit in with society."[106] Magid concludes, "Dr. Johnson might call his views toward technology 'delusional,' but one could also view them as the product of scapegoating. The implications of this distinction are significant: while paranoid schizophrenia suggests the presence of a variety of symptoms and a lack of self-control, Kaczynski may have simply made a choice to become the Unabomber as a response to his personal dissatisfaction with the world."[107]

Differentiating overvalued ideas from delusional thinking is easier said than done and any attempt at valid distinction may be moot. The psychiatrist Tahir Rahman defines an *extreme overvalued belief* as "one that is shared by others in a person's cultural, religious, or subcultural group. The belief is often relished, amplified, and defended by the possessor of the belief and should be differentiated from an obsession or a delusion. The belief grows more dominant over time, more refined and more resistant to challenge.

The individual has an intense emotional commitment to the belief and may carry out violent behavior in its service."[108] A delusion, on the other hand, is commonly regarded as "a fixed, false, and idiosyncratic belief (not shared by others)."[109] But what if a delusion *is* widely held? In late 2019, the alleged mafia hitman Anthony Comello confessed to murdering the mob boss Francesco Cali "because [Cali] was part of the 'deep state,' a member of a liberal cabal working to undermine President Trump."[110] Comello also professed to being an adherent of the QAnon conspiracy cult. The case was reminiscent of events surrounding Cesar Sayoc from a year earlier. An avid Trump supporter, Sayoc mailed multiple pipe bombs to Democratic politicians and media figures in the United States, believing them to also be members of the deep state. Such issues might seem pertinent to the use of the insanity defense, which is based on establishing whether the defendant "at the time of the act, labored under such a defect of reason from disease of the mind as to not know the nature and quality of the act [he/she] was doing, or as to not know what [he/she] was doing was wrong."[111] As the psychiatrist Kenneth Weiss explains, the McNaughten rule (named after the nineteenth-century murder trial of Daniel McNaughten) is essentially about knowing right from wrong, as opposed to being unable to resist an impulse to do something.[112] Being able to differentiate right from wrong can make a difference, at least from the perspective of defendants and their lawyers. Many supporters of former President Trump who took part in the attack on Capitol Hill in 2021 subsequently faced multiple criminal charges. A legal defense mounted by some of them attempted to absolve them of responsibility by essentially saying the only reason they participated in the attack was because "Trump told them to do it." Judges in several cases were quick to dismiss the argument, countering that if such an assertion were true, the defendants couldn't be trusted to exercise their own judgment and as such couldn't be trusted to be allowed out on their own.[113]

Other cases are more clear-cut. Sayoc sent pipe bombs to public officials and members of the public based on what he assumed were their political leanings.[114] He lived in a van festooned in stickers and posters supportive of Donald Trump and condemned news outlets such as CNN. According to his lawyers, Sayoc was a Trump "super fan" who "began to consider

Democrats as not just dangerous in theory, but imminently and seriously dangerous to his personal safety."[115] Sentencing Sayoc to twenty years in prison, the judge ruled that he was not "insane in the technical legal sense of that word . . . [but] he clearly became obsessive and paranoiac, and it was in this state, made still worse by his steroid abuse, that he decided to commit the crimes for which he is now to be sentenced."[116]

CONCLUSIONS

Having read this chapter and the previous two, we can arrive at several conclusions. We can say, with confidence, that there is no one single pathway to terrorism even within groups, let alone across them. The risk factors for involvement are dynamic. They vary considerably even within the same local context. At long last, our understanding of the terrorist has moved beyond crude profiles. This is because we see lots of different people—men, women, and children from all backgrounds and circumstances—becoming involved in terrorism. They join up in different ways, for initially different reasons, and they end up playing different roles. They often end up performing actions that are different than what they imagined for themselves. The cognitive and behavioral sequencing associated with involvement in terrorism remains unclear. It may even be unclear to the terrorists themselves. Some recruits first become ideological, which serves as a stepping stone to involvement with a group and subsequent action; other recruits become ideological only after they engage in violent action. In other words, the sequence does not necessarily follow an orderly or linear path even for members of the same group.

We have also seen there are many consequences to involvement. Interesting things happen when people get into terrorism. People who might initially be drawn to a group for their own distinct cluster of reasons but otherwise have diverse ideas of their own don't necessarily remain this way for very long. The differences among diverse recruits may be flattened out because of continued exposure to the group. How people change because of continued involvement is not something we know much about, but we can say that there will be variability in the qualities experienced by people involved in terrorism and, thus, how the terrorist mindset might look and feel different for various participants. For those who engage in violence, the brutality required for that role doesn't necessarily come overnight. It is learned behavior—in some cases, the product of practice. We've seen in this chapter where such practice leads. The next chapter, however, explains why it may not *always* be the one-way street we assume it is.

5

REINTEGRATION

*"The truth is, most of us discover where we are headed when we arrive.
At that time, we turn around and say, yes, this is obviously where I was
going all along."*

In late August 2020, Brenton Tarrant was sentenced to life in prison without parole for killing fifty-one people in Christchurch, New Zealand, and attempting to kill forty more. Prior to sentencing, a psychiatrist and psychologist were solicited to interview and assess Tarrant with a view to establishing his mental state. Both concluded Tarrant "showed no remorse for his actions" or "concern for the victims or their families."[1] Furthermore, Tarrant demonstrated "a lack of willingness to rehabilitate" and "lack of insight into his offending." The latter, the experts argued, was "proof of his significant risk of further offending."[2] Given what he had done, it's hardly surprising, even to nonexperts. But consider the idea for a moment: What would constitute rehabilitation for someone like him? Are there indicators we would look for? Expressions of remorse, evidence of shame, or a glimmer of humility? Would we feel better about someone's chances of rehabilitation if they renounced their ideological beliefs? If they cooperated with law enforcement? Or, should we really care about this at all? Why would anyone believe the word of someone whose passion and commitment saw him produce a hate-filled manifesto before murdering as many Muslims as he could? If the prospect of rehabilitation for someone like Tarrant seems farfetched, to entertain it seems undeserved at the very least.

At the time of his sentencing, we could characterize Tarrant as disengaged but not deradicalized. They are related yet distinct processes that terrorism researchers have examined for over a decade now. Sometimes they co-occur, and sometimes one happens without the other. There is much debate in academic circles around whether true rehabilitation should be measured in terms of disengagement, deradicalization, or both. But let's first clarify what these terms mean. In the context of terrorism, *disengagement* means stopping one's involvement. That can happen for many reasons, and the result of that stopping might look different from person to person. One terrorist's disengagement might involve arrest, conviction, and imprisonment. For another, it might only occur at the time of their death, whether at their own hand or by opposing forces. But the key focus in disengagement is detecting a change in a person's physical behavior. Disengagement, put simply, means that the person is no longer "doing" terrorism.

Deradicalization implies a change of heart or, more precisely, a change of mind. When recruits no longer believe in what the group is doing, that's a form of psychological disengagement. Their commitment wanes and their emotional attachment to the cause comes undone; they no longer embrace and commit to extreme beliefs (assuming, of course, they once did). While all terrorists disengage at some point, only some experience deradicalization. In general, it can be thought of as a process in which the terrorists' views change in such a way that they become less committed to the ideals of the group or the group itself. It is, put another way, the unraveling of the mindset they once worked so hard to build.

Why are these processes related yet distinct? There are three reasons. First, a terrorist can disengage and then deradicalize. For instance, convicted terrorists might come to realize in prison that while they are no longer physically able to continue participating, they also no longer want to even identify with the cause or movement. They feel that they've had enough and see an opportunity for something else, so they begin putting psychological distance between themselves and the movement. In a way, prison provides the ideal setting for such distancing to happen.[3] The author Alison Jamieson's interviews with former members of the Italian Red Brigades movement revealed how prison provided ex-combatants an opportunity to, in her words, "re-examine the past critically, and to work through individual and collective responsibilities as a prelude to rehabilitation and release."[4]

Second, a person can disengage and not deradicalize. Just because people walk away from terrorism doesn't necessarily mean that they have turned their back on the movement or what it stands for. People disengage for all kinds of reasons, and it is common for imprisoned terrorists to remain fully committed to the cause. In some cases, terrorist movements allow their own rank and file to walk away unscathed. Assuming those groups put measures in place to maintain organizational and operational security, allowing members to take an occasional break can go a long way in preventing burnout and simultaneously retaining valuable human capital.

Last, a terrorist can deradicalize but not necessarily disengage. A person may be an active, engaged, and even *violent* member of a terrorist group and concurrently be deeply disillusioned. They are, for all intents and purposes, de-radicalized, but they may not have yet walked away or been able to do so. Recall Sarah from the previous chapter, who was disillusioned with the movement long before she was able to leave it. Fear of retribution, and lack of alternatives outside the group (including not having access to basic resources), conspired to keep her involved despite her own realization she was no longer the committed soldier she once was. But just as involvement brings both benefits and costs, so too does disengagement. Terrorists who leave a group may embrace the newfound psychological freedoms of disassociation from a stifling movement, yet they may now be without the close bonds forged inside.

Deradicalization is also used to describe a growing number of initiatives worldwide that seek to reduce the risk of reengagement in terrorism. These programs involve a combination of psychological counseling, vocational training, and in some cases restorative justice—meeting with those bereaved or otherwise affected by terrorist violence. The precise recipe for what constitutes an effective terrorist rehabilitation program is far from clear, but in prisons and other places of detention worldwide, the rise of deradicalization programs has been met with a mixture of curiosity, hope, skepticism, and derision in ever-changing measures. And yet, some of these efforts seem to demonstrate real promise.

WALKING AWAY FROM TERRORISM

Disengagement is an important element of terrorist behavior to understand. It was largely ignored for years, perhaps just overshadowed by the focus on understanding how people get into terrorism in the first place. It was incorrectly assumed for years that terrorism was a one-way street. The assumption seemed logical. After all, journeying through a twilight world where the risk of capture or death is likely suggests that stepping into that realm in the first place is a process not easily reversed. But since the mid-2000s, research on how and why people exit terrorism has exploded.[5] There is now even a dedicated academic journal on deradicalization. As the Islamic State ascended in notoriety, the author Graeme Wood proclaimed, "Our ignorance of [IS] is in some ways understandable: It is a hermit kingdom; few have gone there and returned."[6] And yet, how quickly that has changed, with tens of thousands of returnees now back in their home countries or languishing in squalid detention camps. The Islamic State was unique in so many ways, but most terrorist movements eventually fall; that simultaneously poses new security and other challenges for the countries their members once willfully fled while also providing opportunities for us to learn from them.

The research tells us that there is even some diversity in the process and experience of disengagement. It can be sudden or gradual. A single event may act as a catalyst for someone wanting to get out of terrorism. For others, it is a gradual process of weighing alternatives and trying to find the right time and place to make the physical leap. Disengagement can be a voluntary experience, as in when a terrorist decides to leave and does. It can also be involuntary. This could be the case when the police arrest someone, but it can just as easily happen when a member is dismissed from the movement for some infraction, or perhaps that same person falls ill or is injured. Robert White and Terry Falkenberg White once said that terrorist careers end in capture or death.[7] These would constitute dramatically sudden forms of disengagement, with the latter an obviously permanent outcome. But often terrorist groups allow members to just, well, take a break. Perhaps they do so only for some members, but when they do it, it is sometimes to avoid that person becoming burned out. Knowing they are likely to return, the movement may reap the rewards of welcoming back an even more effective operative.[8] We can say, therefore, that it can be short-term, long-term, or permanent disengagement. In her research on how and why Indonesian jihadists quit terrorism, the political scientist Julie Chernov Hwang found disengagement can in some cases even be "conditional."[9] Nearly half of her interviewees were mobilized by local communal conflict; former participants in violence might well be open to reengaging should certain conditions reappear, such as invasion by enemies.[10] It is very important to consider where the risk of reengagement comes from. Considering the broader context and setting is critical when trying to reintegrate former terrorists safely and successfully—in other words, not just placing all the emphasis on what the terrorism scholar Sarah Marsden called the "internal change" of the offender.[11]

With notable exceptions, much of what we know about disengagement is at the level of the individual terrorist.[12] We know far less about what groups do to facilitate or mitigate the process of their members leaving. In some groups, factors at play insulate terrorists from disengagement. In contrast to the IRA, which would routinely allow members to step out every now and again, Andreas Baader allegedly would tell new recruits to the Baader-Meinhof group that the only way out was "feet first" (i.e., with their death), adding, "Whoever is in the group simply has to be tough, has to be able to hold out, and if one is not tough enough, there is not room for him here."[13] An analysis of Islamic State personnel records by researchers at West Point's Combating Terrorism Center suggested that personnel were allowed to leave IS provided they gave an acceptable reason for doing so.[14] The researchers discovered the main reasons given by recruits were "leaving to receive medical treatment" or "family reasons." The latter involved a temporary hiatus with the intention of returning to IS territory with additional family members. One form intriguingly noted that an IS member had "confusion with matters," while another was seemingly allowed to leave because he "could not practice patience."[15]

Thinking back on the lessons learned from the previous two chapters, we could entertain an interesting idea here. We could, hypothetically, distill lessons from that research to reverse engineer what on paper is the psychological recipe for a perfect terrorist. But regardless, everyone who becomes a terrorist will encounter challenges; it is one inevitable consequence of getting involved in terrorism. Even the most dedicated of recruits cannot predict how they will process the experiences associated with involvement and deepening commitment and, ultimately, what will happen to them. Michael "Bommi" Baumann, founder of the German 2 June Movement, recalled in his memoirs how he began to change:

> You start developing the instincts of an animal of prey. After a while, you just run around like a gunman. Any sharp eye could recognize you. It's crazy what you do, always running around with a gun. A man who runs around with a gun anchors his center on the weapon—where you carry it, that's your center. You move so that you can always pull it out any time, anywhere. Today, I can tell with anyone if he's got a gun on him, and where he has it, because you can see how he moves. This crazy concentration, all day long."[16]

Baumann concludes, "[The pressure] always catches up with you."[17] When we considered how the terrorist mindset develops, we saw that some cope better than others with the demands associated with deepening involvement. But while individual terrorists experience their own struggles with commitment, terrorist movements sometimes devise structures that serve as a pressure release valve. Some groups allow dissent to emerge, presumably as a means of stemming more serious problems like defection. This applies not just to their own members but to their supporters, too. In areas controlled by the Islamic State, the movement reportedly allowed members of the public to "report misconduct by its members," which was aided by setting up an actual complaints box at a local mosque.[18]

Even a cursory glance at terrorist careers reveals both the voluntary and involuntary nature of disengagement. This distinction was first recognized in sociological studies of people who walked away from certain roles. Helen Ebaugh's early sociological research involved interviews with nearly sixty ex-nuns, which led her to a deeper exploration of what she termed "role exit."[19] In her 1988 book, *Becoming an Ex*, Ebaugh expanded her interviewee sample to former prisoners, former prostitutes, divorcees, (more) ex-nuns, ex-convicts, retirees, and so on—a broad group whose shared experience was that at some point in their lives they had all exited a role that once defined their lives and identities. For Ebaugh, these "exes" followed similar pathways out. They experienced doubts, which led them to seek out potential alternatives. That was followed by experiencing a critical turning point, whereupon a subsequent decision to leave was made before the person occupied their new role as an "ex." Ebaugh's research raises several fascinating questions for thinking about the terrorist. Would walking away from terrorism involve a similar process? On the face of it, voluntary disengagement from terrorism seems like a risky proposition for all concerned. Even groups that allow members to disengage might not wish to advertise the fact widely. Why risk undermining organizational prestige by letting members know they can also just walk out the door whenever they change their minds? Whether voluntary or involuntary in nature, however, disengagement can happen for many reasons. There's rarely one factor alone that causes someone to disengage, and a person might experience some or all of them, and they might not happen in any specific order. In fact, the principles of multifinality and equifinality may just as easily apply to disengagement as they do to radicalization. Terrorists rarely just walk away. From terrorist memoirs and interviews with former terrorists, disillusionment is a common theme in accounts of disengagement.[20] Chernov Hwang found that, in the case of her Indonesian jihadists, disillusionment on its own rarely culminated in people walking away because "loyalty to the group would often trump disillusionment."[21] But disillusionment itself also occurs for several reasons. It may result from such things as personality clashes with colleagues, jealousy, rivalry, dealing with the stress of living a clandestine life once the initial excitement wears off, and sometimes just plain old boredom. Experiences of disillusionment will naturally vary from person to person, and possibly even from group to group, depending on what structures or internal practices groups put in place to manage challenges. The terrorism expert Michael Kenney noted in his study of the UK-based al Muhajiroun movement that even the most well-run community of practice can produce dissent and acrimony, and his respondents were certainly keen to suggest that such disagreements were, overall, minor.[22] Still, the consequences of devotion are sometimes too much to bear. Activists often just get burned out.[23] "Mujaahid4Life," the Twitter nom de guerre of the Finnish male convert to Islam mentioned in chapter 3, recalled this of his online involvement supporting IS's global propaganda effort: "When I was in that Isis bubble, I was thinking so emotionally. . . . When you're younger you don't have the intellectual capabilities to process it. It was an obsession, just blind devotion."[24]

One of the striking findings from research on disengagement is that the causes of disengagement are often just the same personal and professional issues that can affect most people at some point in their lives—stress, dysfunction, jealousy, squabbling, or people just being fed up and wanting change. The sociologist Mehr Latif and colleagues' study of women in violent racist groups in the United States showed their disillusionment arose from "poor relationships with other white supremacists, violence, or mistreatment of women in the movement."[25] Other reasons included feelings of shame and regret associated with violence they had committed and general dissatisfaction with gender and sexual hierarchies associated with women in general in such groups.[26]

As with just about everything on terrorist behavior, context is everything. Each of the factors associated with disengagement can be understood only in its own specific time and place. For example, terrorists may become disillusioned with the tactics and strategy being pursued by their movement. But that can come from two very different places. For some, disillusionment grows when a group is regarded as going too far—for example, killing too many people or killing children. This breach of what was once considered unlikely or impossible can make members reevaluate their commitment. For others, however, it comes from a feeling of not being able to do anything at all. When terrorist organizations experience major turning points, the risk to organizational cohesion can be profound. The researchers White and White recall how an IRA ceasefire in the mid-1970s undermined the prospect of the movement relaunching its campaign: "Disillusion set in in some quarters, and the return to a normal life tapped the commitment of some IRA members."[27] Alternatively, and in the same context, during the series of ceasefires that took place in the mid-1990s in Northern Ireland, many Irish Republican paramilitaries there gravitated to splinter groups who became even *more* extreme and *more* violent because they felt their progenitors had succumbed to a process that would betray all that they had previously fought for. So, just as disillusionment can be a catalyst for reducing one's commitment, it can also feed commitment, leading to seeking out and embracing ever more extreme outcomes. Disillusionment with one group might lead the member to start or join another.

Despite the newfound knowledge and exciting progress on disengagement processes, there is still much to be done. For example, though there is much research on disengagement from nationalist terror groups, jihadist movements, and the extreme right, very little is known so far about disengagement from the far left.[28] Though many former members of left-wing terror groups such as the German Baader-Meinhof gang and the Italian Red Brigades have long told their stories, and some have even written memoirs, we know relatively little about disengagement from other major left-wing groups across South Asia and Latin America, or indeed the wave of left-wing terrorist actors operating in the United States throughout the 1970s.

REHABILITATION AND REINTEGRATION

As a terrorism researcher, I've often wondered about how much time people spend in terrorist groups. *What does an average career look like? Does it vary by group? Group type? By role?* We can probably assume there is a spectrum. Some members' involvement will be short, and some will stay involved for decades. Furthermore, there are not just career terrorists within movements but also across them. The American University terrorism expert Chelsea Daymon and her colleagues studied career foreign fighters who migrated across different groups.[29] They found that foreign fighters who come back from one terrorist campaign are able to transfer their acquired knowledge, skills, and resources to others. This adaptability makes these careerists, the researchers conclude, far more dangerous than apparent "one-off" terrorists.[30] Studies like this raise questions about what to do with returning foreign fighters—and terrorist prisoners more generally.[31] But how terrorist offenders are processed and managed by the criminal justice system is barely known about let alone understood.

In one of the few studies of terrorism-related sentencing and its guidelines, the legal scholar Stephen Floyd suggests the judicial system holds some deeply problematic assumptions.[32] He illustrates his concerns: "The broad scope of the material support statute treats violent and nonviolent acts alike, resulting in similar sentences for dissimilar crimes," resulting in disproportionate treatment of a wide variety of different types of offender. What may happen, Floyd concludes, is that "a nonviolent, first-time offender who indirectly supports a terrorist act may receive the same criminal history category as a violent offender with a lengthy sentence."[33] The material support statute, he explains, has its origins in the 1993 terrorist attack on New York's World Trade Center. Soon after, Congress passed the 1994 Violent Crime Control and Law Enforcement Act. The Act gave rise to the new offense of "material support to terrorists" while also pushing for terrorists to receive harsher sentences more generally.[34] The result of the subsequent blanket treatment of terrorist offenders, broadly speaking, comes from what Floyd says is the ingrained belief that "terrorists are distinct from other criminals and refractive to rehabilitation."[35] A consequence of all of this, he concludes, is that current approaches to terrorist offenders, at least in the United States, largely "[ignore] the potential for rehabilitation."[36]

Judicial sentencing of terrorist offenders is in disarray for other reasons, and yet again, at the heart of such disarray is the issue of gender. As the legal scholar Natalia Galica explains, because of gender stereotypes, female involvement in terrorism is often framed in a "feminine and submissive light"[37] with the significance of their actions and agency often "infantilized"[38] and "diminished by the media."[39] That same framing can influence judicial sentencing decisions, leading to disproportionate outcomes. Galica compared court sentences between 156 males and 10 females charged with Islamic State–related terrorism offenses in the United States. Her analysis focused on cases where men and women provided material support to terrorist groups (e.g., donating money), as well as those who made false statements to officials—these typically represent some of the "most common charges that both males and females accused of terrorism face."[40] Though the sample is obviously skewed heavily toward men, the average sentence received by women convicted of making false statements to officials was 49.5 months. Males received on average 87.2 months under the same charge. Women convicted on material support charges received on average 86.4 months, compared to 155.2 months for men charged under the same offense. Galica explains, "The rhetoric of the legal professionals involved in the cases demonstrate[s] that the sentencing disparities are due to the notions that women are more naïve, lonely, or innocent than males when it comes to such violent crimes."[41] A correction proposed by Galica is to "categorize the sentences based on the roles the terrorists play in the plot."[42]

Curious to see firsthand how terrorist offenders are managed postsentencing, I visited my first deradicalization program in 2008. I traveled to Saudi Arabia as part of a group of invited guests to see up close what was already in the West being called efforts to reverse radicalism.[43] Our group was about a dozen strong. We were comprised of national security professionals, a few internationally recognizable figures who engineered peace processes in communities afflicted by decades of internecine conflict, assorted retired military figures, and a few others who said very little about who they were and for whom they worked and certainly gave the impression that they did not want to be there. I was one of a handful of academics on the trip invited to tour the Kingdom's rehabilitation facilities. We were given a royal welcome and, amid some extraordinary security, invited to tour the facilities. They were as one would expect—modern, well-resourced, and lavish without being garish. To this day, the Saudi program stands alone in terms of the sheer amount of resourcing available to it. Many other programs run on little more than the goodwill of practitioners already straining under crippling caseloads. Unsurprisingly, the Saudi visit was highly choreographed and our movements were controlled—we saw what we were allowed to see, and that was it. We were whisked from one setting to the next, sometimes within the hour. As part of the trip, our group had the opportunity to meet with several graduates of the program face to face. One memorable evening, during which we dined with former Al-Qaeda members, we received a tour of where the program's art therapy sessions took place. Art therapy was one component of the rehabilitation program that involved classes in vocational training, religious "reeducation," and sports. This room was festooned with art, all created by program participants. In the Western media, the Saudi program was routinely maligned for the idea of curing terrorism by giving jihadists a paintbrush to express their feelings. I shared the skepticism. Who would believe that the key to reforming a terrorist lies in simply providing them with new information, as if mere exposure would now result in them making different choices? The psychologist in me was curious about the different treatment components at the facility: What specific plans for treatment and management were being used here? What does psychotherapy with Al-Qaeda even look like? I didn't shy away from asking the participants about their respective art projects, as well as the director of the art therapy program, himself a psychologist. One participant painted a blazing hot desert scene, and with his permission I snapped a picture of it. When I asked him about it, he told me he wanted to paint Afghanistan because he missed his friends there.

The Saudi authorities put on an impressive show for us, and of course we couldn't help but wonder if what we were observing was real. The Saudis claimed they were seeing tremendous success with their efforts and recidivism was practically nonexistent. But why was recidivism so low? Might it have had something to do with the fact that graduates from the program are provided with jobs and living spaces, helped to find wives, all of which would presumably be withdrawn if there was even a hint of reengagement? Perhaps the provision of those benefits *was* the deradicalization program, not the detailed rehabilitation story projected to impress visitors. Notwithstanding all of that, surveillance by Saudi authorities would likely mitigate any such temptations for graduates to even contact former colleagues in Al-Qaeda, let alone attempt to physically reconnect with them. The program provided a good lesson in thinking very carefully about the issue of recidivism and why it does or does not happen. I visited a very different rehabilitation program in 2018, this time in Somalia where former al-Shabaab members were helped to reintegrate back into the communities they once abandoned. Several "formers" I met mentioned that the risk of them reengaging with al-Shabaab was very low because, they said, if they tried to go back to the movement, they would almost certainly be executed for having left in the first place. Little wonder the postrehabilitation recidivism rate was virtually zero there.

The Saudi program had been in place for at least three years before our visit in 2008. Different programs have since emerged in different countries amid varied circumstances. In some cases, the programs came to exist through the realization that prisons are a place where radicalization can, if left unchecked, get worse, either through indoctrination from other inmates or through deepening commitment of those already convicted for terrorist offenses. A second reason relates to the acknowledgement that many convicted on lower-level terrorist offenses will eventually be released back into the communities from which they came, and it stands to reason that some efforts would ideally be undertaken to try to reduce the risk of reengagement (of whatever type or degree) back into terrorism. That is how it is explained on paper, anyway. Publicly, deradicalization programs are a hard sell. Not only is there often little appetite for them, but in some cases the very idea of rehabilitation is met with reactions that range from skepticism to outright protest. The jihadism expert Aaron Zelin describes how, in early 2017, protests emerged in Tunisia at the prospect of returning foreign fighters. Common refrains included "No return, no freedom for savage (IS) bands" and "No repenting, no pardon for terrorists."[44] A recurring tension exists between selling the idea of rehabilitation and holding terrorists accountable for their past actions.

RECIDIVISM

Policymakers routinely ask if deradicalization programs work. The short answer is that some of them probably do, but nobody can right now be sure because these programs are rarely subject to any kind of evaluation.[45] The Belgian academic and terrorism expert Rik Coolsaet summarized the issue thusly: "Deradicalization programmes often constitute a potpourri of objectives from inclusiveness and prevention of all kinds to repression and counter-narratives."[46] Little wonder, he concludes, why they are so difficult to properly evaluate. Furthermore, when programs appear to be effective, it is not the case for all offenders. A more precise question might be whether deradicalization programs truly reduce the risk of recidivism in program participants (relative to those who do not participate), and, if so, how precisely is that reduction achieved? This might seem like a needlessly finicky argument, but it's important in a practical sense. The main defense offered by successful programs is that they point to low or nonexistent recidivism rates. But to have confidence in such a defense, we should ask, would the risk of recidivism still be low even if an offender did not participate in a deradicalization program? For reasons we do not yet fully understand, the risk of recidivism to violent extremism is *very* low. In the United States, nonterrorist offenders "re-offend at rates between 25 and 83 percent", with similarly high rates in other countries.[47] Typically, "ordinary crime" recidivism rates tend to range from 45 to 55 percent.[48] Compared to ordinary criminals, the recidivism rate for terrorists is much lower. The Spanish terrorism expert Fernando Reinares and colleagues examined 199 cases of jihadist cases from Spain.[49] They detected a 7 percent recidivism rate (fourteen cases, five of which took place in prison). Thomas Renard, director of the International Center for Counter-Terrorism, reviewed 557 cases of jihadist convictions in Belgium over three decades. He found a recidivism rate of just under 5 per cent.[50] When Renard went even further and analyzed results from twelve studies (including some of those mentioned above) that encompassed some three thousand cases of terrorist convictions, he found the overall recidivism rate was 2.9 percent.

These are striking findings. Before we get too carried away, however, let's acknowledge that the results might, at least to some degree, vary depending on how we define *recidivism*—technically speaking, it implies a return to offenses connected to terrorism, whereas reoffending would encompass a far broader set of activities.[51] The criminologist Omi Hodwitz's Terrorism Recidivism Study examined 561 cases of people convicted for terrorist offenses in the United States in the post-9/11 era.[52] She detected an overall recidivism rate of approximately 1.6 percent. That is, only nine people reengaged in activity. Of those, five "recidivated" while still in prison. A closer look, however, found that offenders engaged in behavior that did not, at least on the surface, indicate reengagement in terrorism. One offender violated the terms of his plea agreement by simply accessing the Internet, another "committed fraud by illegally buying food stamps," while another was put back in prison because of "drug possession."[53] Hodwitz found that two of the nine attempted murder postrelease, but neither episode was deemed to be "politically motivated."[54] Within his Belgian sample, Renard found that "no reoffender was involved in a terrorist plot for their second offense."[55] Such findings, if they continue to be replicated elsewhere, suggest that the risk of recidivism to terrorism may even be lower than what already appears in unusually low rates.

The research of Hodwitz, Renard, and others raises important questions about what we mean by recidivism. Renard cautions that because terrorist recidivism studies tend to only be concerned with reoffending into the same type of offense (terrorism), it shouldn't be surprising that, all other things being equal, it would be much lower than ordinary criminal recidivism (which considers subsequent engagement in *any* kind of crime a type of recidivism).[56] So Hodwitz then asks, what might explain the low recidivism rate associated with former terrorists? Specifically, are they actually rehabilitated? Do they take longer to reengage in potential terrorist activity? Or, she wonders, might they subsequently be better skilled at concealing their actions and intentions?[57] In a case study of UK efforts at deradicalizing terrorist offenders, the researcher Douglas Weeks highlighted the case of Usman Khan, the British jihadist who killed two people in London in 2019.[58] Khan had earlier been imprisoned for terrorist offenses, but his sentence was reduced. During Khan's time in prison, he participated in two deradicalization programs.[59] Did authorities allow him to fall through the cracks, or was he, as one journalist argued, "engaged in a long-term effort to con the British authorities"?[60] Despite being exceptionally rare instances of terrorist recidivism, the Khan case, and the few others like it, Weeks explains, fuel public outrage and reignite extensive debate over the merits of deradicalization efforts.[61]

Notwithstanding the distinctions between recidivism and reoffending (broadly), using different data sources may also reveal different findings. With my colleagues Mary Beth Altier and Emma Leonard Boyle, I looked at nearly ninety terrorist autobiographies published over a hundred-year period.[62] We found evidence suggesting a much higher rate of reengagement to terrorism in our sample—over 60 percent in some cases. What we found in that study cannot, nor should it, be used to approximate a recidivism base rate. We had to explicitly repeat that point after one well-known terrorism researcher misinterpreted our findings.[63] But the question here is what might explain why we found a much higher rate in our sample, especially when we deliberately focused on reengagement in terrorism and not just recidivism broadly speaking? It is of course possible that terrorist memoirs tend to be written by people with a long, storied career in terrorism, which often will be characterized by intermittent involvement and commitment over decades. It's equally possible, therefore, that our sample had overrepresentation from those with a lengthier than normal involvement in terrorism.[64]

RISK ASSESSMENT

A cliché in debates on deradicalization is that there's no one-size-fits-all solution. That comment means two different things. First, we should never uncritically look at a program in one country as a potential blueprint for building a program in another. Second, Daymon's findings from the study of career foreign fighters remind us that not all terrorists are created equal. As we've seen in previous chapters, people become involved in terrorism in different ways and for different reasons, and they end up doing very different kinds of things, not all of which (and in many cases, rarely) directly involve violence. Would it stand to reason then that it would be easier to rehabilitate some terrorists compared to others? And if we accepted that premise, would it require us to develop ways to assess differences between terrorists, not just by considering what they did prior to disengagement but whether they reliably signal progress toward rehabilitation?

The concerns raised by both Galica and Floyd around inappropriate and inconsistent sentencing of terrorist offenders should inform efforts at rehabilitation. But if judicial sentencing does not reflect data-driven research on terrorist behavior (at least yet), assessing the potential for rehabilitation can only begin when offenders are assessed for potential risk of future violence or, much more broadly, potential reengagement in terrorist activity. This is easier said than done. On the one hand, research into terrorist risk assessment has flourished in recent years. Multiple risk assessment tools exist (no less than twenty), and at least seven well-known and frequently used tools are commonly used in detention settings.[65] They mostly resemble guided checklists of factors that are either present or absent at the time of their measurement. With a little training (in some cases a few hours), many such tools are designed to be used by people with little if any knowledge of how terrorism works. Without a clear way to channel such checklists into practical guidance on managing any subsequent risk, it can be difficult to see what practical benefit such tools offer apart from supporting the assessor's confidence in his or her decision at the time.[66]

To be fair, mental health practitioners face a profoundly challenging task in assessing terrorist offenders. As the Irish clinical psychologist Kiran Sarma argues, the enormous predictive challenges associated with risk assessment are owed to "the variable nature of terrorism, the low base-rate problem, and the dearth of strong evidence on relevant risk and resilience factors."[67] In an article in *The Journal of Forensic Psychiatry and Psychology*, psychologist Mats Dernevik and colleagues cautioned, "It is unsafe to assume that mental health professionals are able to assess the risk of terrorist violence recidivism." Mental health professionals are those most likely to be positioned to make such assessments, typically in prison settings, but Dernevik and colleagues warn that in many cases there is just not enough known about these issues to reliably recommend action.[68] In 2009, their recommendations to clinicians tasked with making such judgments included the need to develop working knowledge of terrorism, knowledge of research on terrorist psychology, knowledge of the specific political and cultural contexts in which any conflict takes place, and if mental disorder is present, and knowledge of how to interpret its role (if any) in the motivation of the offender's actions. Like I said, easier said than done. And how can any professional be reasonably expected to have knowledge or expertise across these multiple domains—from assessment to mental health, to violent extremism, ideology, history, culture, and so on? To compound matters, as the scholars Caroline Logan and Rachel Sellers asked in the very same journal over a decade later, how can practitioners be expected to make sound judgments and generally engage in good practice when the evidence base informing such decisions is itself so limited?[69] Perhaps the first step is to embrace a more critical perspective on the nature and limitations of the tools used to guide assessment. Risk assessment professionals are constantly concerned about assessing dangerousness; typically, this is about whether an offender is likely to inflict violence. Historically, the forensic researchers Jerrod Brown and Jay Singh argue, that emphasis gave rise to the area of forensic risk assessment grounded in the need to "accurately establish the risk of future offending" through "a growing preference . . . for probabilistic estimates of the risk."[70] This actuarial-type approach, they explain, stood in contrast to assessments based on the professional judgments of experts.[71]

Risk assessment is also concerned with identifying risk and protective factors—i.e., identifying what specifically is likely to cause an increase or decrease in the likelihood of problematic behavior, whether that is violence or something else.[72] It turns out that clinical judgments in some cases offer little predictive success compared to chance guesses. But professionals at least now have a choice between actuarial risk assessment and structured professional judgment. The former involves instruments where respective risk and protective factors and the estimated risk of recidivism are respectively weighted in accordance with known rates. But, as Brown and Singh note, a real challenge lies in how group-based recidivism rates can somehow be applied to the cases of individual patients.[73]

Structured professional judgment (SPJ) represents an increasingly accepted approach to risk assessment of terrorist offenders.[74] Originally devised to improve on actuarial tools, SPJ prioritizes a focus on the individual as opposed to the group, allowing greater flexibility for individual assessors to incorporate contextual factors into their decisions.[75] Here, for example, the person doing the assessment might return a judgment of risk of likely future offending "when combined with case-specific information gained through clinical experience with the client being evaluated."[76] Logan reminds us that SPJ "is an *approach* and not a specific set of risk assessment and management guidance or a particular tool or instrument."[77] On the surface, SPJ seems like a no-brainer approach to assessing terrorist offenders. While he cautions that risk assessment of terrorists doesn't lend itself to a simple formula or "tally of risk factors," the psychologist Randy Borum suggests that "a structured assessment process that is systematic, transparent, and reliant on current evidence would serve the interests of both procedural fairness and substantive security."[78] Terrorism research clearly reveals terrorist offenders to be a very mixed group, with multiple different cohorts emerging even within the same movement over time. Surely such a complex phenomenon requires an equally flexible and dynamic approach to assessing risk emanating from those within? Not so fast—after all, greater flexibility means introducing the kinds of decision-making bias that actuarial tools were designed to weed out.[79] By and large, however, SPJ approaches are generally considered by many practitioners to be the most appropriate tools for risk-assessing terrorist offenders.[80]

There are some additional considerations. The terrorism researchers Nadine Salman and Paul Gill add that we mustn't forget to look at more than just the tools.[81] We must also find ways to provide ongoing education and training for professionals so that they can develop competencies across those different knowledge domains. Salman and Gill kick-started that process by surveying forty-one professionals involved in risk assessment, asking them what training, experience, and general characteristics *they* believe make for a good assessor of risk. Recommendations included having higher-level education, formal professional training (viewed as more important than formal education), and good interpersonal skills to allow for building rapport. The practitioners surveyed also suggested that cases be reviewed by not just one professional but "at least two."[82]

Another theme we've encountered in previous chapters is the danger of allowing dichotomies to control our thinking—that the solution must lie in one approach or interpretation as opposed to the other. No matter whether actuarial or structured professional judgment approaches are used, the lack of theoretical clarity of what constitutes risk and protective factors in a terrorism context will hinder an already complicated task. The future of terrorist risk assessment cannot only be about developing (and validating) population-specific tools to address terrorist offenders but also (if not more so) focusing on developing a better understanding of what respective offenders specifically *do* (or did) as terrorists. The need to consistently build more and more evidence to support such decision-making remains critical. As new research areas emerge, we would do well to consider their relevance for thinking about practical applications. As an example, psychologists have only recently begun to systematically study the topic of humility. Daryl Van Tongeren and colleagues define it as a "trait characterized by both an ability to accurately acknowledge one's limitations and abilities and an interpersonal stance that is other-oriented rather than self-focused."[83] Other researchers have described intellectual humility as involving "an awareness of how incomplete and fallible their views on political and social issues were."[84] Notably, intellectual humility was not associated with intelligence or political affiliation but "strongly linked to curiosity, reflection and open-mindedness."[85] Could such research encourage us to think further about individual-level risk or protective factors for reengagement in terrorism? Despite the challenges in translating and transforming research into practice, some research is ready to inform risk assessment and, indeed, judicial sentencing. In an expansion of his earlier work on what terrorists read, the UK-based terrorism expert Donald Holbrook was able to detect different levels of "extremities" within the various narratives.[86] Holbrook distinguished ideological material into three categories: moderate, fringe, and extreme. He graded material as moderate when it contained no messages endorsing violence or hostility toward others. Material classified as fringe contained "hostile rhetoric toward identified people without explicit endorsement of lethal violence against them," while extreme material contained "support for lethal violence against identified people and/or explicit dehumanizing rhetoric."[87] If taken seriously, the kind of work being done by scholars like Holbrook could provide a foundation for challenging what Stephen Floyd and other criminal justice experts reveal as the highly inconsistent sentencing of terrorist offenders (while also, giving "first-time offenders the chance for disengagement and rehabilitation").[88]

CONCLUSION

Research on disengagement from terrorism has only begun relatively recently, but already it is raising intriguing questions about whether people can be persuaded to leave terrorist groups and whether those who have already left can be persuaded to stay out. In addition to the popular media coverage of deradicalization programs (all of which require rigorous evaluation), stories of small-scale efforts abound. Daryl Davis, a Black musician who suffered a racially motivated attack when he was ten years old, has dedicated his life to engaging with white nationalist extremists in the United States. Davis claims to have effectively helped hundreds of white supremacists disengage by engaging them in simple conversation and, for the most part, listening to what they had to say.[89] Deradicalization programs, which more accurately should be called rehabilitation, reintegration, or risk-reduction programs, can also be effective, but they don't suit everyone.[90] Can anyone, no matter how senior their rank or how committed they might appear, deradicalize? Theoretically, yes. But not everyone wants to, and so not everyone does. Often at the heart of the acrimony that surrounds such programs is the idea that when they work, they only work for lower-ranking members of terrorist groups. We should see this less of an indictment and rather as clear evidence of what works—and at what level. If a reintegration program is to be meaningful, its participants can't just be fringe supporters, but if we assume that many leadership figures, or career foreign fighters, begin as foot soldiers, then we would do well to give such interventions a chance to work if they prove effective at those lower levels. There are lots of unknowns here, of course, but we do not have the luxury of hiding behind imperfect knowledge while we wait for more research to materialize. As a matter of general principle, we should be pragmatic. To criticize deradicalization programs because they seem to work mostly on low-ranking members misses the point. More egregiously, it displays a narrow and misguided view of the benefits to be had of "thinning the herd." No program can be 100 percent successful, and it isn't realistic to expect that of any program—no matter how well resourced it might be. Politically speaking, the consequences of getting it wrong, or having someone fall through the cracks, can be profound. But even when risk assessment professionals get it wrong, it doesn't mean we shouldn't continue to invest in and improve these efforts. If we get it wrong, why did it happen? What were the circumstances in which that assessment occurred and what led to decisions surrounding a particular case? We don't know nearly enough about the inner workings of these programs, let alone how decisions emerge from discussion and deliberation, and we certainly don't know enough about the failures. If something seems to work, we need to know why. If something seems to fail, we also need to know why.

Several basic issues still need to be figured out. In a sense, separating disengagement from deradicalization might seem unnecessary. When the sociologist Helen Ebaugh talked about disengagement, it encompassed both the behavioral part of walking away and the *accompanying* cognitive shifts (or lack thereof). For her, a person's disengagement means "the process of disassociating and disidentifying with the values, ideas, expectations, and social relationships for a given period in his or her life."[91] Ebaugh argues that people who exit roles experience a "hangover identity" from the previous role. The challenge for the "ex" is to assimilate and accommodate that experience into their emerging and future identity. For the ex-terrorist, this is no easy task, and concerns will always linger around whether a disengaged terrorist may be at risk for reengaging. Distinguishing disengagement from deradicalization, and understanding their interrelationship, can be important in ascertaining the level of risk associated with potential reengagement. And yet, even for the repentant former terrorist, there are still enormous barriers to reintegration. The challenge can be overwhelming. First highlighted by the psychologist Max Taylor as far back as 1988, negative mental health consequences are increasingly recognized now as outcomes of participation in terrorism.[92] Guilt and shame can go hand in hand with the stigma of being viewed as nothing more than an ex-terrorist. Only very recently have researchers begun to call attention to in terms of how trauma and toxic stress can be just some of the outcomes of participation in terrorism.[93]

Some criticisms of deradicalization programs are that they don't do anything that you wouldn't expect to see emerge naturally. Surely, the logic goes, it's easy to deradicalize someone who is deeply disillusioned and thinks they might avoid a lengthier prison sentence. Well, yes. And we could extend this further by saying it's easier to deradicalize someone who wants to be deradicalized. The kinds of interventions associated with those programs cannot be expected to work on everyone—if they don't work on the terrorist elites, the tough nuts, maybe that's OK. We must be realistic. Likewise, if we expect 100 percent success even at the level of the lower ranks, then we are equally deluding ourselves on this front. There *will* be failures. The challenge is to understand why and how they occur. Only by doing so can we improve our knowledge of the relevant processes. A current limitation with deradicalization initiatives is, as the Belgian criminologist Sigrid Raets argued, they are "operating in a theoretical vacuum" where research on disengagement isn't necessarily accessible (or translatable) to real-world interventions—at least yet.[94] I remain skeptical of deradicalization programs yet I also support them—I want to see them succeed. Better discussions and partnerships must develop between policy makers, practitioners, program managers, academics, and specialists who know about how to evaluate the effectiveness of such interventions. Such concerns are compounded by what Omi Hodwitz (and many others) point to as the groundswell of terrorist offenders scheduled for release over the coming decades.[95] Whatever the future brings for these programs, opportunities exist in prison settings for better assessment of the risks associated with reengagement in terrorism, which can help, more broadly, in trying to achieve safe reintegration and rehabilitation of former terrorist offenders. In the United States, the growing specter of domestic, homegrown terrorism underscores the fact that terrorist offenders of today and tomorrow will be an increasingly diverse population. If reintegration of terrorist offenders is something that the United States is prepared to seriously consider, it will need to prepare for that diversity. This is not just about figuring out what rehabilitation and reintegration will mean for jihadist terrorist offenders due for release but what release and probation will look like for (among others) some of those who stormed the U.S. Capitol on January 6, 2021.

Many deradicalization initiatives today are managed by state actors and agencies. In practice, non-governmental organizations tend to be better positioned (sometimes with the help of state officials) to make reintegration and rehabilitation happen. For many programs, the real work begins when the former terrorist is allowed reenter society, facing an array of pressing and immediate challenges including stigma, lack of employment, little or no access to a social network, and fear of retribution from former comrades, concerned citizens, or security officials. There are many lessons to be learned from postconflict societies around the world, and these may help create greater awareness of what needs to be done to maximize success in fledgling programs.[96] There will continue to be cases of what the RAND Corporation behavioral scientist Ryan Brown and his colleagues call "self-driven exit," where people are intrinsically motivated to change their situation.[97] Otherwise, effective intervention takes a village. The 2021

RAND report *Violent Extremism in America: Can It Be Stopped?* found that in cases of successful interventions that led to disengagement and deradicalization in American terrorists, those who intervened ranged from life partners, children, other family members, school officials, journalists, and even other former violent extremists.[98] To be successful, future rehabilitation efforts will require cooperation between government bodies and nongovernmental entities, including key roles by certain former members of these same types of violent extremist movements themselves to overcome obstacles to reintegration.[99] But these efforts will need to be informed by data on the social and psychological makeup of the community such efforts are directed toward—everything we have explored in this book until now. In his treatise on what is needed for effective risk assessment of terrorist behavior, the University of Virginia psychologist John Monahan concludes that what is truly needed to build the scientific base of such research is nothing less than an "infrastructure for facilitating access to known groups of terrorists and non-terrorists from the same population."[100] Put simply, if we are to make real progress, we need access to the terrorists.

6

TALKING TO TERRORISTS

"Terrorism does not lend itself easily to research."

ARIEL MERARI AND NEHEMIA FRIEDLAND

n the summer of 2021, the *Journal of Psychiatric Research* published a systematic review of how terrorism and psychiatric disorders might be linked. The research team, led by Margot Trimbur, concluded, "We were not able to identify a significant association between radicalization, terrorism, and psychiatric disorders." They did, however, note that "some research suggests high rates of psychiatric disorders in subgroups of radicalized people and lone-actor terrorists."[1] To those familiar with the field, the findings validated what we already knew. Trimbur and her colleagues couldn't help but observe, however, that almost all of those studies were methodologically shoddy, and as such, "knowledge about psychiatric disorders among [terrorists] remains scarce and contradictory."[2] Almost as striking was that a meager twenty-five articles were deemed eligible for inclusion in their analysis. Trimbur and her team recommended further research but also stressed the urgent need to use "standard psychiatric assessment methods."[3]

The researchers' arguments were unassailable. But the question is how best to respond. Any response to their concerns, in my view, should not just be about doing more research but figuring out how we can make better progress on these issues. In fact, perhaps the question here isn't so much *how* but *where*: Where do we need to go to get better answers to these questions? A full sixteen years earlier, in his review of terrorist psychology research, the neurologist Jeff Victoroff was blunt about what needed to be done: "Scholars must be willing to attempt research that brings them into direct contact with active terrorists, recently active terrorists, or those at risk for becoming terrorists."[4] To dig deeper into psychological processes, it stands to reason that we would want to explore and collect individual experiences. And as we've seen from previous chapters, we might do that by looking through autobiographical accounts or secondhand interviews of terrorists conducted by journalists. We might in some cases be able to access court testimony or diaries (in rare cases) and possibly direct interviews with the person of interest. In this chapter, I present an inevitable argument from both reviewing and being involved in decades of research on terrorist behavior; if we are to make the kinds of progress we truly believe we can make—not just in understanding terrorist minds but in eventually developing evidence-based responses aimed at prevention—we have to do so much more to interview those who are, or were, directly involved in terrorist acts. Furthermore, in contrast to earlier efforts, we need to do it systematically and on a previously unimagined scale.

INTERVIEWING

Over the years, I've conducted dozens of interviews with former terrorists. It always seemed like a lot, at least at the time, and in hindsight, I never felt like it was enough. I even had some luck conducting a few interviews with people I later learned were still involved in terrorism at the time. In other cases, I maintained email correspondence with incarcerated terrorists but found that it really didn't compare with interviewing a terrorist in person.

So, when various opportunities came up to travel to Pakistan, Saudi Arabia, Somalia, and elsewhere to meet with defectors or other former violent extremists (often through deradicalization programs), I found such opportunities too alluring to turn down. I've learned a lot from such meetings, and I always tell my students that it can take a face-to-face meeting with someone who has been involved in terrorism to fully realize they are often not what we think they are. After meeting with several enthusiastic and engaging Islamists in London, author Graeme Wood wrote, "If they had been froth-spewing maniacs, I might be able to predict that their movement would burn out as the psychopaths detonated themselves or became drone-splats, one by one. But these men spoke with an academic precision that put me in mind of a good graduate seminar."[5] The idea of traveling somewhere to meet with someone who had been (or is) involved in terrorism seems foolhardy, if not downright suicidal depending on the context. Sometimes the danger is palpable, and researchers must carefully consider the risks associated with what might result in (from a data collection perspective at least) minimal return. I've sometimes wondered about the merits of certain trips. On one visit to Pakistan's Swat Valley, during which my host came to pick me up from Lahore airport, she remarked as we drove away, "Things are so bad here right now I couldn't even tell you if there is a bomb under our car." I paused before asking, "Um, so maybe we should check?" She just laughed.

Whether you are a researcher or not, consider this question: If you had a chance to meet a terrorist, would you take it? Would you be worried about your safety? Would you be worried about what people might think knowing that you took the time to speak to a terrorist? Would you be concerned about your reputation among friends or professional colleagues? What would you want to talk about? Would you be concerned you might fall under their spell, maybe even sympathize with them? The sociologist Lorne Dawson wrote, "Hypothetically, the information from interviews with terrorists can help to save lives and preserve the social order."[6] To anyone who has navigated an interview with a terrorist, this might be overstating things just a tad. Granted, Dawson said "hypothetically," but still, one might be forgiven for wondering what the point of such discussions might even be, especially if someone is still actively committed to the movement. The sociologist Kathleen Blee bluntly noted that violent extremists can be "disingenuous, secretive, intimidating to researchers, and prone to give evasive or dishonest answers. Standard interviews often are unproductive, yielding more than organizational slogans repeated as personal beliefs."[7] That is not to suggest that some researchers haven't had extraordinary success in field research. Plenty of researchers who study terrorism have undertaken painstaking ethnographic fieldwork.[8] In fact, studies involving terrorism fieldwork have improved so much that even listing them all would fill several pages. Furthermore, as the political violence expert Rachel Schmidt writes, the term *fieldwork* increasingly "means many things. Scholars conduct interviews online, meet former extremists in their own cities, and travel across the world to interview ex-combatants, often in contexts where lines between civilians and insurgents are blurred."[9]

Face-to-face interviews with terrorists (whether active or not) are relatively rare, and because of this, there is a danger of attributing special status to such accounts. As the independent scholar Jamie Khalil wrote in a review of studies involving interviews with terrorists, "Researchers often uncritically accept interviewee responses at face value, overlook key theoretical insights, downplay or neglect potentially important explanatory variables, fail to offer sufficient information about their sampling methods, and deliver findings with inferences beyond what their sample allows."[10] Put simply, just having access to terrorists doesn't necessarily mean that as a researcher you will emerge from that access with good (or useful) data or any new insights. Good scientific practice involves reviewing knowledge about a particular issue (for example, by doing a systematic literature review), identifying research gaps or questions that need to be asked again, and then figuring out a way in which to investigate those questions. Those ways might involve designing an experiment, an online survey, a focus group, an interview, something else entirely, or even a combination of some of these. What we should not do is prioritize the method of inquiry. We don't choose to do a case study, or a set of interviews, and then figure out the rationale for picking that method. We formulate our research questions first and then figure out how best to answer them.

Naturally, because of the relative rarity of interviews, other researchers are keen to hear about the experiences of those who meet with violent extremists—plus it's good scientific practice to not just disclose methodology but to share insights and talk about the practicalities of doing such work. Reflecting on his experience of fieldwork in Southeast Asia, the political scientist Zachary Abuza says that terrorism research in the field "is never easy, nor is it safe, but it is not impossible."[11] We would do well to heed the earlier advice of Jamie Khalil and at the same time acknowledge that data collected through interviews, or fieldwork, might, in the words of the researcher Cerwyn Moore, enhance our understanding, even anecdotally, of issues we can learn about in many ways.[12] But researchers must consider the trade-off. Michael Knights, of the Washington Institute for Near East Policy, cautioned researchers thinking of going to Iraq (during wartime) to first ask themselves if the knowledge they expected to acquire about terrorism there could easily be found right at home? Is the risk of the fieldwork worth it?[13] One day the special status surrounding interviews with terrorists will hopefully no longer exist, and interviews will be regarded as just another (equally) important source of information to be assessed against others. Indeed, Abuza offers some of the best advice to would-be field researchers seeking to interview terrorists: temper your expectations and be ready to receive incomplete, and biased, accounts. He explains, "You have to be extremely patient. Even when I was frustrated beyond belief, I was good humored about it. 'Maybe tomorrow we can talk?' I would say with a smile each time the door was being shut."[14]

The challenges faced by an interviewer will reflect the specific circumstances of not only the setting but also how radicalized the offender is. An active, committed terrorist is likely to unload grievances to the interviewer, parroting propaganda and waxing lyrical about the structural conditions that forced them into action. In my own experience, I consciously decided not to challenge or contradict an interviewee. Little would come of it, and at a minimum it would make an already guarded interviewee more defensive. Challenging a respondent would rightfully lead that person to wonder why someone who requested an interview with them would then question their worldview instead of listening to them. Instead, I allow respondents to say whatever they want to say, even if in some cases that obviously involves them reciting their movement's propaganda. Only after that do I follow the guidance offered by the psychologists Max Taylor and Ethel Quayle from their experiences in Northern Ireland and gently try refocusing the interview onto more psychologically relevant issues.[15]

Aside from training in, and deploying, suitable interview techniques, there are many bigger, broader issues for researchers to consider. The setting in which the interview takes place can matter significantly. It's widely accepted that conflict in Northern Ireland is what researcher Kacper Rekawek called completely overresearched.[16] As Rekawek recalled about his efforts to conduct research on terrorist groups there, "the easy availability of senior *dramatis personae* instantly inspired me to conduct interviews with actual and former members of different organizations, to further enhance my research."[17] Sometimes, it's just a matter of being willing to go, and, echoing the experiences of Zachary Abuza, bang on doors.[18]

But no matter the method, no matter the sincerity of the most professional and ethically minded of researchers, every approach will have bias of some kind. It's very common for terrorism researchers to use a technique called snowball sampling, for instance. This technique involves using one research subject to help find another and so on. Often, it means asking the participant at the end of an interview something like "Do you think there might be anyone else out there who would be willing to talk to me?" I use this approach all the time. Khalil, whose research on terrorism has taken him to multiple countries, cautions that using this technique may result in researchers only accessing additional like-minded participants in the movement.[19] What constitutes "like-minded" is debatable, but if it means people who are willing to talk to researchers, then naturally use of this practice to generate more interviewees represents a type of bias. To be fair, though, as Khalil himself concedes, it's often just a reflection of the practical reality of doing such work.[20] Describing the background to his own research in Northern Ireland, Rekawek explained how he discovered access to the "interview circuit."[21] In this place, interviewees "are usually widely available. . . . Quite often they also socialize together and/or are work colleagues. . . . Getting in touch with them is more than easy and very often they will direct you to their friends, peers, colleagues etc."[22] Like-minded interviewees? Yes, probably, but what researcher wouldn't take advantage of this?

Paying close attention to researchers' experiences in the field is important for reasons other than just data collection or verification. Rachel Schmidt describes multiple, serious ethical challenges encountered during her fieldwork in Colombia. She recalled experiences of "having to lie to an active paramilitary member for my own safety, a participant who was arrested and needed legal help, a participant that was killed by the group he deserted, the return to arms of several commanders of the Revolutionary Armed Forces of Colombia (FARC), sexual harassment by male participants, veiled threats by demobilized commanders, implications that some participants had not actually demobilized, and repeated requests for money, immigration advice, and other forms of assistance."[23] Reading such accounts certainly challenges any notion one might have of terrorism fieldwork being glamorous or fun. Schmidt lamented that the terrorism research community doesn't, for the most part, share their experiences about ethical dilemmas faced in the field. She wonders if it has to do with concerns that it might somehow undermine their professional credibility.[24] Having conducted well over a hundred interviews in Colombia as a graduate student, she calls attention to the broader issue of the lack of guidance on how researchers ought to regulate ongoing contact with research participants once the fieldwork is over. Should the researcher just walk away?

In her own research interviewing militants and their families in Pakistan, the counterterrorism expert Laila Bokhari explains how she made a conscious decision to maintain communication with those she met and interviewed in the field. They include the family members of people whose accounts Bokhari chronicled. Of those who disengaged from terrorism, Bokhari says that their requests to remain anonymous had to do with the fact that they now live in constant fear of being captured by either the authorities or their former comrades.[25] Bokhari acknowledges that such issues raise challenging quandaries for the researcher.[26] Schmidt said she felt similarly torn: "I needed distance from the field to write about it, but the field followed me home in the form of desperate stories and veiled threats, making 'objective' analysis difficult. Cutting off contact, however, was not an option if I wanted to maintain truly informed consent."[27]

Fieldwork has an air of excitement about it, and make no mistake, there is no shortage of narratives pushed out by journalists, researchers, and academics that embellish and romanticize what can be a profoundly risky undertaking. A consequence of this is what Schmidt called "the fetishization of dangerous fieldwork."[28] The experiences of Schmidt, Bokhari and several others illustrate how in many cases, approaches can be made, contacts approached, and with enough patience and perseverance, the careful researcher can soon develop an active network of cooperative interviewees. But both Schmidt and Bokhari decided to share much more about their experiences, admitting they were unafraid to tread across some tricky ground and then actually write about it. Reflecting on her decisions to go speak to Pakistani militants, Bokhari writes that she forced herself to look in the mirror on more than one occasion, telling herself: "Think this thoroughly though . . . Logistically, ethically, morally—it may be a bigger task than you imagine. Do you know what you are fully up against?"[29]

CLOSER TO HOME

In June 2013, I traveled to the FBI Academy in Quantico, Virginia. I'd been there several times before to teach workshops on terrorist psychology to agents in the Behavioral Analysis Unit (BAU). I relished those visits as an opportunity to share findings from academic research but I did them for my own selfish purposes, too. I wanted to learn from those same agents about the kinds of challenges they face in their work in the hope I would become a better, smarter researcher. It's one thing to be familiar with research literature, to talk about radicalization theories, and to teach classes on terrorist psychology in universities. It's another thing entirely to put yourself in the shoes of an agent conducting a threat assessment on someone who may or may not engage in a possible act of terrorism. And make no mistake, I'll take the classroom challenge any day. But the reason I was there that day was to meet with someone with whom I'd been emailing while he was incarcerated in federal custody. I'm going to call him "Ajmal" here. He was a former terrorist recruiter and propagandist jailed for his part in a plot to engage in terrorist activity on U.S. soil. A year earlier, FBI agents had approached me and asked if I'd be willing to offer a view on a case involving a former terrorist who was now struggling with his journey out of terrorism. There were lots of questions surrounding the case. *Did his account seem genuine? Was it normal for him to have doubts? Were those struggles a sign that he might still be on the road to deradicalization?* The agents wanted to know if I would be willing to have some discussions with him about all these issues and more. I said I would help where I could and agreed to be put in touch with Ajmal. When I started interacting with him, he was in his mid-thirties. We corresponded for several months before finally meeting in person. Ajmal and I had agreed in our communications about how meeting face-to-face was preferable so we could continue the discussions we'd started much earlier. Sometimes my emails to him wouldn't be received for a few days, or I'd discover weeks later he'd been moved to another institution. Ajmal was certainly happy to meet with me, and vice versa. The FBI was ready and willing to facilitate. But there was a problem. Prison authorities didn't want me inside the facility where he was incarcerated. Ever resourceful, the FBI decided to explore another option. Why not bring Ajmal out of prison for the day and drive him to Quantico where he and I could spend the day together?

That morning in June, I introduced myself and extended my hand to him, not immediately realizing that his hands were cuffed to a big leather belt around his waist. The restraints allowed him only to clumsily grasp my hands in response. He looked embarrassed. Ajmal wore a jumpsuit, and in addition to the restraints around his wrists, had additional shackles around his ankles. Standing beside him were two security personnel (I didn't know if they were with the FBI or the Federal Bureau of Prisons), as an agent from the BAU chatted with me about finding a room where Ajmal and I could sit and talk. Ajmal remarked to one of the security personnel that his right ankle was hurting him. He asked if the leg restraint could be loosened by one notch. The agent obliged, getting down on one knee to loosen the restraints on both legs. His handcuffs were then removed, and he spent the next few minutes rubbing the impression lines out of his wrists. Ajmal's head was clean shaven, and he sported a neatly trimmed beard.

I said, "It's nice to finally meet you. I've been waiting for this moment for a long time."

"Me too," he responded. "It's very good to see you."

We were asked if we could like some coffee. In unison we responded: "Yes, please." An FBI agent asked Ajmal if he was hungry. He answered, "I am." The agent replied, "All we have here are some donuts, but we can get you something."

Ajmal replied, "No, no, no, that's fine. A donut's fine. I'll take the one with the peanut butter on top." He looked at me and smiled. "That'll at least have some protein." I thought to myself, he hasn't even had breakfast yet and this guy's got charm to burn. No wonder he was a recruiter.

We waited for about five minutes for an interview room to become available. The area was spacious, and I assumed it was a common space. It had a TV (that looked a lot older than I thought it should be), lots of books, and comfortable sofas and chairs throughout. Ajmal sank into a sofa, and I pulled over a chair to be nearer to him, facing him slightly off center. I asked Ajmal about his family. In our correspondence, he would frequently write about the effects of his growing extremism on his family and how he worried about the damage it had done to them. The coffee came and we drank it before eventually proceeding to a small interview room, about thirty feet away from the open area. The room had a round table with four chairs around it. There was another ancient-looking TV (turned off) above us. The door remained cracked open, as the agents left the room. I couldn't hear them but assumed they were back in the common area again. Once the agents left the room, Ajmal looked at me and said, "Thank you for coming. I know you're very busy."

"I am," I responded, "but honestly there's nowhere I'd rather be at the minute than right here."

I let out a long breath. It was time to transition. I began, "I don't know exactly how much time we have, but I'll be here for as long as you're happy to have me here." I asked Ajmal about his thoughts on what we might cover.

"Whatever you want," he said.

"So, you know, before we actually start talking, and I know I've already said this, but I'm confident that nothing you tell me can be used to help reduce your sentence." He nodded before I could even finish the comment, but I made sure he understood I meant this. "Our mutual friends outside helped bring us together to meet, and I know they want to help give you the support you need on your journey, but speaking only for myself, I'm telling you this now, I am not going to lie to you."

Ajmal replied, "I know that, and thank you for restating that, but if I thought you were lying to me at any point, I would stop talking to you."

I nodded along before adding, "I know, and you should know you are under no obligation to speak with me at all. I don't work for the FBI. They helped set up our conversations, but I don't have any influence with them." I clarified, "They'll be curious about how our conversation goes, I suspect."

"I know that," he responded, "but you know something, I'm learning a lot and I have lots of things to think about from our interactions. I'm very grateful for your interest, Professor Horgan."

I thought back on what Ajmal said to me at that moment—"whatever you want" [to talk about]. I *wanted* to talk about everything. What were the circumstances of his conversion to Islam? Did his becoming a convert precede his radicalization? Or was it the other way around? Maybe it was coincidental? Would he tell me more about his personal upbringing and the turmoil he endured at home? Would he tell me how he became fascinated with Anwar al Awlaki while simultaneously developing his own ideas and critiques of al Awlaki's teachings? I wasn't (and am still not) an expert on jihadism, so he and I were never going to have a conversation about ideological doctrine and the intricacies of the meaning of jihad— either in the context of terrorism or outside of it. The psychologist in me was curious about him, the meaning he attributed to his actions, and how he saw the challenges facing him in his ongoing journey away from violent extremism. I knew he was struggling with a variety of deeper personal issues that may have influenced him to get into that world in the first place. I also felt he was trying to figure out what to conceal and what to reveal. He was likely clever enough to realize that others around him were making their own assessments about where precisely he was on that journey. Did he have doubts about the road ahead? Was he concerned about still being seen as too "radical" and would this conspire against him in his sentencing appeal? Alternatively, perhaps his honesty in revealing such inner conflict might convince a judge about his commitment to recovery? This was just the tip of the iceberg of what *I* wanted to talk about.

I knew we'd never have time to cover all those issues even in a full day together, so I decided the best course of action was to first continue building on the rapport we had already established. Doing this might help both of us loosen up. I wanted to kick it off by talking about something I knew he was passionate about—countering violent extremism. This was something he had revealed in his written communications. He was not short of ideas about how he could contribute as a "former." He nodded enthusiastically as I suggested we resume that conversation. I started with a few basic questions about what his thoughts were on the field of countering violent extremism at the time. Ajmal was nervous. He spoke quickly and mostly avoided eye contact. He rubbed his hands together as he jumped from point to point. There was a lot of nervous energy in the room, and I made sure to just give him the time he needed to just breathe. His enthusiasm was infectious. He had plenty to say about it and was very well read. He would routinely pepper our conversation with a mention of this research paper or that research paper. "Yeah, that piece by [Clint] Watts . . . good, very thoughtful stuff. Did you read that other thing he did with [Will] McCants? You should." This went on and on. He was familiar with the debates and the research. He would look at me nodding along, periodically pausing, and say things like, "Sorry, I'm going on too much." He was engaged, passionate about the subject, and once he started to fully relax, we were off to the races. In another hour we had accomplished more than weeks of clunky email correspondence could ever achieve.

All in all, we must have spent the best part of two hours engaging in the academic, "intellectual" discussion about the nature of terrorism and fledgling efforts to prevent it. He enjoyed this. I raised the issue about what he thought a future role for him might be in that process. He had plenty to say on that front, too. He viewed himself as being able to speak to people who are on the road to radicalization. He frequently referred to being able to assist with "a variety of initiatives," including educating different types of audiences about how radicalization works and "helping out" law enforcement. I noticed Ajmal used "we" a lot. I took this to mean he saw a potential alignment of sorts between him and law enforcement, and on more than one occasion he implied that he was helping the FBI with their efforts to think about preventing or disrupting terrorism. I wasn't interested in the specifics of this but acknowledged that he saw himself as having much to offer as someone who had "been through it." He acknowledged that the nature of the threat environment was changing and made some self-deprecating remarks on things: "Well, it may be that what I have to say is out of date or irrelevant, but I still think I can reach the hardcore Salafis, whether on forums or somewhere else."

I was curious about this. I asked him how and where he felt he could be most effective and why. Was it through his intellectual arguments around jihadism, his deep historical knowledge, or was it by the fact that he had had these experiences? He had been a bona fide jihadist recruiter. He had proven his effectiveness in that role. His subsequent incarceration and now ongoing deradicalization meant he was someone with a compelling personal story to tell. Ajmal slowed down a little and chose his words carefully. He acknowledged that he was still working through a lot of issues and that while he was, in his words, "very clear" in his views about violence, he said, "I'm not sure I'm ready to right now draw that line in the sand to say 'Here's what I think and that's that.'" Many formers struggle with doubts even long after their disengagement, and it can be daunting to allow oneself the freedom to express those struggles openly. Ajmal was either now taking a risk, or this was a very calculated move. I asked him what he thought about holding onto that sense of ambiguity. Was he worried this might make people around him suspicious? He answered that he thought the ambiguity was necessary to maintain credibility. Credibility with whom, I wondered. Other terrorists considering disengagement? Or did he mean the FBI? He shifted ever so slightly in his chair, appearing anxious. He acknowledged he was struggling to be truthful about his inner conflict around various positions while at the same time grappling with the fact that he felt he needed to give clear and unambiguous statements to reassure those around him. Shortly after this, Ajmal referred to a document he was writing that would factor into his sentencing appeal. In it, he described in detail his journey out of extremism. At this point Ajmal said, "It would be helpful if you could go through that document and let me know if there are things I should edit out to be able to convey to the BOP [Bureau of Prisons] that I am taking my rehabilitation seriously." I first was surprised that he asked me this (and in the moment did my best to conceal it), and later I would wonder why he felt I might do such a thing for him. When he asked me, I paused for a few seconds before answering that I could not do that. It was now Ajmal's turn to be surprised. I told him I couldn't give him suggestions on what to avoid in navigating his rehabilitation process. This was his journey. I told him I wanted to help him highlight these issues (the ambiguity being one example) because they raise difficult questions. I told him that asking these difficult questions was important. I told him I felt these were things he might want to reflect upon and think about. Ajmal acknowledged this and agreed that was an appropriate step, or (I briefly thought) perhaps he was just disappointed in my answer. He started to choke on his words and apologized.

On more than one occasion, Ajmal suggested he and I were more alike than different. "You know I've read some of what you've written, right? You're kind of like a radical yourself. I imagine some of what you say doesn't go down too well with your academic colleagues." He smiled. "You're actually just like me. We're both radicals." I couldn't help but smile back, and at the same time I admired his approach. Was he consciously trying to flatter me? *Is this how you try to recruit people?* I wondered for the second time that day, though I did not ask him that. Realizing I was sitting there with a grin on my face for what was probably a few seconds too many, I decided it was time to do something different. I challenged him. I asked Ajmal what it might mean to him if people didn't see him the same way he saw himself. What if his intellectual arguments, his insights, and what he had to offer were neither new nor creative, or even relevant? Why did he think fellow travelers who were still radicalized should listen to him at all? I was now the one taking the risks but decided it was worth it. After all, if Ajmal was to pursue this "former" future postrelease, what he would face on the outside would be far less sensitive than the way in which I was broaching this question right now in front of him. What did Ajmal have in his armory to convince those on the outside that he had something to offer efforts to counter violent extremism? The speed with which he answered my question didn't reassure me that he understood what I was getting at, and it made me wonder if I had just fumbled the question altogether. Ajmal argued that it was his idealism that landed him in trouble in the first place. He said he had always felt weighed down by an "inability to see things developing until it was too late." Ajmal now wondered if that same idealism, now centered on the dizzying prospect of helping the FBI prevent terrorist plots in the United States, was so alluring that it might blind him to his responsibilities once out of prison. Would his new mission in the world of countering violent extremism simply take the place of the old one, leaving behind (again) a wife and children in pursuit of new glories?

By this point, Ajmal and I had still only spoken for a few hours. In some ways we had discussed a lot, and in other ways we had just scratched the surface. Ajmal was on a journey, the contours of which he himself was still trying to figure out. He didn't shy away from acknowledging that he was struggling with ambiguity and was trying to figure out not so much "what to say" but rather "the order in which to say things." Meeting him in person was a valuable experience. He was a smart, articulate, and thoughtful person. This impression was consistent with what I had concluded from our correspondence. He seemed very self-aware, used humor and some amount of flattery with me, and was very self-deprecating. He also had a high opinion of himself. He liked impressing me with his knowledge of Islamic concepts and history, and throughout our day together, gave me several examples of when his knowledge impressed those around him. He recalled one day in prison when the staff "called me downstairs to ask about the significance of [an inmate] having a beard." He spoke with gusto about conversations with officers from the New York Police Department, telling them, "Well hey guys, you can stop wasting your time. This [pointing to a diagram in a report] is where I am on your model." He added, "I could see the jaw drop of the expert in the room." Ajmal was playing the role of the expert, and he relished it.

Lunch was unavoidable and it inevitably led to a less productive afternoon. Ajmal was visibly tired after eating, and I didn't feel comfortable being responsible for him sitting there in that state. I started to draw things to a close about an hour after our return. On the long drive back home the next morning, my thoughts turned to next steps. I had been afforded a rare half day in person with Ajmal. But what now? Were we condemned to email once again? I bristled at the thought of it. Could we have more conversations face-to-face? What if we had had more time during this visit? What if we could talk about the offenses for which he was convicted? What if he could take me back to when he first got involved? To how he recruited others? What strategies did he use? It took all but a few seconds for me to wonder about the possibilities of conducting interviews with other terrorist offenders, —and across different ideologies, too. In the case of Sarah mentioned in earlier chapters, with my colleagues Mary Beth Altier, Neil Shortland, and Max Taylor, we illustrated the kinds of insights to be had by speaking to just one single violent extremist. What if we could do this but with a hundred such people? Or a thousand? And even more, what if we could follow Victoroff's advice to "stratify [our] findings according to level and role."[30] Would the FBI support this? If they were able to get access to prisoners in ways academics (so far) could not, maybe they would do such study? Developing an interview guide and codebook wouldn't be hard, I thought. Then it hit me. *The serial killer study.*

GOING TO THE SOURCE

In the early 1970s, the FBI established the Behavioral Science Unit (BSU), which led to the development of "techniques, tactics, and procedures" to support investigative processes across multiple domains.[31] A small group of FBI agents started doing more systematic work to develop a nationwide database on serial killers. In 1977, John Douglas and Robert Ressler began traveling around the country interviewing serial killers in prison to find out, basically, why they did what they did and how they felt before, during, and after doing it.[32] The agents were interested in offender and victim demographics, criminal histories of the offenders, what planning and preparation they did leading up to the crimes, how they behaved during the crime itself and at the scene, and what kinds of things they did after committing the offense. A fictionalized account of the origins of that study was portrayed in the popular television show *Mindhunter*. The real-life study involved interviews with thirty-six serial offenders, with accompanying data on over a hundred of their victims. This study gave the BSU something nobody had before—a baseline, data-driven understanding of how these serial predators operated. Armed with this knowledge, BSU agents could (in theory) derive insights to help solve unsolved crimes that appeared to exhibit similar extreme behaviors.[33] Some of this activity became known as offender profiling and then eventually just profiling. Though the topic enjoys as much popularity as serial killers themselves, the early claims of success in that field are as overstated as they are sensationalized. The popular belief in profiling's efficacy may in part be due to widespread exposure of certain high-profile (successful) cases rather than a serious analysis of all successes and failures.[34]

What struck me in thinking about the early work wasn't just what those agents did but *how* they did it. The FBI investigators would typically travel around the country, teaching classes to local law enforcement before asking about nearby incarcerated serial killers, whom the investigators would subsequently approach for an interview.[35] In hindsight, what might then have seemed like a practical, efficient use of limited resources (and time) for some, to others, also constituted a problem with research sampling. FBI Supervisory Special Agent Robert Morton and his colleagues summarized their limitations: "The sample size of the study was small, consisting of only 36 murderers. This lessens the reliability of the results and diminishes any predictive value of the study."[36] Morton and his team added that another problem lay in the fact that the investigators were relying mostly on the firsthand accounts of the offenders themselves, and as a result there would be all kinds of inherent biases. Scientifically speaking, all these criticisms are perfectly valid. But in acknowledging the limitations of the study it is easy to overlook what they accomplished. The critical lesson from that period was the FBI made a concerted move from what started as "a loose survey" to systematically collect, assemble, and build upon this data.[37] Though the original serial killer research would give way to even more comprehensive and systematic research both within and outside the FBI, it is difficult to overstate the importance of that pioneering research into the motives and methods of America's serial killers. The function of the BSU would eventually be subsumed within other structures at the FBI (there are now various sections within what is called the BAU), though it still exists at the FBI Academy under a different name. The data from the original serial offender study eventually gave rise to a database so voluminous in scope and potentially groundbreaking in its practical utility that it paved the way for a million-dollar research grant that years after the original study would culminate in the Violent Criminal Apprehension Program (ViCAP).[38] ViCAP remains a central repository for serial offender data to this day.

Serial killers and terrorist offenders are certainly different, but they do have a few things in common. They are both associated with not just killing but killing multiple people. Serial killers typically are defined as offenders who kill three or more people over time. Some terrorists also do this, though as we've seen earlier, not all terrorists necessarily engage in violence. The activities of serial killers can span "several jurisdictions . . . [while] offender behaviors may not be consistent among all the cases; and there may be no obvious relationship between the offenders and the victims."[39] These features apply to many terrorist offenders, too. Of course, serial killers and terrorist offenders also differ in several ways. Terrorists may kill several victims over time, but the terrorist's victims are largely incidental; they're not chosen because of their personal qualities or because their selection fulfils a fantasy but because they are thought (by the terrorist) to symbolize and epitomize the source of the terrorist's grievance—or at least, the victim is thought of as a conduit to addressing that grievance. As we have seen in earlier chapters, we would be ill-advised to dismiss personal motivations in terrorist lives, but ideology and identification with a victimized community gives direction, meaning, and urgency to the terrorist in a way that is absent for the serial killer. The serial killer is driven by the need to act upon deeply held private fantasies. The terrorist's fantasies are shared by many and their motives (at least on one level) are far more easily discerned than we might detect from examining the aftermath of a serial killer.

I didn't seek out Ajmal. In a way, he just fell into my lap. I was asked if I would be interested in meeting him, with his informed consent (a point the FBI made before I ever broached the ethics of this), and if after that, I would be willing to offer a perspective on his journey out of extremism. I've been fortunate over the years to just be at the right place at the right time to have such opportunities, and often I grab them. You just never know where they might lead. As a researcher, you can of course also make some things happen. One of the greatest benefits of being an academic is that we can choose what to study. Fed up studying a particular topic? No problem. Just turn to something else. We can also apply for grants to fund research. We don't necessarily need a grant to get access to research subjects, and having a research grant doesn't bring with it any kind of privileged access. What researchers can do is reach out, make contact, and see what happens. But funded research allows us to do so much more with what we have—it allows for things like traveling to multiple locations to collect data, hiring a research assistant, or buying specialized equipment, and it allows us to scale up our research to go beyond individual case studies or library research. But what struck me about the serial killer study was that serial killings are so much rarer than terrorist crimes. If the FBI (or anyone for that matter) could develop such a groundbreaking body of research starting with only thirty-six offenders, why on earth were we not doing the same to conduct interviews with former terrorist offenders while still in prison? Sure, we might have to start small, but given what the original serial killer study eventually gave rise to, it seemed senseless for us not to be doing the same thing with terrorists. There is certainly no shortage of potential subjects. There were (as of early 2023) at least six hundred terrorist offenders in the U.S. prison system.

A criticism often leveled at ethnographic field research is that those types of studies don't meet the kinds of standards required for eligibility in systematic reviews. With some exceptions, the sample sizes are small, there are few controls or none, and methods rarely surpass semistructured interviews. It is easy to be unfair here. Often these features reflect the reality of doing fieldwork in communities affected by conflict, which is in some cases ongoing. Prisons, on the other hand, afford researchers an ideal environment to not just collect detailed data on offenders and their crimes but to do so systematically and even across other offender groups for comparison. There was clear precedent, not just from the original serial killer study, but with terrorist actors in other jurisdictions. We might recall the 1986 study conducted by the psychiatrists H. J. Lyons and Helen Harbinson in Northern Ireland where they were able to compare detailed records of politically motivated murderers with prisoners who were not politically motivated. The veteran journalist Chris Ryder, who wrote a book about the Northern Ireland Prison Service, wrote in 2000 that the terrorist prisoners "didn't show remorse because they rationalized it very successfully, believing that they were fighting for a cause. [They], generally speaking, did not want to be seen by a psychiatrist; they feel there is nothing wrong with them, but they did co-operate."[40] Another success story comes from Israel, where the psychologist Ariel Merari compared fifteen Palestinian prisoners, each of them a failed suicide bomber, to a control group of twelve Palestinian terrorists convicted for other terrorist offenses.[41] In an interview with the terrorism researcher John Morrison, the renowned criminologist Gary LaFree lamented the lack of access to terrorist prisoners:

> One of my personal frustrations, and this has been a problem more in the United States than in other parts of the world, is getting access to prison populations. We had funding to do a project on the U.S. Bureau of Prisons 7 or 8 years ago and we got all the way through the human subjects issues etc. etc., and were eventually turned away. . . . This would be a fantastically interesting group to have information from. Yet the government has so far not allowed that to happen.[42]

If we are to make the kind of progress necessary to fill in the knowledge and research gaps identified in the preceding chapters, we need to have such access.[43] It would also allow us to directly compare, for example, the behaviors, experiences, and thinking patterns that might exist between novice and expert terrorists. The benefits would quickly become apparent, and we already have frameworks prepared to deploy in collecting data. For example, the criminologist David Keatley and colleagues used crime script analysis to compare twenty-four violent extremists with sixteen nonviolent extremists.[44] Crime script analysis starts with the assumption that offenders operate along certain "scripts" when they are planning and engaging in criminal activity.[45] In other words, there might be certain things that a criminal does a few days before a planned crime is to be committed, certain steps that are followed in the hours or minutes before it, certain ways in which the actual crime itself is executed, and certain patterns that follow the offense. Such fine-grained accounts are sometimes found in terrorist autobiographies, but the depth and quality of such accounts varies tremendously. To not only rigorously collect such data, but also to do the kinds of systematic comparisons Keatley and his colleagues (and Lyons and Harbinson years earlier) were able to do, allow for any emergent differences to be considered as serious hypotheses—such as Keatley and his team finding that a history of ostracization distinguished the violent extremist sample from the nonviolent extremists. As well, the violent offenders often suffered bullying in their early childhoods.[46] Without this type of systematic comparison, we can only speculate what distinguishes violent extremists (or other extremists) from nonviolent extremist (or other offender) populations.

Gang members would seem to represent another very important comparison here. The criminologists Scott Decker and David Pyrooz argue the broader point that research on gangs (of where there is over a hundred years' worth) can greatly inform the study of terrorism.[47] After all, gangs and terrorist groups have much in common. Both are organized entities characterized by strict group dynamics whose members live semiclandestine lives fraught with risk and illegality. For members, experiences run from initial recruitment to deepening commitment and demonstrations of loyalty to disengagement. Decker and Pyrooz recommend paying close attention to how gangs operate in prison because, just like their terrorist counterparts, imprisonment can be the setting for increasing and expanding membership. However, another obvious parallel here is that prison is a setting in which both gang members and terrorist offenders can be approached, interviewed and compared. This doesn't quite equate to a control group per se, but the point is that the comparison is valuable, and it can help strengthen (or otherwise challenge) the validity of findings that suggest real differences exist. We can't just dismiss studies without a control group; instead, we ought to be mindful that they, like all studies, simply have limitations that need to be considered by everyone, from other researchers and practitioners to policy makers, eager to learn about a particular issue.

There are more benefits to be had. Prison settings offer ideal opportunities for reinterviewing. Morrison and Chernov Hwang both emphasize how, in their respective research in Northern Ireland and Indonesia, being able to reinterview people led to greater insights into their respondents' life course trajectories into and out of the movement; in a more basic sense, it also enhanced a sense of trust (or at the very least, familiarity) between interviewee and interviewer.[48]

Outside of the United States, several researchers have begun to illustrate what is possible once they get access to prison settings. One of the most detailed accounts of interviews with terrorist prisoners so far comes from the Belgian researcher Lana De Pelecijn. For her then-ongoing PhD research on violent extremism, she wrote in 2021 that she had already managed to conduct twenty-one detailed interviews with former terrorists across different ideologies.[49] De Pelecijn is one of the few researchers who has taken the time to produce transparent guidance about the interviewing process as she experienced it. For her, this involved making initial contact, often via a brief letter followed by (if the potential interviewee is willing) an introductory meeting.[50] Her recommendations to other researchers proved invaluable. Don't underestimate just how promising the act of writing a letter might be, she urges. She describes one of her respondents' reply to her: "When I read your letter, I was very surprised that a Western woman is interested in me and my story. Even my own lawyer behaves distantly towards me."[51] That led to the prisoner agreeing to meet with her, during which De Pelecijn explained her project in more detail and was able to ask (in person) if the prisoner would agree to tell their story. Not everyone will want to sit and talk to a researcher, of course. De Pelecijn also says it's important to understand why subjects would *not* want to engage. Many of those she approached with a letter of introduction told her they were either traumatized from their experiences, or in some cases, their personal situations remained too sensitive because of ongoing legal issues. All in all, she concludes, after imparting much practical advice, "conducting interviews . . . is a very time-consuming, fragile, and sometimes even highly stressful process."[52] Nevertheless, she succeeded in gaining access as well as the prisoners' cooperation. Her experiences demonstrate that what should be done can in fact be done.

CONCLUSION

Lorne Dawson's 2019 essay on terrorist motivations argues for "securing more interviews with terrorists and treating what they say about their motivations as a serious source of insight into how and why people become terrorists."[53] It is increasingly clear that the conceptual and theoretical obstacles facing terrorism researchers are easier to overcome than the practical barriers preventing the kind of cooperative engagement that awaits us. Ajmal *wanted* to talk. He wanted to tell his story. The more former terrorists I speak with postrelease, the more they reinforce this. As researchers, we seek out people to talk to us about their experiences as terrorists. As former terrorists, they want to be heard. I am often asked this question: "How do you know they aren't lying?" Well, I don't. At least not entirely. If the interviewee's identity is known (perhaps we have read their memoir or seen or read about them on the news), good interviewers will be prepared. They will be very familiar with the person's case, their experiences, and the offenses for which they were charged and ultimately convicted. A good interview will allow for some triangulation to be done—checking data from one source against another. Discrepancies might arise, but just because they exist doesn't mean an interviewee is lying. We should also remember that interviews are not interrogations. Academics are not in the business of gathering intelligence. We do not cultivate informants or sources, and we don't identify coconspirators in the hope of prosecuting terrorist offenders, as would a criminal investigator or counterintelligence agent.[54] Our goal is neither to break someone nor elicit a confession. It is, for all intents and purposes, to have a conversation but not just any old conversation. Instead, the conversation is one that is planned and guided by theory and other research, and it is conducted in such a way to elicit the most reliable information possible under the circumstances. Our critical task is to find ways to facilitate an opening—to arrange a situation in which an interviewee feels comfortable offering their perspective on what the researcher is curious to learn about. Interviewing is not some magical skill. The techniques associated with effective interviewing can be learned and improved with time and experience. There are no trade secrets. Any apparent sleight of hand is merely the result of practice, which helps smooth transitions from topic to topic. Successful interviewers don't just know how to ask probing questions; they also know how and when to just shut up and listen. As the former FBI agent Joe Navarro once wrote, "To successfully interview terrorists, the interviewer must be willing to listen more than he talks."[55] And while academic interviewers are not interrogators, both groups can learn from each other. Adopting specific, deliberate strategies increases the likelihood of an interviewee cooperating, engaging, and disclosing. Navarro concludes, "Every great interviewer will tell you, what really works is first and foremost . . . being humane."[56] And this isn't some misty-eyed principle either. It is grounded in scientific research—it *works*. Building rapport with interviewees leads respondents to be more inclined to cooperate and may even enhance the accuracy of the information being recalled.[57]

The preceding chapters here are a testament to the fact that no informed student would deny the progress made by psychological research on terrorism in recent years. In some cases, especially around questions of motivation, there's plenty to debate. It sometimes feels like we've come a long way only to know what *doesn't* explain terrorism. But such is scientific progression. As we've seen from the research showcased earlier, we know so much about who becomes involved in terrorism, and why, that we could only speculate about twenty years ago. As the researchers Paul Gill, Bart Schuurman, John Morrison, and others have all remarked, the once-characteristic lament of lack of primary data in the field has since given way to an acknowledgment that things *have* improved. The challenge that lies ahead of us isn't about producing more of the same. It's about finding ways to verify and validate what we think we know, both within and across samples, cohorts, and other similar comparison groups.

Given the subject matter we're concerned about in this book, interviews with terrorists continue to remain vitally important. If anything, the continued success of psychological research on terrorism requires us to conduct interviews on a scale never seen before. This is the only way in which we can better test what theories we currently have, as well as validate what we think we know about multiple questions surrounding terrorist behavior. The lack of systematic, controlled interviews is nothing less than a major bottleneck for the potential that lies ahead in the psychology of terrorist behavior. Doing so within the prison system has multiple benefits, yet in the United States, the barriers to entry seem insurmountable, largely because access is so strictly controlled; even basic inquiries about access can take months to receive a response. And as my experiences, and those of Gary LaFree, John Monahan, and many others illustrate, holding discussions with the prison authorities for even *years* at a time can result in nothing. It can be a lot easier to contact and interview someone who was convicted and has since been released from prison than it is to get agreement from prison authorities for access to people who are incarcerated. The sociologist Pete Simi and his colleagues have had great success in recruiting and interviewing former violent extremists in this way.[58] It doesn't mean that an account of involvement from a long-disengaged terrorist is necessarily any more truthful than one from a recently convicted terrorist; rather, such interviews may be easier to secure in a practical sense. The case for access can hardly be more important. The urgency with which policymakers and practitioners require actionable knowledge to prevent, disrupt, or otherwise intervene to reduce the risk of terrorist action is at odds with the quality of evidence that is currently available to them. So, what do we need to do to change that? That's the burning question. Part of the solution (and it is only a part) must involve access to terrorist populations in prison settings, and as researchers, we must advocate for this to happen. Prisons offer an ideal setting in which some of the major methodological and theoretical shortcomings associated with inferences about terrorist motivation may be overcome.

Terrorism studies no longer suffer from lack of data. Quite the contrary. Nor do we need more theories on terrorism. Now is the time to test what we think we know. We urgently need to strengthen our knowledge base on terrorist offenders by conducting systematic, controlled research with them. The benefits would not be limited to enhancing scientific knowledge but would help provide an evidence base for actionable knowledge that will inform operational practice. Given what the FBI was able to do with knowledge from thirty-six serial predators, the possibilities of what might come from accessing even a fraction of incarcerated terrorist offenders are tantalizing.

7

CHASING STORMS

"I see little more effectiveness in the average clinical psychiatrist stepping out to help manage a complex social situation than in ancient times when the local priest was called in to shake his fist at the clouds to drive them away."

DAVID HUBBARD

The preceding six chapters have introduced us to a challenging social problem, the very essence of which we rarely judge in a consistent way. We know far more about who participates in the various activities that constitute terrorism than about what motivates them. We know that a critical feature of terrorism today is the diversity of opportunities for involvement, which in turn leads to the development of diverse experiences and mindsets. We've seen welcome attention devoted to not only how and why people get involved but also how and why they leave, and we have arrived at an inevitable conclusion about what is needed for us to make real breakthroughs in the psychology of terrorism—far from needing more theories about why terrorists do what they do, we need to test what theories we have with the kinds of large-scale, systematic interviewing that has reaped benefits in other domains. The lack of such activity, especially in prison settings, poses a serious bottleneck in the psychology of terrorism, and we must address it.

All in all, just about every chapter up to now has highlighted the complexity of terrorist behavior and terrorism itself. In this final chapter, I want to do the opposite—simplify it. I want to do so in a way that might provide a useful and memorable way to think about terrorism and the ways in which people engage in it. My goal in doing this, through an analogy, is not just to simply give you yet another metaphor for thinking about terrorism; I also want to cement some of the key lessons learned in the previous chapters. I want to trace what I believe are the outer limits of what we can currently achieve, given both what we know and the resources currently available to us. I firmly believe that we cannot fully explain terrorism. I suspect, though I will not be around to say so, we will reach the same conclusion in fifty years. I still maintain that we have a far better understanding today than ever before about who becomes involved (and how) and the kinds of things they subsequently do. Our efforts to better describe terrorist behavior are paying off. We are identifying the pathways and tracing the processes. We are pinpointing what we believe to be the risk factors and what we must do to validate them as potential indicators. To reuse Noémie Bouhana's analogy from the preface, we have managed to connect several of the pieces of the puzzle. Some have required a little more pressure to unite than we expected, and we must not be deterred by how many more pieces might remain in the box. Rather, we must be encouraged. The picture *is* taking form.

STORM FRONT

The city of Joplin lies in the southwest corner of the state of Missouri. Known to many as "JoMo," its population is just over fifty thousand. The city's website clarifies it is not, in fact, named after the legendary composer

Scott Joplin.[1] On May 22, 2011, a tornado tore through Joplin, the third to strike the city since 1971, but this was nothing like the previous two.[2] The damage was catastrophic. It claimed 161 lives, destroyed over two thousand homes, a thousand cars, and many local businesses were completely leveled.[3] That tornado is generally viewed as the worst in modern times to hit the United States.[4] Beyond the devastation, it served as reminder that despite all the technology available to forecasters, such events could still cause a major death toll.[5] A major factor in why the casualty rate was so high was the simple "lack of awareness of the approaching tornado."[6] Efforts to understand them—how they form, behave, and affect their surrounding environment—are critical to help provide communities with valuable extra minutes of warning time when faced with an advancing tornado. There is a deeply complex science around tornado forecasting, and the ability to provide such warnings, based on models of such rare events, requires scientific analysis of data derived from multiple sources, such as satellites, weather balloons, and weather stations.[7] The average warning time people can now expect is about fourteen minutes.[8]

In the days that followed the Joplin disaster, a group of researchers from the U.S. National Institute of Standards and Technology carried out a ground-level investigation to ascertain just how members of the public reacted to the various emergency warnings issued prior to the tornado's arrival.[9] They also collected data on damage to vegetation, structures, and building design, all with a view to identifying better ways to prepare for future such events. Such investigations are common. Sarah Horton, a UK-based tornado chaser, said in an interview with *Wired* magazine that she is part of a "bank of people who are willing to go out whenever there is severe weather damage and . . . investigate it."[10] She led research into a tornado in the United Kingdom that impacted Surrey in December 2019. That study involved several days of fieldwork. The areas associated with the most damage from tornadoes are often the focus of most of the media coverage, but Horton and her team argue that such locations typically only represent a small piece of the overall damage done.[11] A critical source of information in such cases is not only the volunteer storm researchers and enthusiasts but also eyewitnesses and even people with their own weather station technology.[12] That tornado became, in Horton's words, a good example of "citizen science," with multiple local media groups in the community quickly collecting and collating the various data.[13]

D. K. Lilly, a scientist at the National Center for Atmospheric Research, defined a tornado as "an element of frequent disaster-causing potential whose basic internal dynamics are largely unknown."[14] Lilly continues, "The unsatisfactory state of knowledge is mainly due to the difficulty of making quantitative observations on a phenomenon which is rare in occurrence at any given location, short-lived, and highly destructive to ordinary instruments and other human fabrications."[15] On these issues alone, tornadoes share several similarities with terrorism. Additionally, both are dramatic, newsworthy phenomena provoking fear and fascination and have the potential to be highly destructive to property and life. Their destructive power is apparent not just from damage surveys but also as it happens. Damage can vary in size and intensity, and mindful of Horton's point, often extends far beyond the immediate impact area. Despite the potential damage, however, tornadoes, just like terrorist events, are rare. And because they are rare, they appear largely unpredictable. Both terrorism and tornadoes are difficult to study directly, and this in turn makes them almost impossible to model. Consequently, efforts at risk management (through warnings, for example) can be challenging. The behavior associated with each phenomenon is complex, and whether we are talking about terrorism or tornadoes, both are respectively shaped by even more complex, higher-level dynamics (whether social unrest or supercells)—in essence, both are symptoms of underlying conditions. Furthermore, let's not overlook the obvious appropriateness to use a tornado to visualize at least some terrorism-related dynamics: a tornado is a violent spiral, and the psychologist Max Taylor described in 1988 how spiraling is one critical psychological quality of terrorism whether it reflects an individual's increasing commitment or the process of "reciprocal" radicalization where one group or movement feeds off another (and vice versa), escalating the intensity or lethality of a conflict.[16]

There are further parallels. As we have seen in previous chapters, to a select few, the allure of terrorism is irresistible. It is no different for tornadoes. The 1996 disaster movie *Twister* popularized the subculture of storm chasers. In that film, two rival teams race around Oklahoma in heavily customized vehicles in search of tornadoes. Each group is on a quest to beat the other to release probes up inside a tornado funnel so they can collect data on the tornado's internal dynamics. The fictional account portrayed storm chasers as close-knit oddballs whose enthusiasm to get their hands dirty was matched only by their passion to unravel the mysteries of the phenomenon itself. *Twister* earned nearly half a billion dollars at the box office. So insatiable was the public's appetite that Discovery Channel commissioned a documentary-style reality show called *Storm Chasers*. The Storm Prevention Center distinguishes chasers from spotters—spotters are essentially local observers who report relevant information to the National Weather Service. Chasers, on the other hand, are mobile, sometimes following or intercepting storms many miles away. The motives of chasers vary from genuine scientific curiosity to an interest in weather photography to selling footage to media outlets.[17]

At the individual level, tornadoes and terrorism thus share apparent similarities. For different reasons, they both attract different types of people. But there is more to it: just like terrorism, those drawn to tornadoes come through different pathways, with different resources at their disposal, and engage at sometimes vastly different levels. The individual experience with the phenomenon is different—what is seen and felt by the distant spotter will differ from the experience of the chaser. Both, in turn, constitute very different experiences than that faced by staff at the National Weather Service working from a distance with input from satellite imagery. The exposure each has to the phenomenon reflects their respective roles or, rather, the different levels and distances at which they experience the phenomenon. What scientific analysts from the National Oceanic and Atmospheric Administration (NOAA) measure about a tornado from satellite imagery doesn't necessarily eclipse what ground-level storm chasers feel and vice versa. Both experiences are valid and equally meaningful to the respective participants.[18]

Terrorism is no different. No single experience can characterize the terrorist mind or involvement—it will vary depending on who the person is, what precisely they do, how they feel about it, and how and where they do it. The person who sits behind a keyboard and manages an extremist message board may feel excitement and a sense of purpose and mission in doing what they do in a way that is no less meaningful than that experienced by the battlefield fighter, despite the distinct nature of their respective experiences.

I'm mindful of stretching this analogy beyond its limits, so let's be careful here. If done right, analogies help. They can illuminate, burning an image into the minds of observers trying to understand what is going on or how something works. Some can be memorable. The author Graeme Wood, in *The Way of the Strangers*, said of an Islamic State recruiter he interviewed, "They were fishers of men, and as I watched them work, I saw that they were trawling on a commercial scale."[19] And perhaps more importantly, analogies and metaphors can help us define lines of inquiry. Thinking about tornadoes clarifies that it's one thing to try to explain where, when, and why tornado *events* happen. It's another task entirely to understand how, why, where, and when *people* engage with them (let alone that they all seem to do it in very different sorts of ways and at different levels). This is a critical conceptual distinction if we want to think more deeply about what motivates terrorists and what we do in studying them. Some overlap between events and processes affecting those who participate is inevitable because many who chase tornadoes will do so with some readiness. They have some expectation of what awaits and purposefully seek it out. Others just happen to be in the right place at the right time. Others still find their opportunities for exposure are shaped simply by bad luck—getting caught up in the extreme winds, or impacted by the damage, again simply by being in the wrong place at the wrong time.

Tornado dynamics, and their inherent complexity, might help us think about the dynamics of individual movement into and out of terrorism. When tornadoes form, objects in their path can be subject to very different outcomes. Tornadoes typically carry objects up into the sky, and they might land anywhere from very short distances from where they were picked up to great distances away. The NOAA reports that tornadoes routinely toss paper "over a hundred miles away."[20] Thinking about objects as participants, there is a multiplicity of pathways and actor differentiation, each of whose pathways, observations, and experiences might be fundamentally different from person to person. In both terrorism and tornadoes, it is the phenomenon that attracts the people—all of whom have their own roles, resources, and respective expectations around their interactions (whether distant or proximal) with that phenomenon. Tornado dynamics, even at their most rudimentary, would appear to involve both multifinality and equifinality. Where precisely objects (or people) end up, and how, is often due to powerful forces outside of their control. The damage associated with tornadoes is, of course, often a function of not just wind speed but what precisely that wind is carrying. Terrorism is no different—it's not enough to simply have people involved. They must be capable of inflicting damage. Several examples from previous chapters illustrate that the competent performance of individual terrorists can be central to the overall effectiveness of even the best resourced and committed terrorist groups.

The comparison is valuable for another reason, briefly alluded to earlier. This point has more to do with identifying the outer limits of our academic boundaries. Tornadoes don't just appear out of nowhere. They are caused by thunderstorms, which in turn develop under certain atmospheric conditions. Explaining why tornadoes form (e.g., from supercells) does not tell us anything about why, or how, people are drawn to tornadoes. Similarly, explaining the complex causes that give rise to terrorist violence doesn't tell us anything about why, or how, people are drawn to engage in acts of violent extremism. Although I've already made this distinction before, I'll stress it again here—*it doesn't have to*. Explanations (or descriptions) of how, why, when, and where people become involved in terrorism might stand separate and distinct from explanations about how, why, where, and when conflict within and between societies might emerge. Recognizing such distinctions might seem to undermine the case for terrorism needing to be an area of multidisciplinary engagement—it should not. Rather, recognizing these boundaries can clarify the role (and limits) of different perspectives in the study of terrorism. I don't mean calling for restrictions on where disciplines like psychology, or political science, ought to be relevant—I am less concerned with academic preciousness than

I am about seeing the potential benefits of recognizing where disciplinary boundaries (and relevance) lie. Bouhana memorably characterized violent extremism today as a "wicked problem,"[21] something so messy and complicated that it seems utterly impossible to fix. She writes, "The perception of the problem itself is contentious and malleable: definitions are disputed or elusive. Because there are no boundaries, it is impossible to say where the problem stops and where the solution begins. Interventions have unintended consequences on other, interlocking problems. The very claim that there is a problem may be challenged."[22] A good model of terrorism, even a good analogy, should embrace its complexity, not shy away from it. It should acknowledge boundaries, forcing clarity around what precisely can be explained, and how.

DESCRIPTION

A recurring theme in previous chapters has been about placing a premium on both accurately and reliably *describing* terrorist behavior and those who engage in it. Only the foolhardy would rush in to try to explain terrorism. The political scientist Marcus Kreuzer argued that the point of good description in the social sciences is to find out "just like journalists, *who* the central actors were, *how* they behaved, under *what* circumstances, and *when* and *where* their actions took place."[23] Throughout this book, we have explored who becomes involved in terrorism, what their behavior entails, and how they perform while engaging in this behavior—all across different settings and environments. There is broad consensus that no terrorist personality exists, but that is not the same as suggesting that personality doesn't matter. When tornadoes happen, most people might be expected to run away. Others might hide. Some step outside with caution to take a closer look, and others rush toward it—not content with merely looking, they want to *feel* it, to be part of it. The issue is that personality alone cannot explain much, if anything, about why the phenomenon happens. It might reveal more about why certain people are attracted to the phenomenon in particular ways—for instance, why some want to get closer to the action than others.

And perhaps we can extend this just a little further. Any student of terrorism will quickly realize that many models of terrorism exist, and they are not equal. Every model, without exception, has its limitations. As described in previous chapters, the psychologists Clark McCauley and Sophia Moskalenko produced what is probably the most popular model of radicalization, which initially characterized the problem as a pyramid, and in subsequent work presented the notion of there being two pyramids—one characterizing radicalization up from a wider base toward a narrow apex of extreme opinions, the other radicalization also from a wider base up toward a narrow apex of extreme action. Their fellow psychologist Randy Borum suggests their model "may or may not actually elucidate *mechanisms* of radicalization; instead, they may just describe different precipitants or contributing factors."[24] But that is not necessarily a bad thing. Borum acknowledges, as do the authors themselves, that "there is no empirical evidence [that] suggests that any of them are sufficient conditions for engaging in terrorist activity."[25] All in all, Jeff Victoroff concludes that these various attempts to explain terrorism, though seemingly relevant, await "better substantiation."[26] Indeed, this is true of the many influential models in circulation underpinned with analysis that Borum says is little more than "anecdotal and unsystematic."[27] It can be easy to read such statements, especially this late in the book, and conclude that progress has not been made. That would be inaccurate, and the studies referred to in previous chapters ought to constitute evidence of just what has been accomplished. But what such critical reviews highlight is the gaps in our thinking, and thus (in theory) a roadmap for building better linkages between parts of the process. Offering some guidance, Victoroff points to a major obstacle in early research—the lack of control groups and the failure to use "validated psychological instruments."[28] These, he implies, still hold the keys to progress, and I unreservedly agree with his observation. McCauley and Moskalenko concede that "most terrorism research . . . is not ready for formal modeling" that can predict outcomes.[29] Not right now, anyway. Even the most ambitious studies of terrorists, which rarely use control groups, involve mere hundreds of subjects. The more careful approaches to understanding terrorism, in the words of the researcher Tyler Evans and colleagues, resemble more of an "exploratory exercise in theory building, not an explanatory approach to theory testing."[30] One might assume there's consensus in academia about what constitutes a good model, but that, too, would be incorrect. At a minimum, a good model probably should make a complex problem easy to understand and memorable. That is, of course, a double-edged sword. We can reduce the complexity of a problem so much that a neat analogy or metaphor might mislead more than inform. A good model *should* be informed by empirical evidence. Perhaps just as important, it ought to be amenable to refinement. The emergence of new contradictory data on a particular issue might ultimately complicate a model such that it spells the end of the metaphor, but it might still be a step in the right direction as far as developing an accurate picture of the phenomenon as a result. A good model probably should have some predictive ability, and finally, it (or its creator) ought to emphasize and clarify realistic expectations of its users.

Tornadoes might prove a neat comparison to terrorism, though (for now) I will stop short at suggesting it constitutes the basis of a model. There is also, frequently, no clear delineation between these: analogies and metaphors frequently pass for (or at least are proposed as) models, and sometimes vice versa. Providing an analogy between tornadoes and terrorism isn't my attempt to explain terrorism per se; it only describes how an appreciation of tornado dynamics may illuminate critical qualities both of terrorism itself and the motivation and behavior of its participants at multiple levels. If anything, the point of this comparison is precisely to show that the perspectives and data presented throughout this book *cannot* explain terrorism. To explain it is not the point, at least from psychological perspectives. The greatest benefits from the comparison, beyond the obvious power of the visual metaphor of terrorism as a tornado (and perhaps vice versa), are an appreciation of these three factors

- The complexity of individual dynamics into, through, and out of the phenomenon. Acknowledging the diversity and complexity of both the phenomenon as well as its participants will help us appreciate how multiple actors come to the same end point, as well as how multiple actors can come to very different end points.

- The undeniable role of time and place in providing the opportunities for exposure and, thus, engagement.

- The boundary lines—attempting to trace the dynamics of involvement, spiraling, exit, and so on is not the same as trying to explain how the phenomenon forms in the first place. Highlighting boundaries is not about calling for restrictions; rather, it suggests areas of concentration and focus on what, as observers, we are respectively equipped to do.

Ultimately, to understand involvement in terrorism, we must appreciate how individual factors (e.g., demographics, personality, and individual drivers) interact with group or organizational dynamics, which in turn are shaped by social, political, historical, ideological, and cultural factors, which in turn are shaped, or in some cases triggered by, key events or influential figures. This has essentially been the goal of some five decades of psychological research on terrorism. After reviewing, in great depth, the various prevailing theories and evidence at our disposal, Victoroff gets straight to the point: *Why has the behavioral science community so far failed to mass a persuasive body of evidence in this domain?* We could answer him in many ways. We can equally identify the practical obstacles that prevent us from being able to systematically collect and compare data in data-rich environments like prisons. To echo Randy Borum, we can ask better questions.[31] Well, we have. We can pursue better quality data by building datasets and making them more and more rigorous and transparent as we go. We have also done that. Victoroff concludes, "A new model is needed, one that accommodates the multiplicity of forces at work to arrive at plausible and testable *consilience*—that is, a unified theory that is explanatory across levels of analysis and examples of terrorist activity."[32] A review of literature in 2021 (a full sixteen years after Victoroff's) by the psychologist Ángel Gómez and his colleagues concluded that while many earlier models in the literature helped better our understanding of the factors driving involvement, they have not explained how those various factors work in relation to each other.[33] That is easier said than done and made even more challenging by the fact that there is so much more to do to validate what we think we already know. There is no way we will accomplish this without significant investment in the kinds of work I described in the previous chapter—we must conduct as many interviews with as many terrorist offenders as possible. The time for us to do this has arrived.

We will one day get there, I hope. What we continue to struggle with is a way to acknowledge (and concede to) terrorism's complexity in a way that is simultaneously robust for the science, satisfactory to the scientists, resistant to the critics, and memorable to the policymakers. But intermittent gloomy forecasts about the health of terrorism research continue to be proven inaccurate. Surveys of the literature, as well as of researchers themselves, assert the opposite.[34] In a series of interviews with forty-three terrorism experts for his podcast, *Talking Terror*, John Morrison found optimism among researchers about what the future holds.[35] Terrorism research shines so brightly that it may be experiencing its "golden age."[36] Yes, Morrison reminds us, we have a long way to go, but I am mindful of Van Gogh, who is credited with the notion that great progress is merely "a succession of little things that are brought together."[37]

Encouraging you to think about tornadoes is not about me offering just another cute analogy that promises much but doesn't deliver. A benefit to that analogy is that it reduces the sense that terrorism is a special problem. My point in going to other areas is not to necessarily advocate for interdisciplinary thinking; rather, it is to steal insights found elsewhere to think more creatively about my own perspective. I'm acutely aware of the dangers of stagnation, of getting locked into predictable ways of thinking, as well as better appreciating what my discipline is unable to explain. There's always a risk for researchers to spout self-serving clichés just as terrorists themselves do. So how do we advance psychological perspectives on terrorism by not only getting more psychologists involved, but also individually learning to think in new ways? I'm not sure that's what people intended when they called for interdisciplinary research, but thinking more clearly about the boundary lines and their relevance (i.e., *how* and *where*) ought to be an important element for us to seriously consider it. Perhaps some disciplinary humility (on all sides) might be better arrived at by clarifying at what levels of the phenomenon our respective disciplines might be best focused. The psychologist may not be able to tell you where the tornadoes will touch down, but we might be better positioned than most disciplines to help understand how people behave when they see them, why and how people are drawn to them in different ways, for different reasons, and for those who do dare to get close, why they don't have much (if any) control over how they are tossed around by those violent winds.

CONCLUSION

Terrorism today isn't like just one tornado. We are witnessing the rapid development of multiple, sometimes overlapping, tornadoes touching down in places we least expect and causing more damage than we could ever imagine. Their force envelops men, women, and children, some of whom impacted on the periphery while others get violently swept up, ending up in a place far from where they started; some of the victims survive but many don't. Some get swept up simply because of where they live. They didn't seek it out. The storm arrived at their doorstep. They may not have had sufficient fortification to protect them from being unwittingly sucked in, but nevertheless, it happened. Others come from far away, on purpose, to get closer, to feel the power and intensity of an experience that calls to them. They are prepared to face the risks involved despite the uncertainty of how those winds will suck them in and toss them out, maybe even kill them in the process. Some, having survived, go back and seek it out again. What are career foreign fighters if not habitual storm chasers? For five decades now we have searched for clues as to those select few who seek out these storms. But the search for answers around why people seek out tornadoes doesn't tell us anything about how and why they form in the first place. And perhaps, after all is said and done, that's just fine. We don't have to try to explain it all, at least not alone. And psychology cannot now, nor will it ever, explain terrorism. The challenge for those of us interested in the storm chasers is to better describe, understand, and ultimately explain how, why, where, and when the select few are willing to risk their lives in pursuit of a few fleeting moments with something much bigger and more awe-inspiring than they realize—until, often, it is just too late. If we can achieve this, we will one day be in a far better position to do something about it. Description *must* be our goal for now. It is fundamentally still about the "who, when, where and how, and its answers furnish the raw material for theorizing and explaining."[38] Like tornadoes, terrorism is highly unpredictable. Its aftermath, in part, is impacted by what we do in pursuit of minimizing its impact on us. All too often, however, we fail to act until it is too late. We reel from the shock, we take stock, mourn the dead, and rebuild. There are no easy answers, but there are things we can do. We can get better at spotting the warning signs. We can prepare for their arrival. We can fortify our barriers. We can educate the public about their inherent dangers.

Science takes time, no matter how impatient we are in the interim for solutions. In any field of human endeavor, it can take a lot of time and effort to arrive at what seems obvious only in hindsight. Who today would doubt the link between smoking and lung cancer? Yet the history of that realization is replete with major, systematic studies over several decades, hundreds of thousands (even millions) of research subjects, and an unwavering sense of the importance of finding answers. The gaps I and many others have highlighted will all one day be filled. And in the meantime, there is so much promise on display. Terrorism researchers have finally begun to use lab experiments to explore key research questions. As the communication scholar and terrorism expert Kurt Braddock teases, "The possibilities are endless."[39] Amid all this, researchers today face additional serious challenges that will impede such progress if left unchecked. We live in an age of widespread disbelief, along with a mistrust of evidence, expertise, and public institutions, and of course, we are suffocating under an avalanche of disinformation—in the United States at least, this has become nothing less than a public health crisis. Researchers will face new obstacles in not just doing research but translating such research for a public, many of whom may not necessarily be receptive to its findings.

Throughout this book, I highlighted many of the challenges involved in studying terrorists. I want to end on an optimistic note. Thinking back over my twenty-five years in terrorism research, I cannot help but take comfort in how the field has matured. A long-standing tradition of terrorism researchers is to complain—to moan about how hard their research is to do, to groan about how we don't have enough data, enough funding, enough collaborators, enough buy-in from practitioners, etc. Well, no more, or at least not as much. Over the past two decades the volume of research on terrorism, available funding, and resources, as well as those studying it, have increased exponentially. For those of us who've been doing this for a while, I think few of us could have predicted its sustained growth and expansion but also its maturity. The *quality* of evidence both available to, and being generated by, researchers is better than ever. A consequence of this is that the standards expected and required of terrorism researchers have increased. We're seeing researchers become far more transparent about their assumptions, methods, and data, and early evidence suggests a greater willingness to share data and make it available for replication elsewhere. We're seeing far more substantive discussion of professional issues, such as the importance of ethics in terrorism research, and how researchers can better protect themselves from some of the dangers of doing research, in a way we haven't seen before.

A couple of years ago I read an article by the terrorism researcher Bart Schuurman where, just like I had once done, he reflected on trends in terrorism research. Schuurman lamented that the field was for a long time what he called "event driven," which means research tends to follow in the wake of current events and crises.[40] In a field like terrorism studies, this is probably to be expected. Each major event, such as 9/11, or successive wave of terrorism is going to see a concomitant surge in focus on the issue of the day. Again, why should we expect anything else? A downside (which he echoes in his review) is that we become so fixated on what's in front of us that we fail to see what might be "just over the horizon."[41] This tension is also evident around funding of terrorism research. Funders tend to want to support research on what they think is relevant right now as opposed to what terrorism experts say might be coming. A consequence of this is that we may well be unprepared for future events.

And yet, signs of progress in terrorism research are all around us. Throughout this book, I've reflected a focus on studies of terrorists and thus indirectly have offered thoughts on psychological research on terrorism. Walter Reich, whose 1990 edited book, *Origins of Terrorism*, was a cornerstone contribution to psychological research on terrorism, warned that psychologists might privately feel that *their* discipline is in some way superior to others.[42] And yet, thirty years later, in a searing review of research on terrorists, the Irish psychologists Orla Lynch and Carmel Joyce contend that a significant amount of psychological research on terrorism "could be described as tokenism and would be readily disputed, perhaps even rejected, if attempts were made to publish it in key psychological journals."[43] Terrorism has been around for a lot longer than the discipline of psychology, but psychology is steadily making up for lost time. In 2017 I had the opportunity to guest edit a special issue of the journal *American Psychologist*, the flagship periodical of the American Psychological Association. With my colleague Neil Shortland, we assembled some of the most exciting new research on terrorism to showcase not just what we have done but what possibilities lie ahead. Similar big-picture explorations have unfolded in other disciplines.[44] Recall from the previous chapter how the criminologists Scott Decker and David Pryooz argued that a hundred years of gang research would, if carefully considered, inform research on terrorism.[45] The researchers say that questions about group structures, marginalization, membership bonds, and role exit have all been widely explored in an area of research with a long history. They also concede that despite the much longer time span of research on gangs, even gang researchers are far from either "broad or final consensus."[46] A breakthrough in gang research, they argue, came when the field was able to combine multiple methods with multiple data sources, allowing for what researchers call triangulation— that is, for researchers to be able to "describe the group from multiple perspectives and more fully assess the reliability and validity of information."[47] Other criminologists concur.[48] Once more, it may be that we achieve a better appreciation of who becomes involved in what *type* of terrorist activity than thinking of terrorism and terrorist as the seemingly simple categories those labels imply. Certainly, broadening the focus would allow us to know if, for example, involvement in one type of activity represents a stepping stone to something more serious.[49]

Let us conclude with a quote from Professor David Clarke, a psychologist who teaches at the University of Nottingham in England: "It is relatively easy to do rigorous research on tidy, well-formed, often trivial behaviors. It's also relatively easy to do work on important problems in a way that's hand-waving and inconclusive. The trick is to get the best of both worlds; to do research which is rigorous and conclusive on big, real-world problems, which are often messy, ill-formed and not very neatly designed for research purposes."[50] For terrorism researchers, what greater challenge can we face?

ACKNOWLEDGMENTS

This book is the culmination of my collaboration with many people who have helped me along the way. I continue to benefit from Max Taylor's support and wisdom. I thank my Georgia State University colleagues including Gabe Kuperminc, Katharina Meredith, Tony Lemieux, Carol Winkler, and Shamieca Shine. I am grateful for the unwavering friendship and support of Barry Coughlan, Joe Reinkemeyer, Louise Pygman, Kurt Braddock, Mick Williams, Graeme Steven, Linn and Jonah Pitts, Brian Swords, Catherine Perkins, Darrin Schnur, Nate Anthony, and the Westview crew. Dan Piper and the Reinkemeyer brothers dragged me off to the most incredible places when I needed it most—you will never make a fly fisherman out of me, gentlemen, but I am grateful that you try. Throughout this book I draw on published research I've produced with dozens of colleagues. In no particular order I am grateful to Max Taylor, Kurt Braddock, Paul Gill, John Morrison, Mary Beth Altier, Emma Leonard Boyle, Daniel Koehler, Gary LaFree, Larry Rubin, Tore Bjorgo, Dipak Gupta, Orla Lynch, Michael Boyle, Stevan Weine, Chelsea Daymon, Heidi Ellis, Saida Abdi, Ron Schouten, Bart Schuurman, Neil Shortland, Katerina Papatheodorou, Katharina Meredith, Michael Kenney, Jesse Morton,

ACKNOWLEDGMENTS

Mick Williams, Jessica Stern, Emily Corner, James Silver, Shaun Walsh, Suzzette Abbasciano, Bill Evans, Sam Hunter, J. M. Berger, Ari Fodeman, Daniel Snook, Andrew Silke, Donald Holbrook, Scott Kleinmann, Jamie Khalil, Martine Zeuthen, and Noémie Bouhana.

Graeme Wood helped me work out some ideas related to the Islamic State. I benefited from Mark Fallon's investigatory wisdom. Ashley Powers shared with me her material on John Walker Lindh. Michele Grossman provided me a platform at AVERT to test out some ideas from an early draft. Prashansa Dickson and Priyam Joshi helped with sources and endnotes. Kim Locke generously shared key source material, John Wyman, Matt Collier, Mond Mugiya, and others at the FBI's Behavioral Analysis Unit-1 (past and present) allowed me to benefit from their experiences in the field and provided me opportunities to try out new ideas. I have benefited from the counsel of Emma Barrett, Rik Legault, John Picarelli, Ajmal Aziz, Ross Owens, and Michael Brown. I am grateful to my editor, Caelyn Cobb, and Monique Briones, at Columbia University Press, and to the two anonymous reviewers whose comments on the first draft were most helpful.

I could not have written this book without the relentless support of my family. J.J., Lhotse, and Nuptse helped despite themselves. As for Bo, bless him, he tries. Kris, on the other hand, helps more than she will ever realize.

NOTES

PREFACE

1. Peter Finn, "Germans Studied Brains of Radical Group's Leaders," *Washington Post*, November 19, 2002.
2. Bernhard Bogerts, Maria Schöne, and Stephanie Breitschuh, "Brain Alterations Potentially Associated with Aggression and Terrorism," *CNS Spectrums* 23, no. 2 (2018): 129.
3. Paul Hoffman, "3 Jailed German Terrorists Reported Suicides as Hostages from Hijacked Plane Fly Home," *New York Times*, October 19, 1977.
4. Finn, "Germans Studied Brains."
5. Finn, "Germans Studied Brains."
6. John Hooper, "The Dead Guerrillas, the Missing Brains and the Experiment," *Guardian*, November 18, 2002.
7. Constance Holden, "Fuss Over Terrorist's Brain," *Science* 298, no. 5598 (2002): 1551.
8. Holden, "Fuss Over Terrorist's Brain," 1551.
9. Rob Broomby, "Mystery Over German Guerrilla's Brain," *BBC News*, November 9, 2002.
10. Mark Landler, "German Radical's Daughter Seeks Brain Kept After Suicide," *New York Times*, November 12, 2002.
11. Landler, "Brain Kept After Suicide."
12. Bogerts et al., "Brain Alterations," 129.
13. Noémie Bouhana, October 21, 2019, http://twitter.com/noemie_bouhana: "After a lecture earlier this week, I was asked (again) what the value of theory really was to an applied field such as ours. It seems to me that chasing any form of knowledge without theory is like trying to solve a vast puzzle without a picture and starting from the middle."

14. Alex P. Schmid, "Comments on Marc Sageman's Polemic 'The Stagnation in Terrorism Research,'" *Terrorism & Political Violence* 26, no. 4 (2014): 593.

15. Tracy Kidder and Richard Todd, *Good Prose: The Art of Nonfiction* (New York: Random House, 2013), 36.

16. Tanjil Rashid, "Inside the Jihadi Mind—Can Fiction Match (or Even Better) an Insider's Account?" *Financial Times*, February 8, 2019.

17. Alexander Meleagrou-Hitchens, *Incitement: Anwar Al-Awlaki's Western Jihad* (Cambridge, MA: Harvard University Press, 2020), 3.

18. Quassim Cassam, *Extremism: A Philosophical Analysis* (London: Routledge, 2021), 89.

1. WHAT IS TERRORISM?

1. Greg Miller and Souad Mekhennet, "Murder in the Atlas Mountains," *Washington Post*, June 21, 2019.

2. "Murders of Louisa Vesterager Jespersen and Maren Ueland," Wikipedia, last modified September 19, 2021, https://en.wikipedia.org/wiki/Murders_of_Louisa_Vesterager_Jespersen _and_Maren_Ueland.

3. Lucia I. Suarez Sang, "ISIS Supporters Who Beheaded Scandinavian Hikers in Morocco Sentenced to Death," *Fox News*, July 18, 2019.

4. Bill Bostock, "The Killing of Two Scandinavian Backpackers in Morocco Has Been Declared an 'Act of Terror' as Officials Investigate an ISIS-Style Beheading Video," *Insider*, December 20, 2018.

5. Miller and Mekhennet, "Murder in the Atlas Mountains."

6. Miller and Mekhennet, "Murder in the Atlas Mountains"; "Morocco Suspect Admits Killing Scandinavian Hiker," *BBC News*, May 31, 2019.

7. "Morocco Suspect Admits Killing Scandinavian Hiker"; Ruth Maclean, "Moroccan Court Orders Death Penalty for Jihadists Who Beheaded Tourists," *Guardian*, July 18, 2019.

8. AFP, "Mother of Danish Student Suspected Killed by Jihadists Demands Death Penalty," *Guardian*, July 11, 2019.

9. Maclean, "Moroccan Court Orders Death Penalty for Jihadists Who Beheaded Tourists."

10. Suarez Sang, "ISIS Supporters Who Beheaded Scandinavian Hikers in Morocco Sentenced to Death."

11. Miller and Mekhennet, "Murder in the Atlas Mountains."

12. Edward Mendelson, "The Complete Works of Primo Levi," *New York Times*, November 23, 2015.

13. "Alek Minassian Tells Police About His Feelings Towards Women," *CTV News Toronto*, September 27, 2019.

14. "Transcript of Video Linked to Santa Barbara Mass Shooting," *CNN*, May 27, 2014.

15. "Transcript of Video Linked to Santa Barbara Mass Shooting."

16. The book was posted online as a PDF. Copy in author's possession.

17. Joseph Lombardo, "LVMPD Criminal Investigative Report of the 1 October Mass Casualty Shooting," Las Vegas Metropolitan Police Department, August 3, 2018, https://www.lvmpd.com/en-us/Documents/1-October-FIT-Criminal-Investigative-Report-FINAL_080318.pdf.

18. Lombardo, "LVMPD Criminal Investigative Report."

19. U.S. Department of Justice, Federal Bureau of Investigation, "Key Findings of the Behavioral Analysis Unit's Las Vegas Review Panel (LVRP)," United States Federal Bureau of Investigation, 2018, https://www.hsdl.org/?view&did=820782.

20. U.S. Department of Justice, "Key Findings of the Behavioral Analysis Unit's Las Vegas Review Panel (LVRP)."

21. Lombardo, "LVMPD Criminal Investigative Report," 20.

22. Vanessa Romo, "Police End Las Vegas Shooting Investigation; No Motive Found," *NPR*, August 3, 2018.

23. Lombardo, "LVMPD Criminal Investigative Report," 125.

24. Institute for Economics and Peace, Global Terrorism Index 2018: Measuring the Impact of Terrorism, Sydney, November 2018, https://www.visionofhumanity.org/wp-content/uploads/2020/10/Global-Terrorism-Index-2018.pdf.

25. Institute for Economics and Peace, Global Terrorism Index 2018.

26. Institute for Economics and Peace, Global Terrorism Index 2018, 45.

27. Institute for Economics and Peace, Global Terrorism Index 2018, 81.

28. Virginia Page Fortna, "Is Terrorism Really a Weapon of the Weak? Debunking the Conventional Wisdom," *Journal of Conflict Resolution* 67, no. 4 (August 2022).

29. Matthew J. Dolliver and Erin M. Kearns, "Is It Terrorism? Public Perceptions, Media, and Labeling the Las Vegas Shooting," *Studies in Conflict & Terrorism* (August 2019): 1–19.

30. Erin M. Kearns, Allison E. Betus, and Anthony F. Lemieux, "Why Do Some Terrorist Attacks Receive More Media Attention Than Others?" *Justice Quarterly* 36, no. 6 (2019): 985–1022.

31. Joseph Silverstein, "Dylann Roof Was Obsessed with Trayvon Martin, Wanted to Save the 'White Race': Friend," *New York Daily News*, June 20, 2015.

32. Ravi Satkalmi and John Miller, "We Work for the N.Y.P.D. This Is What We've Learned About Terrorism," *New York Times*, September 11, 2019.

33. Satkalmi and Miller, "We Work for the N.Y.P.D."

34. Satkalmi and Miller, "We Work for the N.Y.P.D."

35. "UK Courts Hand Far-Right Extremists Lighter Online Crime Sentences Than Islamists," *Arab News*, January 19, 2020.

36. Graham Macklin, "The El Paso Terrorist Attack," *CTC Sentinel* 12, no. 11 (December 2019): 5.

37. Masood Farivar, "2019 'Deadliest' Year for Domestic Terrorism, Says FBI Director," *VOA News*, February 5, 2020.

38. Farivar, "2019 'Deadliest' Year for Domestic Terrorism."

39. "Hate Groups Reach Record High," *SPLC*, February 19, 2019.

40. Nicolò Scremin, "Why an Agreed Definition of Terrorism Matters," *International Counter-Terrorism Review* 1, no. 2 (2020): 6.

41. Scremin, "Why an Agreed Definition of Terrorism Matters," 6.

42. Scremin, "Why an Agreed Definition of Terrorism Matters," 11.

43. Wojciech Kaczkowski, Ayse Lokmanoglu, and Carol Winkler, "Definitions Matter: A Comparison of the Global Terrorism Database and the U.S. Governmental Reports of Terrorist Incidents in Western Europe, 2002–2016," *Cambridge Review of International Affairs* (December 2019): 55–72.

44. Kaczkowski et al., "Definitions Matter," 8–9.

45. Kaczkowski et al., "Definitions Matter," 11.

46. U.S. Department of Homeland Security, Strategic Framework for Countering Terrorism and Targeted Violence (Washington, DC), September 2019.

47. Strategic Framework for Countering Terrorism and Targeted Violence, 2.

48. Douglas Walton, "Persuasive Definitions and Public Policy Arguments," *Argumentation and Advocacy* 37, no. 3 (2001): 117–32.

49. Donald Trump, May 31, 2020, http://twitter.com/realDonaldTrump): "The United States of America will be designating ANTIFA as a Terrorist Organization."

50. Jason M. Blazakis and Colin P. Clarke, "Why Trump Can't Designate Antifa as a Terrorist Organization," *Slate*, June 1, 2020.

51. William James, "On a Certain Blindness in Human Beings" in *Talks to Teachers on Psychology and to Students on Some of Life's Ideals* (Cambridge, MA: Harvard University Press, 1983).

52. Neil MacFarquhar and Adam Goldman, "A New Face of White Supremacy: Plots Expose Danger of the 'Base,'" *New York Times*, January 22, 2020.

53. Mack Lamoureux and Ben Makuch, "FBI Arrests Members of Neo-Nazi Group, Including Canadian Soldier Hiding in US," *VICE News*, January 16, 2020.

54. Hannah Allam, "2019 Marks a Turning Point in How the U.S. Confronts Domestic Terrorism," *NPR*, December 26, 2019.

55. Clare S. Allely, *The Psychology of Extreme Violence: A Case Study Approach to Serial Homicide, Mass Shooting, School Shooting and Lone-Actor Terrorism* (London: Routledge, 2020).

2. WHO BECOMES A TERRORIST?

1. Marcus Kreuzer, "The Structure of Description: Evaluating Descriptive Inferences and Conceptualizations," *Perspectives on Politics* 17, no. 1 (2019): 122.

2. "Man Licked Deodorant in a Walmart for Coronavirus Prank Video, Authorities Say," *CBS News*, March 25, 2020.

3. Jarrod Clay, "Pennsylvania Grocery Store Out More Than $35,000 After Woman Intentionally Coughs on Food," *Local 12 News*, March 25, 2020; WKRC, "Woman Charged After Coughing on $35,000 Worth of Produce at Grocery Store," *Local 12 News*, March 28, 2020.

4. Clare Hymes, "Justice Department Says Intentionally Spreading Coronavirus Could Violate Anti-Terrorism Laws," CBS News, March 25, 2020.

5. GianCarlo Canaparo and Zack Smith, "We Don't Need Terrorism Charges to Prosecute Those Who Cough to Spread COVID-19," *Heritage Foundation*, April 7, 2020.

6. Jessica Pishko, "The FBI Accused Him of Terrorism. He Couldn't Tie His Shoes," *Esquire*, September 8, 2016.

7. Pishko, "The FBI Accused Him of Terrorism."

8. Pishko, "The FBI Accused Him of Terrorism."

9. Pishko, "The FBI Accused Him of Terrorism."

10. Pishko, "The FBI Accused Him of Terrorism."

11. Pishko, "The FBI Accused Him of Terrorism."

12. Pishko, "The FBI Accused Him of Terrorism."

13. Shawn Pogatchnik, "IRA Proxy Bombings Kill 6 Troops, Civilian: Northern Ireland: The Attack by the Terrorist Group Is the Deadliest Against British Forces in Two Years," *Los Angeles Times*, October 25, 1990.

14. "Murder at the Airport: The Brazen Attack on Kim Jong Nam," *Reuters*, April 1, 2019.

15. Shafi Md Mostofa and Natalie J. Doyle, "Profiles of Islamist Militants in Bangladesh," *Perspectives on Terrorism* 13, no. 5 (2019): 112–29.

16. Mostafa and Doyle, "Profiles of Islamist Militants in Bangladesh," 116.

17. Lorenzo Vidino and Seamus Hughes, "ISIS in America: From Retweets to Raqqa," Program on Extremism, George Washington University (December 2015): ix.

18. Vidino and Hughes, "ISIS in America," ix.

19. "GW Extremism Tracker: Terrorism in the United States," Program on Extremism, George Washington University (December 2018).

20. "GW Extremism Tracker: Terrorism in the United States," Program on Extremism, George Washington University (June 2020).

21. Lorne Dawson, "A Comparative Analysis of the Data on Western Foreign Fighters in Syria and Iraq: Who Went and Why?" *International Centre for Counter-Terrorism*, February 2021, 2.

22. John Horgan and John F. Morrison, "Here to Stay? The Rising Threat of Violent Dissident Republicanism in Northern Ireland," *Terrorism & Political Violence* 23, no. 4 (2011): 642–69.

23. Horgan and Morrison, "Here to Stay?" 654.

24. Fernando Reinares, "Who Are the Terrorists? Analyzing Changes in Sociological Profile among Members of ETA," *Studies in Conflict & Terrorism* 27, no. 6 (2004): 473.

25. Leonard Weinberg and William Lee Eubank, "Neo-Fascist and Far Left Terrorists in Italy: Some Biographical Observations," *British Journal of Political Science* 18, no. 4 (1988): 531–49.

26. Weinberg and Eubank, "Neo-Fascist and Far Left Terrorists in Italy," 538.

27. Mauricio Florez-Morris, "Joining Guerrilla Groups in Colombia: Individual Motivations and Processes for Entering a Violent Organization," *Studies in Conflict & Terrorism* 30, no. 7 (2007): 615–34.

28. Jon Lewis, Seamus Hughes, Oren Segal, and Ryan Greer, "White Supremacist Terror: Modernizing Our Approach to Today's Threat," Program on Extremism, George Washington University (April 2020): 13.

29. Carol García-Calvo, Fernando Reinares, and Álvaro Vicente, "National Extraction, Geographical Origin and Migratory Ancestry Among Jihadists in Spain," *Studies in Conflict & Terrorism* (July 2020): 798–823.

30. Robin Simcox and Emily Dyer, "Al-Qaeda in the United States: A Complete Analysis of Terrorism Offenses," *Henry Jackson Society*, February 26, 2013.

31. Marc Sageman, *Understanding Terror Networks* (Philadelphia: University of Pennsylvania Press, 2004), 92.

32. Lorenzo Vidino, Francesco Marone, and Eva Entenmann, *Fear Thy Neighbor: Radicalization and Jihadist Attacks in the West* (ISPI: Milan, 2017).

33. Fernando Reinares, "The Madrid Bombings and Global Jihadism," *Survival* 52, no. 2 (2010): 87.

34. Reinares, "The Madrid Bombings and Global Jihadism," 88.

35. Jeanine de Roy van Zuijdewijn and Edwin Bakker, "Analysing Personal Characteristics of Lone-Actor Terrorists: Research Findings and Recommendations," *Perspectives on Terrorism* 10, no. 2 (2016): 43.

36. Marc Smith, Tracy Connor, and Richard Engel, "The ISIS Files: What Leaked Documents Reveal About Terror Recruits," *NBC News*, April 18, 2016.

37. Paul Gill and John Horgan, "Who Were the Volunteers? The Shifting Sociological and Operational Profile of 1240 Provisional Irish Republican Army Members," *Terrorism & Political Violence* 25, no. 3 (2013): 435–56.

38. Reinares, "Who Are the Terrorists?" 477.

39. Justin C. Altum, "Anti-Abortion Extremism: The Army of God," *Chrestomathy: Annual Review of Undergraduate Research at the College of Charleston* 2 (2003): 6.

40. Ayla Hammond Schbley, "Toward a Common Profile of Religious Terrorism: Some Psychosocial Determinants of Christian and Islamic Terrorists," *Police Practice and Research* 7, no. 4 (2006): 280.

41. Kathleen Blee, "Becoming a Racist: Women in Contemporary Ku Klux Klan and Neo-Nazi Groups," *Gender and Society*, 10, no. 6 (1996): 686.

42. Schbley, "Toward a Common Profile of Religious Terrorism," 280.

43. Jytte Klausen, Tyler Morrill, and Rosanne Libretti, "The Terrorist Age-Crime Curve: An Analysis of American Islamist Terrorist Offenders and Age-Specific Propensity for Participation in Violent and Nonviolent Incidents," *Social Science Quarterly* 97, no. 1 (2016): 31.

44. Jason Burke, "Khalid Masood Was a Convert with a Criminal Past. So Far, So Familiar," *Guardian*, March 25, 2017.

45. John Horgan, Mia Bloom, Chelsea Daymon, Wojciech Kaczkowski, and Hicham Tiflati, "A New Age of Terror? Older Fighters in The Caliphate," *CTC Sentinel* 10, no. 5 (2017): 13–14.

46. Horgan et al., "A New Age of Terror?" 14.

47. Horgan et al., "A New Age of Terror?" 14.

48. Horgan et al., "A New Age of Terror?" 17.

49. Horgan et al., "A New Age of Terror?" 18.

50. John Horgan, Max Taylor, Mia Bloom, and Charlie Winter, "From Cubs to Lions: A Six Stage Model of Child Socialization Into the Islamic State," *Studies in Conflict & Terrorism* 40, no. 7 (2017): 645–46.

51. Global Coalition to Protect Education from Attack (GCPEA), "Education Under Attack 2020," accessed May 24, 2023, https://eua2020.protectingeducation.org.

52. Cited by Gill and Horgan, "Who Were the Volunteers?" 442.

53. Horgan et al., "From Cubs to Lions," 646.

54. John Horgan, "The Lost Boys," *CREST Security Review* (Spring 2017): 10–13.

55. Feriha N. Peracha, Raafia R. Khan, Arooj Ahmad, Sadia J. Khan, Sahar Hussein, and Haroon Rashid Coundry, "Socio Demographic Variables in the Vulnerable Youth Predisposed Towards Militancy (Swat, Pakistan)," *Psychiatry, Psychology and Law* 19, no. 3 (2012): 439–47.

56. Peracha et al., "Socio Demographic Variables," 441.

57. Peracha et al., "Socio Demographic Variables," 441.

58. Anti-Defamation League, "Feuerkrieg Division (FKD)," 2020, October 7, 2019, https://www.adl.org/resources/backgrounders/feuerkrieg-division-fkd.

59. Michael Kunzelman and Jari Tanner, "He Led a Neo-Nazi Group Linked to Bomb Plots. He Was 13," *Associated Press*, April 11, 2020.

60. "Teenage Neo-Nazi from Cornwall Is UK's Youngest Terror Offender," *BBC News*, February 1, 2021.

61. Jessica Davis, Leah West, and Amarnath Amarasingam, "Measuring Impact, Uncovering Bias? Citation Analysis of Literature on Women in Terrorism," *Perspectives on Terrorism* 15, no. 2 (2021): 58–76.

62. Alexander Meleagrou-Hitchens, Seamus Hughes, and Bennett Clifford, *Homegrown: ISIS in America* (New York: I. B. Taurus, 2021).

63. Weinberg and Eubank, "Neo-Fascist and Far Left Terrorists in Italy," 531–49.

64. Weinberg and Eubank, "Neo-Fascist and Far Left Terrorists in Italy," 545.

65. Blee, "Becoming a Racist," 680.

66. Blee, "Becoming a Racist," 681.

67. Blee, "Becoming a Racist," 681.

68. Blee, "Becoming a Racist," 682.

69. Reinares, "Who Are the Terrorists?" 467.

70. Reinares, "Who Are the Terrorists?" 468.

71. Reinares, "Who Are the Terrorists?" 471.

72. Julia Chernov Hwang, *Why Terrorists Quit: The Disengagement of Indonesian Jihadists* (Ithaca, NY: Cornell University Press, 2018).

73. Blee, "Becoming a Racist," 682.

74. See especially Reed Wood, *Female Fighters: Why Rebel Groups Recruit Women for War* (New York: Columbia University Press, 2019).

75. Aaron Y. Zelin, *Your Sons Are at Your Service: Tunisia's Missionaries of Jihad* (New York: Columbia University Press, 2020), 228.

76. Lizzie Dearden, "Safiyya Shaikh: How an Unemployed Mother Ran an International Isis Propaganda Network," *Independent*, July 3, 2020.

77. Jason Warner and Hilary Matfess, "Exploding Stereotypes: The Unexpected Operational and Demographic Characteristics of Boko Haram's Suicide Bombers," August 19, 2017, Combating Terrorism Center at West Point.

78. Warner and Matfess, "Exploding Stereotypes," iv, 35.

79. Jason Warner and Ellen Chapin, "Targeted Terror: The Suicide Bombers of Al-Shabaab," February 13, 2018, Combating Terrorism Center at West Point.

80. Warner and Chapin, "Targeted Terror," 5.

81. Warner and Chapin, "Targeted Terror," 30, 28–29.

82. Warner and Chapin, "Targeted Terror," 32.

83. Charles A. Russell and Bowman H. Miller, "Profile of a Terrorist," *Studies in Conflict & Terrorism* 1, no. 1 (1977): 17–34.

84. Russell and Miller, "Profile of a Terrorist," 17.

85. Russell and Miller, "Profile of a Terrorist," 17.

86. Gregory Cumming and Stephen Sayles, "The Symbionese Liberation Army: Coming Together, 1973," *History Compass* 9, no. 6 (2011): 486.

87. Cumming and Sayles, "The Symbionese Liberation Army," 487.

88. William Rosenau, "'Our Backs Are Against the Wall': The Black Liberation Army and Domestic Terrorism in 1970s America," *Studies in Conflict & Terrorism* 36, no. 2 (January 2013): 177.

89. Thomas Strentz, "A Terrorist Psychosocial Profile: Past and Present," *FBI Law Enforcement Bulletin* 57 (1988): 13.

90. Strentz, "A Terrorist Psychosocial Profile," 17.

91. Weinberg and Eubank, "Neo-Fascist and Far Left Terrorists in Italy," 540.

92. Graeme Wood, *The Way of the Strangers: Encounters with the Islamic State* (New York: Penguin Random House, 2017), 146, 147.

93. Wood, *The Way of the Strangers*, 296.

94. Diego Gambetta and Steffen Hertog, *Engineers of Jihad: The Curious Connection Between Violent Extremism and Education* (Princeton, NJ: Princeton University Press, 2016).

95. Gambetta and Hertog, *Engineers of Jihad*, 127.

96. Steffen Hertog, "Engineers of Jihad," Carnegie Endowment for International Peace, September 1, 2009.

97. Robert S. Leiken and Steven Brooke, "The Quantitative Analysis of Terrorism and Immigration: An Initial Exploration," *Terrorism & Political Violence* 18, no. 4 (2006): 511.

98. Hertog, "Engineers of Jihad."

99. This point was also made by Quassim Cassam, *Extremism: A Philosophical Analysis* (London: Routledge, 2021), 176.

100. For example, Hugues Lagrange, "Diego Gambetta and Steffen Hertog, *Engineers of Jihad: The Curious Connection Between Violent Extremism and Education*," *European Sociological Review*, 33, no.1 (February 2017): 161–64.

101. Lagrange, "Diego Gambetta and Steffen Hertog, *Engineers of Jihad*," 164.
102. Hertog, "Engineers of Jihad."
103. Bundesamt für Verfassungsschutz, *Analyse Der Den Deutschen Sicherheitsbehörden Vorliegenden Informationen Über Die Radikalisierungshintergründe Und-Verläufe Der Personen, Die Aus Islamistischer Motivation Aus Deutschland in Richtung Syrien Ausgereist Sind*, Ständige Konferenz der Innenminister und senatoren der Linder, 2016.
104. Bernhard Bogerts, Maria Schöne, and Stephanie Breitschuh, "Brain Alterations Potentially Associated with Aggression and Terrorism," *CNS Spectrums* 23, no. 2 (2018): 131.
105. Rosenau, "Our Backs Are Against the Wall," 177.
106. Rosenau, "Our Backs Are Against the Wall," 183.
107. Wood, *The Way of the Strangers*, xxiii.
108. Michael S. Schmidt, "Canadian Killed in Syria Lives on as Pitchman for Jihadis," *New York Times*, July 15, 2014.
109. Vidino et al., *Fear Thy Neighbor*, 11.
110. Graeme Wood, "What ISIS Really Wants," *Atlantic*, March 15, 2015.
111. Simon Cottee, "Why It's So Hard to Stop ISIS Propaganda," *Atlantic*, March 2, 2015.
112. Brian Dodwell, Daniel Milton, and Don Rassler, "The Caliphate's Global Workforce: An Inside Look at the Islamic State's Foreign Fighter Paper Trail," *Combating Terrorism Center at West Point*, April 18, 2016, iv.
113. Dodwell et al., "The Caliphate's Global Workforce," 12.
114. Dodwell et al., "The Caliphate's Global Workforce," iv.
115. Gill and Horgan, "Who Were the Volunteers?" 441.
116. Gill and Horgan, "Who Were the Volunteers?" 441.
117. Rodger Shanahan, "Typology of Terror: The Backgrounds of Australian Jihadis," *Australasian Policing* 12, no. 1 (2020): 32–38.
118. Weinberg and Eubank, "Neo-Fascist and Far Left Terrorists in Italy," 532.
119. Blee, "Becoming a Racist," 686.
120. Blee, "Becoming a Racist," 686.
121. Strentz, "A Terrorist Psychosocial Profile," 13–19.
122. Strentz, "A Terrorist Psychosocial Profile," 15.
123. Strentz, "A Terrorist Psychosocial Profile," 15.
124. Strentz, "A Terrorist Psychosocial Profile," 16.
125. Kathleen Belew, "Opinion: Why 'Stand Back and Stand By' Should Set Off Alarm Bells," *New York Times*, October 2, 2020.
126. Strentz, "A Terrorist Psychosocial Profile," 18.
127. Dodwell et al., "The Caliphate's Global Workforce," iv.
128. Francisco Gutiérrez-Sanín, "Telling the Difference: Guerrillas and Paramilitaries in the Colombian War," *Politics and Society*, 36, no. 1 (2008): 6.
129. A pioneering study in this area is from Arie Perliger, Gabriel Koehler-Derrick, and Ami Pedahzur, "The Gap Between Participation and Violence: Why We Need to Disaggregate Terrorist 'Profiles,'" *International Studies Quarterly* 60, no. 2 (2016): 220–29.

130. Paul Gill, John Horgan, and Paige Deckert, "Bombing Alone: Tracing the Motivations and Antecedent Behaviors of Lone-Actor Terrorists," *Journal of Forensic Sciences* 59, no. 2 (2014): 425–35.

131. Gill, Horgan, and Deckert, "Bombing Alone," 431.

132. Strentz, "A Terrorist Psychosocial Profile," 432.

133. De Roy van Zuijdewijn and Bakker, "Analysing Personal Characteristics of Lone-Actor Terrorists," 42–49.

134. De Roy van Zuijdewijn and Bakker, "Analysing Personal Characteristics of Lone-Actor Terrorists," 44.

135. De Roy van Zuijdewijn and Bakker, "Analysing Personal Characteristics of Lone-Actor Terrorists," 44.

136. John Horgan, Neil Shortland, Suzette Abbasciano, and Shaun Walsh, "Actions Speak Louder Than Words: A Behavioral Analysis of 183 Individuals Convicted for Terrorist Offenses in the United States from 1995 to 2012," *Journal of Forensic Sciences* 61, no. 5 (2016): 1228–37.

137. John Horgan, Neil Shortland, and Suzette Abbasciano, "Towards a Typology of Terrorism Involvement: A Behavioral Differentiation of Violent Extremist Offenders," *Journal of Threat Assessment and Management* 5, no. 2 (2018): 84–102.

138. Horgan et al., "Towards a Typology of Terrorism Involvement," 91.

139. For example, see Horgan et al., "Towards a Typology of Terrorism Involvement," 96–97.

140. Simcox and Dyer, "Al-Qaeda in the United States."

141. Audrey Alexander, "Cruel Intentions: Female Jihadists in America," Program on Extremism, George Washington University (November 2016).

142. Alexander, "Cruel Intentions," vii.

143. Horgan et al., "Towards a Typology of Terrorism Involvement," 86.

144. Horgan et al., "Towards a Typology of Terrorism Involvement," 87.

145. Strentz, "A Terrorist Psychosocial Profile," 14.

146. Ariel Merari, "Academic Research and Government Policy on Terrorism," *Terrorism & Political Violence* 3, no. 1 (1991): 88.

147. Jeff Victoroff, "The Mind of the Terrorist: A Review and Critique of Psychological Approaches," *Journal of Conflict Resolution* 49, no. 1 (2005): 7.

148. Merari, "Academic Research and Government Policy on Terrorism," 91.

149. Merari, "Academic Research and Government Policy on Terrorism," 93.

150. Merari, "Academic Research and Government Policy on Terrorism," 92.

151. Bart Schuurman, "Non-Involvement in Terrorist Violence: Understanding the Most Common Outcome of Radicalization Processes," *Perspectives on Terrorism* 14, no. 6 (2020): 14; also see Leena Malkki, "Learning from the Lack of Political Violence: Conceptual Issues and Research Designs," *Perspectives on Terrorism* 14, no. 6 (2020): 27–36.

152. "Individuals Referred to and Supported Through the *Prevent* Programme, England and Wales, April 2018 to March 2019," *Home Office Statistical Bulletin* 32 (2019), 19.

153. "Individuals Referred to and Supported Through the *Prevent* Programme," 12.

3. MOTIVATION

The chapter epigraph comes from John McCain and Mark Salter, *Faith of My Fathers: A Family Memoir* (New York: Penguin Random House, 2016), 348.

1. David Cooke and Caroline Logan, "Violent Extremism: The Practical Assessment and Management of Risk," in *Terrorism Risk Assessment Instruments*, ed. Raymond R. Corrado, Gunda Wössner, and Ariel Merari (Amsterdam: IOS, 2021), 99–115.

2. Alexander Meleagrou-Hitchens, *Incitement: Anwar Al-Awlaki's Western Jihad* (Cambridge, MA: Harvard University Press, 2020), 5–6.

3. Pico Iyer, "Introduction," in Peter Matthiessen, *The Snow Leopard* (Toronto: Penguin Canada, 2008), xxi–xxii.

4. Iyer, "Introduction," xxii.

5. Maxwell Taylor, *The Terrorist* (London: Brassey's, 1988).

6. John Horgan, *The Psychology of Terrorism*, 2nd ed. (New York: Routledge, 2014).

7. Gerard Saucier, Laura Geuy Akers, Seraphine Shen-Miller, Goran Knežević, and Lazar Stankov, "Patterns of Thinking in Militant Extremism," *Perspectives on Psychological Science* 4, no. 3 (May 2009): 256–71.

8. Randy Borum, "Rethinking Radicalization," *Journal of Strategic Security* 4, no. 4 (2011): 1–6.

9. Randy Borum, "Radicalization Into Violent Extremism I: A Review of Social Science Theories," *Journal of Strategic Security* 4, no. 4 (2011): 9.

10. Alexander Meleagrou-Hitchens, Seamus Hughes, and Bennett Clifford, "The Travelers: American Jihadists in Syria and Iraq," Program on Extremism, George Washington University (February 2018): 5–6.

11. Meleagrou-Hitchens, Hughes, and Clifford, "The Travelers," 6.

12. Graeme Wood, "What ISIS Really Wants," *Atlantic*, March 15, 2015.

13. G. M. Bailey and Phil Edwards, "Rethinking 'Radicalisation': Microradicalisations and Reciprocal Radicalisation as an Intertwined Process," *Journal for Deradicalization* 10 (2017): 255.

14. Tara Brady, "Jihad Jane: This Story Has Nothing to Do with Religion," *Irish Times*, February 16, 2020.

15. Mauricio Florez-Morris, "Joining Guerrilla Groups in Colombia: Individual Motivations and Processes for Entering a Violent Organization," *Studies in Conflict & Terrorism* 30, no. 7 (2007): 631.

16. Florez-Morris, "Joining Guerrilla Groups in Colombia," 620.

17. Alison Jamieson, *The Heart Attacked: Terrorism and Conflict in the Italian State* (London: Marion Boyars, 1989).

18. Fathali M. Moghaddam and Margaret J. Hendricks, "The Psychology of Revolution," *Current Opinion in Psychology* 35 (2020): 7–11.

19. Sara Elizabeth Williams "The Bullied Finnish Teenager Who Became an Isis Social Media Kingpin—and Then Got Out," *Newsweek*, June 5, 2015.

20. Brady, "Jihad Jane."

21. Jonathan Kenyon, Jens Binger, and Christopher Baker-Beall, "Exploring the Role of the Internet in Radicalisation and Offending of Convicted Extremists," HM Prison & Probation Service (2021), 10, https://assets.publishing.service.gov.uk/government/uploads /system/uploads/attachment_data/file/1017413/exploring-role-internet-radicalisation.pdf.

22. Ciarán O'Connor, "Hatescape: An In-Depth Analysis of Extremism and Hate Speech on TikTok," Institute for Strategic Dialogue, August 24, 2021.

23. Rodger Shanahan, "Commentary: When Is Mental Illness an Excuse for Terrorism?" Lowy Institute, November 21, 2019.

24. Donald Holbrook, "What's on the Terrorists' Bookshelves?" paper presented at the European Counter Terrorism Centre (ECTC) Advisory Network on Terrorism and Propaganda conference, Europol Headquarters, The Hague, April 9–10, 2019.

25. Holbrook, "What's on the Terrorists' Bookshelves?" 7.

26. Thomas Hegghammer, *The Caravan: Abdallah Azzam and the Rise of Global Jihad* (Cambridge: Cambridge University Press, 2020), 481.

27. Hegghammer, *The Caravan*, 482.

28. Jacob Davey and Julia Ebner, "'The Great Replacement': The Violent Consequences of Mainstreamed Extremism," Institute for Strategic Dialogue, July 7, 2019, 4.

29. Shauna M. Bowes, Thomas H. Costello, Winkie Ma, and Scott O. Lilienfeld, "Looking Under the Tinfoil Hat: Clarifying the Personological and Psychopathological Correlates of Conspiracy Beliefs," *Journal of Personality* 89, no. 3 (2021): 422–36.

30. Bowes et al., "Looking Under the Tinfoil Hat."

31. Clark McCauley and Sophia Moskalenko, "Some Things We Think We've Learned Since 9/11: A Commentary on Marc Sageman's 'The Stagnation in Terrorism Research,'" *Terrorism & Political Violence* 26, no. 4 (2014): 603.

32. Wood, "What ISIS Really Wants."

33. Borum, "Radicalization Into Violent Extremism I," 8.

34. For example, see Faiza Patel, "Rethinking Radicalization," Brennan Center for Justice at New York University School of Law (August 2011); Randy Borum, "Radicalization Into Violent Extremism II: A Review of Conceptual Models and Empirical Research," *Journal of Strategic Security* 4, no. 4 (2012): 37–62.

35. Noémie Bouhana and Per-Olof H. Wikström, Al Qai'da-Influenced Radicalisation: A Rapid Evidence Assessment Guided by Situational Action Theory (London: UK Home Office, 2011).

36. Fathali Moghaddam, "The Staircase to Terrorism: A Psychological Explanation," *American Psychologist* 60, no. 22 (2005): 161–69.

37. Clark McCauley and Sophia Moskalenko, "Mechanisms of Political Radicalization: Pathways Toward Terrorism," *Terrorism & Political Violence* 20, no. 3 (2008): 415–33.

38. Clark McCauley and Sophia Moskalenko, "Understanding Political Radicalization: The Two-Pyramids Model," *American Psychologist* 72, no. 3 (2017): 205.

39. Borum, "Radicalization into Violent Extremism I," 31.

40. Alessandro Orsini, "What Everybody Should Know About Radicalization and the DRIA Model," *Studies in Conflict & Terrorism* (2020): 1–33.

41. Michael A. Hogg, "From Uncertainty to Extremism: Social Categorization and Identity Processes," *Current Directions in Psychological Science* 23, no. 5 (2014): 338–42.

42. Hogg, "From Uncertainty to Extremism," 339.

43. Hogg, "From Uncertainty to Extremism," 339.

44. Hogg, "From Uncertainty to Extremism," 338.

45. Hogg, "From Uncertainty to Extremism," 340.

46. For information on the surveys, see Oluf Gøtzsche-Astrup, "Personality Moderates the Relationship Between Uncertainty and Political Violence: Evidence from Two Large US Samples," *Personality and Individual Differences* 139 (2019): 102–9.

47. Jeff Victoroff, "The Mind of the Terrorist: A Review and Critique of Psychological Approaches," *Journal of Conflict Resolution* 49, no. 1 (2005): 36; Borum, "Radicalization into Violent Extremism I,"; see also Borum, "Rethinking Radicalization."

48. Victoroff, "The Mind of the Terrorist," 9.

49. Victoroff, "The Mind of the Terrorist," 9.

50. Tom Burgis, "The Making of a French Jihadi," *Financial Times*, January 26, 2015.

51. Candice Feiring and Michael Lewis, "Equifinality and Multifinality: Diversity in Development from Infancy into Childhood," paper presented at the Biennial Meeting of the Society for Research in Child Development, Baltimore, MD, April 23–26, 1987.

52. Feiring and Lewis, "Equifinality and Multifinality," i.

53. Borum, "Radicalization Into Violent Extremism II"; Corner, Bouhana, and Gill, "The Multifinality of Vulnerability Indicators in Lone-Actor Terrorism."

54. H. A. Lyons and H. J. Harbinson, "A Comparison of Political and Non-Political Murderers in Northern Ireland, 1974–84," *Medicine, Science and the Law* 26, no. 3 (1986): 195.

55. Lyons and Harbinson, "A Comparison of Political and Non-Political Murderers in Northern Ireland," 194.

56. Lyons and Harbinson, "A Comparison of Political and Non-Political Murderers in Northern Ireland," 197.

57. Lyons and Harbinson, "A Comparison of Political and Non-Political Murderers in Northern Ireland," 197.

58. Lyons and Harbison, "A Comparison of Political and Non-Political Murderers in Northern Ireland," 194.

59. Joshua D. Freilich, Steven M. Chermak, and Jeff Gruenewald, "The Future of Terrorism Research: A Review Essay," *International Journal of Comparative and Applied Criminal Justice* 39, no. 4 (2015): 353–69321.

60. Freilich, Chermak, and Gruenewald, "The Future of Terrorism Research," 362.

61. Emily Corner, Helen Taylor, Isabelle Van Der Vegt, Nadine Salman, Bettina Rottweiler, Florian Hetzel, Caitlin Clemmow, Norah Schulten, and Paul Gill, "Reviewing the Links Between Violent Extremism and Personality, Personality Disorders, and Psychopathy," *Journal of Forensic Psychiatry & Psychology* (2021): 19.

62. Paul Gill, Caitlin Clemmow, Florian Hetzel, Bettina Rottweiler, Nadine Salman, Isabelle Van Der Vegt, and Zoe Marchment, "Systematic Review of Mental Health Problems and Violent Extremism," *Journal of Forensic Psychiatry & Psychology* 32, no. 1 (2021): 51–78.

63. Gill et al., "Systematic Review of Mental Health Problems and Violent Extremism," 58.

64. Lorne Dawson, "A Comparative Analysis of the Data on Western Foreign Fighters in Syria and Iraq: Who Went and Why?" February 10, 2021, International Centre for Counter-Terrorism – The Hague, 3.

65. Benedict Carey, "A Theory About Conspiracy Theories," *New York Times*, September 28, 2020.

66. Alex P. Schmid, "Comments on Marc Sageman's polemic 'The Stagnation in Terrorism Research,'" *Terrorism & Political Violence* 26, no. 4 (2014): 587–88.

67. Kathleen Blee, *Understanding Racist Activism: Theory, Methods, and Research* (London: Routledge, 2017), 131.

68. Kathleen Blee, "Becoming a Racist: Women in Contemporary Ku Klux Klan and Neo-Nazi Groups," *Gender & Society* 10, no. 6 (1996): 687.

69. For example, see Tyler Evans, Daniel J. Milton, and Joseph K. Young, "Choosing to Fight, Choosing to Die: Examining How ISIS Foreign Fighters Select Their Operational Roles," *International Studies Review* 23, no. 3 (2021): 515; Brian Dodwell, Daniel Milton, and Don Rassler, "The Caliphate's Global Workforce: An Inside Look at the Islamic State's Foreign Fighter Paper Trail," Combating Terrorism Center at West Point, April 18, 2016.

70. Evans et al., "Choosing to Fight, Choosing to Die," 6, 7.

71. Canadian Security Intelligence Service, "Mobilization to Violence (Terrorism) Research: Key Findings," Intelligence Assessments Branch (2018).

72. Nate Rosenblatt, "The Architects of Salvation: How IS Foreign Fighter Recruitment Hubs Emerged in Tunisia," Program on Extremism, George Washington University, September 2019.

73. Rosenblatt, "The Architects of Salvation," 4.

74. Rosenblatt, "The Architects of Salvation," 4.

75. Rosenblatt, "The Architects of Salvation," 5.

76. Bouhana and Wikström, *Al Qai'da–Influenced Radicalisation: A Rapid Evidence Assessment Guided by Situational Action Theory*.

77. Rik Coolsaet, "Radicalization: The Origins and Limits of a Contested Concept," in *Radicalisation in Belgium and the Netherlands: Critical Perspectives on Violence and Security*, ed. Nadia Fadil, Martijn de Koning, and Francesco Ragazzi, 29–51 (London: I. B. Tauris, 2019), 32.

78. Rosenblatt, "The Architects of Salvation," 17.

79. Rosenblatt, "The Architects of Salvation," 18.

80. Florez-Morris, "Joining Guerrilla Groups in Colombia," 625.

81. Blee, "Becoming a Racist," 689.

82. Radicalisation Awareness Network, "(Young) Women's Usage of Social Media and Lessons for Preventing Violent Extremism," conclusion paper, November 24, 2020, 1; also see Moghaddam and Hendricks, "The Psychology of Revolution."

83. Karen Jacques and Paul J. Taylor, "Male and Female Suicide Bombers: Different Sexes, Different Reasons?" *Studies in Conflict & Terrorism* 31, no. 4 (2008): 319.

84. Jacques and Taylor, "Male and Female Suicide Bombers," 322.

85. Cited in Ayla Hammond Schbley, "Toward a Common Profile of Religious Terrorism: Some Psychosocial Determinants of Christian and Islamic Terrorists," *Police Practice and Research* 7, no. 4 (2006): 279.

86. Schbley, "Toward a Common Profile of Religious Terrorism," 279.

87. John Horgan, *Walking Away from Terrorism* (London: Routledge, 2009), 105.

88. Thomas Hegghammer, "Should I Stay or Should I Go? Explaining Variation in Western Jihadists' Choice Between Domestic and Foreign Fighting," *American Political Science Review* 107, no. 1 (2013): 1–15.

89. "Start and Run a Militia," *Militia News*, accessed May 26, 2003, http://militianews.com /start-and-run-a-militia.

90. Evans et al., "Choosing to Fight, Choosing to Die."

91. Victoroff, "The Mind of the Terrorist," 28.

92. Robert Young Pelton, "Transcript of John Walker Interview," *CNN*, July 4, 2002.

93. Kati Marton, cited in Victoroff, "The Mind of the Terrorist," 28.

94. Graeme Wood, "The American Climbing the Ranks of ISIS," *Atlantic*, January 25, 2017.

95. Spencer Hsu and Rachel Weiner, "In Sentencing Regretful Capitol Protestor, Federal Judge Rebukes Republicans," *Washington Post*, June 24, 2021.

96. Tom Dreisbach, "Conspiracy Charges Bring Proud Boys' History of Violence into Spotlight," *NPR*, April 9, 2021.

97. Victoroff, "The Mind of the Terrorist," 35.

98. Victoroff, "The Mind of the Terrorist," 35.

99. Borum, "Radicalization into Violent Extremism I," 26.

100. Corner et al., "Reviewing the Links Between Violent Extremism and Personality, Personality Disorders, and Psychopathy," 3.

101. Bjørn Ihler, June 3, 2021, http://twitter.com/bjornih.

102. Blee, "Becoming a Racist," 695.

103. Blee, "Becoming a Racist," 695.

104. Stephen King, *On Writing: A Memoir of the Craft* (New York: Scribner, 2000), 18.

105. Victoroff, "The Mind of the Terrorist," 4.

106. James L. Knoll and Ronald W. Pies, "Moving Beyond 'Motives' in Mass Shootings," *Psychiatric Times* 36, no. 1 (January 2019).

107. Knoll and Pies, "Moving Beyond 'Motives' in Mass Shootings," 1.

108. U.S. Secret Service National Threat Assessment Center, "Protecting America's Schools: A U.S. Secret Service Analysis of Targeted School Violence," U.S Department of Homeland Security, November 2019.

109. U.S. Secret Service National Threat Assessment Center, "Protecting America's Schools," iii–iv.

110. U.S. Secret Service National Threat Assessment Center, "Protecting America's Schools," iv.

111. Randy Borum and Terri D. Patterson, "Juvenile Radicalization Into Violent Extremism: Investigative and Research Perspectives," *Journal of the American Academy of Child & Adolescent Psychiatry* 58, no. 12 (2019): 1147.

112. Ayca Altay, Melike Baykal-Gürsoy, and Pernille Hemmer, "Behavior Associations in Lone-Actor Terrorists," *Terrorism & Political Violence* (2020): 26.

113. Masood Farivar, "2019 'Deadliest' Year for Domestic Terrorism, Says FBI Director," *VOA News*, February 5, 2020.
114. Aaron Y. Zelin, *Your Sons Are at Your Service: Tunisia's Missionaries of Jihad* (New York: Columbia University Press, 2020), 220.
115. Thomas Strentz, "A Terrorist Psychosocial Profile: Past and Present," *FBI Law Enforcement Bulletin* 57 (1988): 17.
116. Dodwell, Milton, and Rassler, "The Caliphate's Global Workforce."
117. Donald Holbrook, "The Terrorism Information Environment: Analysing Terrorists' Selection of Ideological and Facilitative Media," *Terrorism & Political Violence* 33, no. 4 (2021): 714.

4. MINDSET

The chapter epigraph comes from Ayla Hammond Schbley, "Toward a Common Profile of Religious Terrorism: Some Psychosocial Determinants of Christian and Islamic Terrorists," *Police Practice and Research* 7, no. 4 (2006).
1. William Wan and Brittany Shammas, "Why Americans Are Numb to the Staggering Coronavirus Death Toll," *Washington Post*, December 21, 2020.
2. Lori Hinnant, "Paris Attacks Suspect: Deaths of 130 'Nothing Personal,'" *Associated Press*, September 15, 2021.
3. Julia Ebner, "Dark Ops: Isis, the Far-Right and the Gamification of Terror," *Financial Times*, February 14, 2020.
4. Graham Macklin, "The El Paso Terrorist Attack: The Chain Reaction of Global Right-Wing Terror," *CTC Sentinel* 12, no. 11 (2019): 3.
5. Elizabeth Segran, "These 3 Women Are the Accused Boston Bomber's Biggest Fans," *Refinery 29*, March 4, 2015.
6. Segran, "These 3 Women Are the Accused Boston Bomber's Biggest Fans."
7. Meredith Bennett-Smith, "Dzhokhar Tsarnaev Fan Club: Boston Bombing Suspect Gets Support from Girls, #Freejahar Following," *Huffington Post*, May 15, 2013.
8. Maxwell Taylor, *The Terrorist* (London: Brassey's, 1988).
9. Jerrold M. Post, *Military Studies in the Jihad Against the Tyrants: The Al-Qaeda Training Manual* (Montgomery, AL: USAF Counterproliferation Center, 2004).
10. Post, *Military Studies*, 28.
11. H. H. A. Cooper, "What Is a Terrorist: A Psychological Perspective," *Legal Medical Quarterly* 1, no. 1 (1977): 18.
12. Cooper, "What Is a Terrorist," 28.
13. Tara West, "'You Are Forgiven': ISIS Murderers Hug Victims Before Stoning Them to Death for Being Gay," *INQUISITR*, November 28, 2016.
14. Carol Winkler, Kareem ElDamanhoury, Aaron Dicker, and Anthony F. Lemieux, "Images of Death and Dying in ISIS Media: A Comparison of English and Arabic Print Publications," *Media, War & Conflict* 12, no. 3 (2018): 248–62.

15. West, "You Are Forgiven."
16. Johannes Lang, "The Limited Importance of Dehumanization in Collective Violence," *Current Opinion in Psychology* 35 (2020): 17.
17. Lang, "The Limited Importance of Dehumanization," 17.
18. Nour Kteily and Emile Bruneau, "Backlash: The Politics and Real-World Consequences of Minority Group Dehumanization," *Personality and Social Psychology Bulletin* 43, no. 1 (2017): 87–104.
19. Brian Resnick, "The Dark Psychology of Dehumanization, Explained," *VOX*, March 7, 2017.
20. Lang, "The Limited Importance of Dehumanization," 18.
21. Lang, "The Limited Importance of Dehumanization," 18.
22. Johannes Lang, "Questioning Dehumanization: Intersubjective Dimensions of Violence in the Nazi Concentration and Death Camps," *Holocaust and Genocide Studies* 24, no. 2 (2010): 225.
23. Lang, "Questioning Dehumanization," 225.
24. Lang, "Questioning Dehumanization," 240.
25. Dan Barry, "You've Got the Wrong Idea about Martin McDonagh," *New York Times*, March 4, 2020.
26. Alessandro Orsini, "What Everybody Should Know About Radicalization and the DRIA Model," *Studies in Conflict & Terrorism* (2020): 4.
27. Sean O'Callaghan, *The Informer* (London: Corgi, 1999).
28. Lang, "The Limited Importance of Dehumanization," 17.
29. Lang, "Questioning Dehumanization," 231.
30. Lang, "Questioning Dehumanization," 234.
31. Herbert G. Kelman, "Violence Without Moral Restraint: Reflections on the Dehumanization of Victims and Victimizers," *Journal of Social Issues* 29, no. 4 (1973): 35.
32. Lang, "Questioning Dehumanization," 232.
33. Kelman, "Violence Without Moral Restraint," 46.
34. Taylor, *The Terrorist*, 168.
35. Theo Padnos, "Dark Powers," *New York Times Book Review*, June 6, 2021.
36. H. A. Lyons and H. J. Harbinson, "A Comparison of Political and Non-Political Murderers in Northern Ireland, 1974–84," *Medicine, Science and the Law* 26, no. 3 (1986).
37. Michael Weiss and Hassan Hassan, *ISIS: Inside the Army of Terror*, 3rd ed. (New York: Regan Arts, 2020), 46.
38. Etienne Wenger-Trayner and Beverly Wenger-Trayner, "Communities of Practice: A Brief Introduction," Wenger-Trayner.com, April 15, 2015.
39. Wenger-Trayner and Wenger-Trayner, "Communities of Practice."
40. Karsten Hundeide, "Becoming a Committed Insider," *Culture & Psychology* 9, no. 2 (2003): 107–27.
41. Christoffer Carlsson, Amir Rostami, Hernan Mondani, Joakim Sturup, Jerzy Sarnecki, and Christofer Edling, "A Life-Course Analysis of Engagement in Violent Extremist Groups," *The British Journal of Criminology* 60, no. 1 (2020): 74–92.

42. Seyward Darby, *Sisters in Hate: American Women on the Front Lines of White Nationalism* (London: Hachette, 2020), 49.

43. Kelman, "Violence Without Moral Restraint," 49.

44. Anni Sternisko, Aleksandra Cichocka, and Jay J. Van Bavel, "The Dark Side of Social Movements: Social Identity, Non-Conformity, and the Lure of Conspiracy Theories," *Current Opinion in Psychology* 35 (2020): 1–6.

45. Sternisko, Cichocka, and Van Bavel, "The Dark Side of Social Movements," 2.

46. Sternisko, Cichocka, and Van Bavel, "The Dark Side of Social Movements," 1.

47. Michael A Hogg, "From Uncertainty to Extremism: Social Categorization and Identity Processes," *Current Directions in Psychological Science* 23, no. 5 (2014): 339.

48. Jamie Bartlett and Carl Miller, *The Power of Unreason: Conspiracy Theories, Extremism and Counter-Terrorism* (London: Demos, 2010), 4.

49. Bartlett and Miller, *The Power of Unreason*, 5.

50. Michael Kenney, *From Pablo to Osama: Trafficking and Terrorist Networks, Government Bureaucracies, and Competitive Adaptation* (University Park: Pennsylvania State University Press, 2007), 145.

51. Michael Kenney, *From Pablo to Osama*, 145.

52. Michael Kenney, *From Pablo to Osama*, 57.

53. Tom Dreisbach, "Conspiracy Charges Bring Proud Boys' History of Violence Into Spotlight," *NPR*, April 9, 2021.

54. John Horgan, Max Taylor, Mia Bloom, and Charlie Winter, "From Cubs to Lions: A Six Stage Model of Child Socialization Into the Islamic State," *Studies in Conflict & Terrorism* 40, no. 7 (2017): 645–64.

55. Chief Coroner, "Inquests Arising from the Deaths in the London Bridge and Borough Market Terror Attack," Royal Courts of Justice, November 1, 2019, 23.

56. Chief Coroner, "Inquests Arising," 23.

57. Chief Coroner, "Inquests Arising," 24.

58. Randy Borum, "Radicalization Into Violent Extremism I: A Review of Social Science Theories," *Journal of Strategic Security* 4, no. 4 (2011): 22.

59. L. R. Rambo, quoted in Borum, "Radicalization into Violent Extremism I," 23.

60. Mauricio Florez-Morris, "Joining Guerrilla Groups in Colombia: Individual Motivations and Processes for Entering a Violent Organization," *Studies in Conflict & Terrorism* 30, no. 7 (2007): 631.

61. Florez-Morris, "Joining Guerrilla Groups," 631.

62. Neil MacFarquhar and Adam Goldman, "A New Face of White Supremacy: Plots Expose Danger of the 'Base,'" *New York Times*, January 22, 2020.

63. Jason Warner and Ellen Chapin, "Targeted Terror: The Suicide Bombers of Al-Shabaab," February 13, 2018, Combating Terrorism Center at West Point.

64. Florez-Morris, "Joining Guerrilla Groups," 628.

65. Florez-Morris, "Joining Guerrilla Groups," 625.

66. Gina Vale, "Piety Is in the Eye of the Bureaucrat: The Islamic State's Strategy of Civilian Control," *CTC Sentinel* 13, no. 1 (2020): 34–40.

67. Nathan Smith and Emma C. Barrett, "Psychology, Extreme Environments, and Counter-Terrorism Operations," *Behavioral Sciences of Terrorism and Political Aggression* 11, no. 1 (2019): 51.
68. Smith and Barrett, "Psychology, Extreme Environments," 51.
69. Daniel Koehler, "Violent Extremism, Mental Health and Substance Abuse Among Adolescents: Towards a Trauma Psychological Perspective on Violent Radicalization and Deradicalization," *The Journal of Forensic Psychiatry & Psychology* 31, no. 3 (2020): 455–72.
70. Maurice A. J. Tugwell, "Guilt Transfer," in *The Morality of Terrorism: Religious and Secular Justifications*, 2nd ed., ed. David Rapoport and Yonah Alexander (New York: Columbia University Press, 1989), 275–89.
71. Tugwell, "Guilt Transfer," 276.
72. Paul Wilkinson, "The Laws of War and Terrorism," in *The Morality of Terrorism*, ed. Rapoport and Alexander, 314.
73. Don Liddick, "Techniques of Neutralization and Animal Rights Activists," *Deviant Behavior* 34, no. 8 (2013): 618–34.
74. Gresham M. Sykes and David Matza, "Techniques of Neutralization: A Theory of Delinquency," *American Sociological Review* 22, no. 6 (1957): 664–70.
75. Liddick, "Techniques of Neutralization."
76. Joby Warrick, *The Triple Agent: The Al-Qaeda Mole Who Infiltrated the CIA* (New York: Vintage, 2011).
77. Post, "Military Studies," 60.
78. Post, "Military Studies," 98.
79. John Horgan, Mary Beth Altier, Neil Shortland, and Max Taylor, "Walking Away: The Disengagement and De-Radicalization of a Violent Right-Wing Extremist," *Behavioral Sciences of Terrorism & Political Aggression* 9, no. 2 (2017): 69.
80. Dale G. Larson and Robert L. Chastain, "Self-Concealment: Conceptualization, Measurement, and Health Implications," *Journal of Social & Clinical Psychology* 9, no. 4 (1990): 439.
81. Tom Frijns, Catrin Finkenauer, Ad A. Vermulst, and Rutger C. M. E. Engels, "Keeping Secrets from Parents: Longitudinal Associations of Secrecy in Adolescence," *Journal of Youth & Adolescence* 34, no. 2 (2005): 137–48; Daniel J. Potoczniak, Mirela A. Aldea, and Cirleen DeBlaere, "Ego Identity, Social Anxiety, Social Support, and Self-Concealment in Lesbian, Gay, and Bisexual Individuals," *Journal of Counseling Psychology* 54, no. 4 (2007): 447; Anna-Kaisa Newheiser and Manuela Barreto, "Hidden Costs of Hiding Stigma: Ironic Interpersonal Consequences of Concealing a Stigmatized Identity in Social Interactions," *Journal of Experimental Social Psychology* 52 (2014): 58–70; Peter Suedfeld, "Harun al-Rashid and the Terrorists: Identity Concealed, Identity Revealed," *Political Psychology* 25, no. 3 (2004): 479–92; Dong Wook Shin, Jong Hyock Park, So Young Kim, Eal Whan Park, Hyung Kook Yang, Eunmi Ahn, Seon Mee Park, Young Joon Lee, Myong Cheol Lim, and Hong Gwan Seo, "Guilt, Censure, and Concealment of Active Smoking Status Among Cancer Patients and Family Members After Diagnosis: A Nationwide Study," *Psycho-Oncology* 23, no. 5 (2014): 585–91.

82. Clayton R. Critcher and Melissa J. Ferguson, "The Cost Of Keeping It Hidden: Decomposing Concealment Reveals What Makes It Depleting," *Journal of Experimental Psychology: General*, 143 (2014): 721–35.

83. Smith and Barrett, "Psychology, Extreme Environments, 51, 54.

84. Aimen Dean, quoted in Smith and Barrett, "Psychology, Extreme Environments," 54.

85. Anita E. Kelly and Kevin J. McKillop, "Consequences of Revealing Personal Secrets," *Psychological Bulletin* 120, no. 3 (1996): 450–65.

86. Post, "Military Studies," 101.

87. Zelin, *Your Sons Are at Your Service*, 264.

88. Mack Lamoureux, Ben Makuch, and Zachary Kamel, "How One Man Built a Neo-Nazi Insurgency in Trump's America," *VICE News*, October 7, 2020.

89. Khachig Tölölyan, "Cultural Narrative and the Motivation of the Terrorist," in *Inside Terrorist Organizations*, ed. David C. Rapoport (London: Frank Cass, 1988), 230.

90. Patricia C. Jackman, Rebecca M. Hawkins, Shaunna M. Burke, Christian Swann, and Lee Crust, "The Psychology of Mountaineering: A Systematic Review," *International Review of Sport & Exercise Psychology* (2020):18.

91. Jackman et al., "The Psychology of Mountaineering," 18.

92. Jackman et al., "The Psychology of Mountaineering," 19.

93. Jackman et al., "The Psychology of Mountaineering," 31.

94. Jackman et al., "The Psychology of Mountaineering."

95. Lorne Dawson, "A Comparative Analysis of the Data on Western Foreign Fighters in Syria and Iraq: Who Went and Why?" International Centre for Counter-Terrorism – The Hague, February 2021, 3.

96. Emily Corner and Paul Gill, "A False Dichotomy? Mental Illness and Lone-Actor Terrorism," *Law & Human Behavior* 39, no. 1 (2015): 23.

97. Roger Cohen, "Highest French Court Rules Killer of Jewish Woman Cannot Stand Trial," *New York Times*, April 17, 2021.

98. Cohen, "Highest French Court Rules Killer of Jewish Woman Cannot Stand Trial."

99. Adam K. Magid, "The Unabomber Revisited: Reexamining the Use of Mental Disorder Diagnoses as Evidence of the Mental Condition of Criminal Defendants," *Indiana Law Journal* 84, no. 5 (2009): 2.

100. Magid, "The Unabomber Revisited," 2.

101. Magid, "The Unabomber Revisited," 2.

102. Sally Johnson, "Psychiatric Competency Report of Dr. Sally C. Johnson, Sept. 11, 1998," in *United States District Court for the Eastern District of California—United States of America, Plaintiff vs. Theodore John Kaczynski, Defendant. CR. NO. S-96-259 GEB ORDER* (1998): 44, 45.

103. Johnson, "Psychiatric Competency Report," 31.

104. Johnson, "Psychiatric Competency Report," 44.

105. Magid, "The Unabomber Revisited," 9.

106. Magid, "The Unabomber Revisited," 9.

107. Magid, "The Unabomber Revisited," 10.

108. Tahir Rahman, "Extreme Overvalued Beliefs: How Violent Extremist Beliefs Become 'Normalized,'" *Behavioral Sciences* 8, no. 1 (2018): 10.
109. Rahman, "Extreme Overvalued Beliefs," 3.
110. Ali Watkins, "Accused of Killing a Gambino Mob Boss, He's Presenting a Novel Defense," *New York Times*, December 6, 2019.
111. Kenneth J. Weiss, "Assassins in London and Washington Force Changes in the Insanity Defense," *Psychiatric Times* 37, no. 3 (March 2020).
112. Weiss, "Assassins in London and Washington Force Changes in the Insanity Defense."
113. Zoe Tillman, "They Said Trump Told Them to Attack the Capitol. Judges Are Keeping Them in Jail Anyway," *Buzzfeed News*, May 6, 2021.
114. Mimi Roach, "Pipe-Bomber Cesar Sayoc's Lawyers Named Trump in Their Defense. They Won't Be the Only Ones," *NBC News*, August 7, 2019.
115. Roach, "Pipe-Bomber Cesar Sayoc's Lawyers Named Trump in Their Defense."
116. Roach, "Pipe-Bomber Cesar Sayoc's Lawyers Named Trump in Their Defense."

5. REINTEGRATION

The chapter epigraph comes from Bill Watterson, "Some Thoughts on the Real World by One Who Glimpsed It and Fled," Kenyon College commencement, May 20, 1990.
1. Marine Lourens, "'No Remorse' and 'Narcissistic': The Psychology of the Christchurch Mosque Shooter," *Stuff*, August 27, 2020.
2. Lourens, "'No Remorse' and 'Narcissistic.'"
3. Andrew Silke and Tinka Veldhuis, "Countering Violent Extremism in Prisons: A Review of Key Recent Research and Critical Research Gaps," *Perspectives on Terrorism* 11, no. 5 (2017): 2–11.
4. Alison Jamieson, "Identity and Morality in the Italian Red Brigades," *Terrorism & Political Violence* 2, no. 4 (1990): 520.
5. Julie Chernov Hwang, *Why Terrorists Quit: The Disengagement of Indonesian Jihadists* (Ithaca, NY: Cornell University Press, 2018); Daniel Koehler, *Understanding Deradicalization: Methods, Tools and Programs for Countering Violent Extremism* (London: Routledge, 2016); Daniel Koehler, "Disengaging from Left-Wing Terrorism and Extremism: Field Experiences from Germany and Research Gaps," *Studies in Conflict & Terrorism* (2021): 1–21; Douglas Weeks, "Lessons Learned from U.K. Efforts to Deradicalize Terror Offenders," *CTC Sentinel* 14, no. 3 (2021): 33–39; Mary Beth Altier, Christian N. Thoroughgood, and John Horgan, "Turning Away from Terrorism: Lessons from Psychology, Sociology, and Criminology," *Journal of Peace Research* 51, no. 5 (2014): 648–50.
6. Graeme Wood, "What ISIS Really Wants," *Atlantic*, March 15, 2015.
7. Robert W. White and Terry Falkenberg White, "Revolution in the City: On the Resources of Urban Guerrillas," *Terrorism & Political Violence* 3, no. 4 (1991): 100–32.
8. John Horgan, *Walking Away from Terrorism* (London: Routledge, 2009).
9. Chernov Hwang, *Why Terrorists Quit*, 7.

10. Chernov Hwang, *Why Terrorists Quit*, 15.
11. Sarah V. Marsden, *Reintegrating Extremists: Deradicalisation and Desistance* (London: Palgrave Macmillan, 2017), 3, 5.
12. Omar Ashour, *The De-radicalization of Jihadists: Transforming Armed Islamist Movements* (London: Routledge, 2009); John F. Morrison, *The Origins and Rise of Dissident Irish Republicanism: The Role and Impact of Organizational Splits* (New York: Bloomsbury, 2013); Audrey Kurth Cronin, *How Terrorism Ends: Understanding the Decline and Demise of Terrorist Campaigns* (Princeton, NJ: Princeton University Press, 2009).
13. Jerrold M. Post, "Prospects for Nuclear Terrorism: Psychological Motivations and Constraints," *Journal of Conflict Studies* 7, no. 3 (1987): 51.
14. Brian Dodwell, Daniel Milton, and Don Rassler, "The Caliphate's Global Workforce: An Inside Look at the Islamic State's Foreign Fighter Paper Trail," April 18, 2016, Combating Terrorism Center at West Point.
15. Dodwell, Milton, and Rassler, "The Caliphate's Global Workforce," 36.
16. Bommi Baumann, "The Last Phase," in *Terrorism: Critical Concepts in Political Science Volume 3*, ed. David Rapoport (London: Routledge, 2006), 397.
17. Bauman, "The Last Phase," 396.
18. Mara Redlich Revkin and Ariel I. Ahram, "Perspectives on the Rebel Social Contract: Exit, Voice, and Loyalty in the Islamic State in Iraq and Syria," *World Development* 132 (2020), 6.
19. Helen Rose Fuchs Ebaugh, *Becoming an Ex: The Process of Role Exit* (Chicago: University of Chicago Press, 1998).
20. Altier, Thoroughgood, and Horgan, "Turning Away from Terrorism"; Mary Beth Altier, Emma Leonard Boyle, Neil D. Shortland, and John Horgan, "Why They Leave: An Analysis of Terrorist Disengagement Events from Eighty-Seven Autobiographical Accounts," *Security Studies* 26, no. 2 (2017): 305–32.
21. Chernov Hwang, *Why Terrorists Quit*, 8.
22. Michael Kenney, "A Community of True Believers: Learning as Process Among 'The Emigrants,'" *Terrorism & Political Violence* 32, no. 1 (2020): 57–76.
23. Tore Bjorgo and John Horgan, *Leaving Terrorism Behind: Individual and Collective Disengagement* (London: Routledge, 2009).
24. Sara Elizabeth Williams, "The Bullied Finnish Teenager Who Became an Isis Social Media Kingpin—and Then Got Out," *Newsweek*, June 5, 2015.
25. Mehr Latif, Kathleen Blee, Matthew DeMichele, Pete Simi, and Shayna Alexander, "Why White Supremacist Women Become Disillusioned, and Why They Leave," *The Sociological Quarterly* 61, no. 3 (2020): 367–88.
26. Latif et al., "Why White Supremacist Women Become Disillusioned," 377.
27. White and White, "Revolution in the City," 119.
28. Koehler, "Disengaging from Left-Wing Terrorism and Extremism," 5. Also note that Steven Windisch and colleagues at the University of Nebraska, Omaha, compared disengagement between left-wing and right-wing violent extremists. Their preliminary work has found that the different types of groups have more in common than not. See Steven

Windisch, Gina Scott Ligon, and Pete Simi, "Organizational [Dis]trust: Comparing Disengagement Smong Former Left-Wing and Right-Wing Violent Extremists," *Studies in Conflict & Terrorism* (2017).

29. Chelsea Daymon, J. H. de Roy van Zuijdewijn, and David Malet, "Career Foreign Fighters: Expertise Transmission Across Insurgencies," Washington, DC: RESOLVE Network, April 2020.

30. Daymon, van Zuijdewijn, and Malet, "Career Foreign Fighters," 2.

31. Koehler, *Understanding Deradicalization*; Daniel Koehler, "Violent Extremism, Mental Health and Substance Abuse Among Adolescents: Towards a Trauma Psychological Perspective on Violent Radicalization and Deradicalization," *The Journal of Forensic Psychiatry & Psychology* 31, no. 3 (2020): 455–72; Marsden, *Reintegrating Extremists*.

32. Stephen Floyd, "Irredeemably Violent and Undeterrable: How Flawed Assumptions Justify a Broad Application of the Terrorism Enhancement, Contradict Sentencing Policy, and Diminish U.S. National Security," *Georgetown Law Journal Online* 109 (2021): 142–72.

33. Floyd, "Irredeemably Violent and Undeterrable," 143.

34. Floyd, "Irredeemably Violent and Undeterrable," 142.

35. Floyd, "Irredeemably Violent and Undeterrable," 144.

36. Floyd, "Irredeemably Violent and Undeterrable," 145.

37. Natalia Galica, "Lifting the Veil: The Impact of Framing on Sentencing Disparities Between Males and Females Convicted of Terrorism since the Rise of ISIS," *UIC John Marshall Law Review* 53, no. 1 (2019): 114.

38. Galica, "Lifting the Veil," 125.

39. Galica, "Lifting the Veil," 124.

40. Galica, "Lifting the Veil," 127.

41. Galica, "Lifting the Veil," 161.

42. Galica, "Lifting the Veil," 155.

43. Amanda Ripley, "Reverse Radicalism," *Time*, March 13, 2008.

44. Zelin, *Your Sons Are at Your Service*, 266.

45. John Horgan, Katharina Meredith, and Katerina Papatheodorou, "Does Deradicalization Work?" in *Radicalization and Counter-Radicalization: Sociology of Crime, Law and Deviance* 25, ed. Derek M. D. Silva and Mathieu Deflem (Bingley: Emerald Publishing, 2020), 9–20; John Horgan, "Deradicalization Programs: Recommendations for Policy and Practice," Washington, DC: RESOLVE Network, August 2021.

46. Rik Coolsaet, "Radicalization: The Origins and Limits of a Contested Concept," In *Radicalisation in Belgium and the Netherlands: Critical Perspectives on Violence and Security*, ed. Nadia Fadil, Martijn de Koning and Francesco Ragazzi (London: I. B. Tauris, 2019), 47.

47. Christopher Wright, "An Examination of Jihadi Recidivism Rates in the United States," *CTC Sentinel* 12, no. 10 (2019): 26.

48. Mary Beth Altier, Emma Leonard Boyle, and John Horgan, "Returning to the Fight: An Empirical Analysis of Terrorist Reengagement and Recidivism," *Terrorism & Political Violence* 33, no. 4 (2019): 836–60.

49. Fernando Reinares, Carola García-Calvo, and A. Vicente, "Yihadismo Y Prisiones: Un Análisis Del Caso Español," *Análisis del Real Instituto Elcano* 123 (2018).

50. Thomas Renard, "Overblown: Exploring the Gap Between the Fear of Terrorist Recidivism and the Evidence," *CTC Sentinel* 13, no. 4 (2020): 19–29.

51. Wright, "An Examination of Jihadi Recidivism Rates," 27.

52. Omi Hodwitz, "The Terrorism Recidivism Study (TRS): Examining Recidivism Rates for Post-9/11 Offenders," *Perspectives on Terrorism* 13, no. 2 (2019): 56.

53. Hodwitz, "The Terrorism Recidivism Study," 60.

54. Hodwitz, "The Terrorism Recidivism Study," 60.

55. Renard, "Overblown," 26.

56. Renard, "Overblown," 27.

57. Hodwitz, "The Terrorism Recidivism Study," 61.

58. Weeks, "Lessons Learned from U.K. Efforts."

59. Weeks, "Lessons Learned from U.K. Efforts," 34.

60. Ceylan Yeginsu, "Portrait of London Bridge Killer, in His Own Words," *New York Times*, December 5, 2019.

61. Weeks, "Lessons Learned from U.K Efforts," 33.

62. Mary Beth Altier, Emma Leonard Boyle, and John Horgan, "Returning to the Fight: An Empirical Analysis of Terrorist Reengagement and Recidivism," *Terrorism & Political Violence* 33, no. 4 (2019): 836–60.

63. Mary Beth Altier, Emma Leonard Boyle, and John Horgan, "On Re-Engagement and Risk Factors," *Terrorism & Political Violence* 33, no. 4 (2021): 868–74.

64. Altier, Boyle, and Horgan, "On Re-Engagement and Risk Factors."

65. Liesbeth van der Heide, Marieke van der Zwan, and Maarten van Leyenhorst, "The Practitioner's Guide to the Galaxy—A Comparison of Risk Assessment Tools for Violent Extremism," International Centre for Counter-Terrorism – The Hague (September 2019).

66. Caroline Logan and Rachel Sellers, "Risk Assessment and Management in Violent Extremism: A Primer for Mental Health Practitioners," *The Journal of Forensic Psychiatry & Psychology* 32, no. 3 (2020): 2.

67. Kiran M. Sarma, "Risk Assessment and the Prevention of Radicalization from Nonviolence Into Terrorism," *American Psychologist* 72, no. 3 (2017): 278.

68. Mats Dernevik, Alison Beck, Martin Grann, Todd Hogue, and James McGuire, "The Use of Psychiatric and Psychological Evidence in the Assessment of Terrorist Offenders," *The Journal of Forensic Psychiatry & Psychology* 20, no. 4 (2009): 513.

69. Logan and Sellers, "Risk Assessment and Management."

70. Jerrod Brown and Jay P. Singh, "Forensic Risk Assessment: A Beginner's Guide," *Archives of Forensic Psychology* 1, no. 1 (2014): 50.

71. Brown and Singh, "Forensic Risk Assessment," 50.

72. Brown and Singh, "Forensic Risk Assessment," 50.

73. Brown and Singh, "Forensic Risk Assessment," 52–53.

74. Logan and Sellers, "Risk Assessment and Management"; John Monahan, "The Individual Risk Assessment of Terrorism," *Psychology, Public Policy, and Law* 18, no. 2 (2012): 167–205.

75. Brown and Singh, "Forensic Risk Assessment," 54.
76. Brown and Singh, "Forensic Risk Assessment," 54.
77. Caroline Logan, "Violent Extremism: The Assessment and Management of Risk," *CREST Security Review* (April 2021): 18.
78. Randy Borum, "Assessing Risk for Terrorism Involvement," *Journal of Threat Assessment & Management* 2, no. 2 (2015): 79, 63.
79. Brown and Singh, "Forensic Risk Assessment," 54.
80. Van der Heide, van der Zwan, and van Leyenhorst, "The Practitioner's Guide to the Galaxy," 7.
81. Nadine Salman and Paul Gill, "Terrorism Risk Assessment: What Makes a 'Good' Risk Assessor?" *CREST Security Review* 11 (2021): 14–15.
82. Salman and Gill, "Terrorism Risk Assessment," 15.
83. Daryl R. Van Tongeren, Don E. Davis, Joshua N. Hook, and Charlotte van Oyen Witvliet, "Humility," *Current Directions in Psychological Science* 28, no. 5 (2019): 463–68.
84. Benedict Carey, "Be Humble, and Proudly, Psychologists Say," *New York Times*, October 21, 2019.
85. Carey, "Be Humble, and Proudly."
86. Donald Holbrook, "The Terrorism Information Environment: Analysing Terrorists' Selection of Ideological and Facilitative Media," *Terrorism & Political Violence* 33, no. 4 (2021): 697–719.
87. Holbrook, "The Terrorism Information Environment," 701.
88. Floyd, "Irredeemably Violent and Undeterrable," 169.
89. Nicholas Kristof, "Defeating Racism One Conversation at a Time: [Op-Ed]," *New York Times*, June 27, 2021.
90. Marsden, *Reintegrating Extremists*; John Horgan and Kurt Braddock, "Rehabilitating the Terrorists? Challenges in Assessing the Effectiveness of De-radicalization Programs," *Terrorism & Political Violence* 22, no. 2 (2010): 267–91.
91. Ebaugh, *Becoming an Ex*, 10.
92. Maxwell Taylor, *The Terrorist* (London: Brassey's, 1988).
93. Koehler, "Violent Extremism, Mental Health and Substance Abuse Among Adolescents"; Michael Niconchuk, "Whose Vulnerability? Trauma Recovery in the Reintegration of Former Violent Extremists," Washington, DC: RESOLVE Network, June 2021.
94. Sigrid Raets, "The We in Me: Considering Terrorist Desistance from a Social Identity Perspective," *Journal for Deradicalization* 13 (2017): 1.
95. Hodwitz, "The Terrorism Recidivism Study," 56.
96. Altier, Boyle, and Horgan, "Returning to the Fight."
97. Ryan Andrew Brown, Todd C. Helmus, Rajeev Ramchand, Alina I. Palimaru, Sara Weilant, Ashley L. Rhoades, and Lisa Hiatt, *Violent Extremism in America: Interviews with Former Extremists and Their Families on Radicalization and Deradicalization* (Santa Monica, CA: RAND, 2021).
98. Brown et al., *Violent Extremism in America*, 58.
99. Marsden, *Reintegrating Extremists*, 87.
100. Monahan, "Risk Assessment of Terrorism," 167.

6. TALKING TO TERRORISTS

The chapter epigraph comes from Ariel Merari and Nehemia Friedland, "Social Psychological Aspects of Political Terrorism," in *International Conflict and National Public Policy Issues: Applied Social Psychology Annual*, vol. 6, ed. S. Oscamp (Beverly Hills, CA: Sage, 1985), 348.

1. Margot Trimbur, Ali Amad, Mathilde Horn, Pierre Thomas, and Thomas Fovet, "Are Radicalization and Terrorism Associated with Psychiatric Disorders? A Systematic Review," *Journal of Psychiatric Research* 141 (2021): 214.
2. Trimbur et al., "Are Radicalization and Terrorism Associated with Psychiatric Disorders?" 214.
3. Trimbur et al., "Are Radicalization and Terrorism Associated with Psychiatric Disorders?" 214.
4. Jeff Victoroff, "The Mind of the Terrorist: A Review and Critique of Psychological Approaches," *Journal of Conflict Resolution* 49, no. 1 (2005): 36.
5. Graeme Wood, "What ISIS Really Wants," *Atlantic*, March 15, 2015.
6. Lorne L. Dawson, "Taking Terrorist Accounts of Their Motivations Seriously," *Perspectives on Terrorism* 13, no. 5 (2019): 74.
7. Kathleen Blee, "Becoming a Racist: Women in Contemporary Ku Klux Klan and Neo-Nazi Groups," *Gender & Society* 10, no. 6 (1996): 687.
8. John F. Morrison, "Analyzing Interviews with Terrorists," Washington, DC: RESOLVE Network, November 2020.
9. Rachel Schmidt, "When Fieldwork Ends: Navigating Ongoing Contact with Former Insurgents," *Terrorism & Political Violence* 33, no. 2 (2021): 312.
10. James Khalil, "A Guide to Interviewing Terrorists and Violent Extremists," *Studies in Conflict & Terrorism* 42, no. 4 (2017): 429.
11. Zachary Abuza, "Researching Militant Groups in Southeast Asia," in *Conducting Terrorism Field Research*, ed. Adam Dolnik (London: Routledge, 2013), 158.
12. Cerwyn Moore, "A Practical Guide to Research on Terrorism in the North Caucasus," in *Conducting Terrorism Field Research*, 126.
13. Michael Knights, "Conducting Field Research on Terrorism in Iraq," in *Conducting Terrorism Field Research*, 104.
14. Abuza, "Researching Militant Groups," 158–59.
15. Max Taylor and Ethel Quayle, *Terrorist Lives* (London: Brassey's, 1994).
16. Kacper Rekawek, "Conducting Field Research on Terrorism in Northern Ireland," in *Conducting Terrorism Field Research*, 169.
17. Rekawek, "Conducting Field Research on Terrorism," 171.
18. Abuza, "Researching Militant Groups," 158
19. Khalil, "A Guide to Interviewing Terrorists," 433.
20. Khalil, "A Guide to Interviewing Terrorists," 433.
21. Rekawek, "Conducting Field Research on Terrorism," 171.
22. Rekawek, "Conducting Field Research on Terrorism," 172.

23. Schmidt, "When Fieldwork Ends," 313.
24. Schmidt, "When Fieldwork Ends," 312.
25. Laila Bokhari, "Face to Face with My Case Study," in *Conducting Terrorism Field Research*, 101.
26. Bokhari, "Face to Face," 101.
27. Schmidt, "When Fieldwork Ends," 317.
28. Schmidt, "When Fieldwork Ends," 316.
29. Bokhari, "Face to Face," 92.
30. Victoroff, "The Mind of the Terrorist," 6.
31. John E. Douglas, Ann W. Burgess, Allen G. Burgess, and Robert K. Ressler, *Crime Classification Manual: A Standard System for Investigating and Classifying Violent Crime*, 3rd ed. (Hoboken: Wiley, 2013), 67.
32. Douglas et al., *Crime Classification Manual*, 68.
33. Scott A. Bonn, "The Birth of Modern Day Criminal Profiling," *Psychology Today*, May 26, 2015.
34. Brent Snook, Richard M. Cullen, Craig Bennell, Paul J. Taylor, and Paul Gendreau, "The Criminal Profiling Illusion: What's Behind the Smoke and Mirrors?" *Criminal Justice & Behavior* 35, no. 10 (2008): 1257–76.
35. Robert J. Morton, Jennifer M. Tillman, and Stephanie J. Gaines, *Serial Murder: Pathways for Investigations* (Quantico, VA: Federal Bureau of Investigation, 2014), 5.
36. Morton, Tillman, and Gaines, *Serial Murder*, 5.
37. Andrew Whalen, "'Mindhunter' True Story: How the FBI Profiles the Real Serial Killers and Crimes Behind the Netflix Series," *Newsweek*, May 29, 2019.
38. Bonn, "The Birth of Modern Day Criminal Profiling."
39. Morton, Tillman, and Gaines, *Serial Murder*, 4.
40. Chris Ryder, *Inside the Maze: The Untold Story of the Northern Ireland Prison Service* (London: Methuen, 2000), xiii.
41. Ariel Merari, *Driven to Death: Psychological and Social Aspects of Suicide Terrorism* (New York: Oxford University Press, 2010).
42. Morrison, "Analyzing Interviews with Terrorists," 13.
43. John Monahan, "The Individual Risk Assessment of Terrorism," *Psychology, Public Policy, & Law* 18, no. 2 (2012): 167.
44. D. A. Keatley, S. Knight, and A. Marono, "A Crime Script Analysis of Violent and Nonviolent Extremists," *Studies in Conflict & Terrorism* (2021): 5.
45. Keatley, Knight, and Marono, "A Crime Script Analysis," 4.
46. Keatley, Knight, and Marono, "A Crime Script Analysis," 11.
47. Scott H. Decker and David C. Pyrooz, "'I'm Down for a Jihad': How 100 Years of Gang Research Can Inform the Study of Terrorism, Radicalization and Extremism," *Perspectives on Terrorism* 9, no. 1 (2015): 104–12.
48. Morrison, "Analyzing Interviews"; Chernov Hwang, *Why Terrorists Quit*.
49. Lana De Pelecijn, Stef Decoene, and Wim Hardyns, "Research Note: 'If I Said I Trust You, I Would Be Lying'—Reflections and Recommendations for Conducting Interviews with (Violent) Extremist Prisoners," *Journal for Deradicalization* 27 (2021): 284–310.

50. De Pelecijn, Decoene, and Hardyns, "Research Note," 286.
51. De Pelecijn, Decoene, and Hardyns, "Research Note," 292.
52. De Pelecijn, Decoene, and Hardyns, "Research Note," 293.
53. Dawson, "Taking Terrorist Accounts of Their Motivations Seriously," 75.
54. Joe Navarro, *Hunting Terrorists: A Look at the Psychopathology of Terror* (Springfield: Charles C. Thomas, 2013), 92.
55. Navarro, *Hunting Terrorists*, 107.
56. Navarro, *Hunting Terrorists*, 105.
57. Allison Abbe and Susan E. Brandon, "The Role of Rapport in Investigative Interviewing: A Review," *Journal of Investigative Psychology & Offender Profiling* 10, no. 3 (2013): 244–45.
58. Pete Simi, Kathleen Blee, Matthew DeMichele, and Steven Windisch. "Addicted to Hate: Identity Residual Among Former White Supremacists," *American Sociological Review* 82, no. 6 (2017): 1167–87.

7. CHASING STORMS

The chapter epigraph comes from David G. Hubbard, "Terrorism and Protest," *Legal Medical Quarterly* 2, no. 3 (1978): 188–97.

1. Joplin, Missouri—Fact Sheet for City, https://www.joplinmo.org/Fact-Sheet-for-City; Joplin, Missouri—History of Joplin, http://www.joplinmo.org/173/History-of-Joplin
2. "2011 Joplin Tornado," Wikipedia, last modified May 31, 2023, https://en.wikipedia.org/wiki/2011_Joplin_tornado.
3. "Joplin, Missouri," Wikipedia, last modified May 30, 2023, https://en.wikipedia.org/wiki/Joplin,_Missouri.
4. Lynn Iliff Onstot, "Fact Sheet – City of Joplin," May 22, 2011, http://www.joplinmo.org/DocumentCenter/View/1985/Joplin_Tornado_factsheet?bidId.
5. Jonathan Erdman, "Joplin's EF5 Tornado: What Our Meteorologists Haven't Forgotten 10 Years Later," *The Weather Channel*, May 21, 2021.
6. Erica D. Kuligowski, Franklin T. Lombardo, Long T. Phan, and David P. Jorgensen, "'It Hit Just Right Then, and Everything Started Flying': Lessons Learned from the May 22, 2011 Joplin, MO Tornado," *Natural Hazards Observer* (September 2014): 4.
7. Roger Edwards, "The Online Tornado FAQ," Storm Prediction Center, https://www.spc.noaa.gov/faq/tornado/, last modified February 19, 2023.
8. Kuligowski et al., "It Hit Just Right Then, and Everything Started Flying."
9. Kuligowski et al., "It Hit Just Right Then, and Everything Started Flying," 1.
10. Chris Baraniuk, "Tornado Investigators Are Unlocking the UK's Extreme Weather Secrets," *Wired*, August 25, 2021.
11. Sarah L. Horton, Matthew R. Clark, and Peter J. Kirk, "Investigating the Surrey Tornado of 21 December 2019," *Weather* 76, no. 12 (December 2021): 1–9.
12. Horton et al., "Investigating the Surrey Tornado," 1.
13. Horton et al., "Investigating the Surrey Tornado," 8.

14. D. K. Lilly, "Tornado Dynamics," National Center for Atmospheric Research, NCAR manuscript no. 69–117 (1969).
15. Lilly, "Tornado Dynamics," 1.
16. Maxwell Taylor, *The Terrorist* (London: Brassey's, 1988).
17. Roger Edwards, "The Online Tornado FAQ."
18. I am grateful to Paul Gill for this observation.
19. Wood, *The Way of the Strangers: Encounters with the Islamic State* (New York: Penguin Random House, 2017), 34.
20. Roger Edwards, "The Online Tornado FAQ."
21. Noémie Bouhana, "The Moral Ecology of Extremism: A Systemic Perspective," paper prepared for the UK Commission for Countering Extremism (July 2019).
22. Bouhana, "The Moral Ecology of Extremism," 5.
23. Marcus Kreuzer, "The Structure of Description: Evaluating Descriptive Inferences and Conceptualizations," *Perspectives on Politics* 17, no. 1 (2019): 122–39.
24. Randy Borum, "Radicalization Into Violent Extremism I: A Review of Social Science Theories," *Journal of Strategic Security* 4, no. 4 (2011): 28.
25. Borum, "Radicalization Into Violent Extremism I," 28.
26. Jeff Victoroff, "The Mind of the Terrorist: A Review and Critique of Psychological Approaches," *Journal of Conflict Resolution* 49, no. 1 (2005): 30.
27. Randy Borum, "Radicalization Into Violent Extremism II: A Review of Conceptual Models and Empirical Research," *Journal of Strategic Security* 4, no. 4 (2012): 38.
28. Victoroff, "The Mind of the Terrorist," 9.
29. Clark McCauley and Sophia Moskalenko, "Some Things We Think We've Learned Since 9/11: A Commentary on Marc Sageman's 'The Stagnation in Terrorism Research,'" *Terrorism & Political Violence* 26, no. 4 (2014): 601–6.
30. Tyler Evans, Daniel J. Milton, and Joseph K. Young, "Choosing to Fight, Choosing to Die: Examining How ISIS Foreign Fighters Select Their Operational Roles," *International Studies Review* 23, no. 3 (2021): 512.
31. See Borum, "Radicalization into Violent Extremism I," 16.
32. Victoroff, "The Mind of the Terrorist," 35.
33. Ángel Gómez, Mercedes Martínez, Francois Alexi Martel, Lucía López-Rodríguez, Alexandra Vázquez, Juana Chinchilla, Borja Paredes, Mal Hettiarachchi, Nafees Hamid and William B. Swann, "Why People Enter and Embrace Violent Groups," *Frontiers in Psychology* 11 (January 2021), https://doi.org/10.3389/fpsyg.2020.614657.
34. Bart Schuurman, "Topics in Terrorism Research: Reviewing Trends and Gaps, 2007–2016," *Critical Studies on Terrorism* 12, no. 3 (2019): 463–80; John F. Morrison, "Talking Stagnation: Thematic Analysis of Terrorism Experts' Perception of the Health of Terrorism Research," *Terrorism & Political Violence* (2020): 1–21.
35. Morrison, "Talking Stagnation."
36. Andrew Silke and Jennifer Schmidt-Petersen, "The Golden Age? What the 100 Most Cited Articles in Terrorism Studies Tell Us," *Terrorism & Political Violence* 29, no. 4 (2017): 692–712.

37. Morrison, "Talking Stagnation," 17.

38. Kruezer, "The Structure of Description," 122.

39. Kurt Braddock, "A Brief Primer on Experimental and Quasi-Experimental Methods in the Study of Terrorism," *International Centre for Counter-Terrorism Policy Brief* (January 2019).

40. Schuurman, "Topics in Terrorism Research," 463.

41. Schuurman, "Topics in Terrorism Research," 465.

42. Walter Reich (ed.), *Origins of Terrorism: Psychologies, Ideologies, Theologies, States of Mind* (Washington, DC: Woodrow Wilson Center Press, 1990).

43. Orla Lynch and Carmel Joyce, *Applied Psychology: The Case of Terrorism and Political Violence* (London: Wiley, 2019), 1–2.

44. Joseph K. Young and Michael G. Findley, "Promise and Pitfalls of Terrorism Research," *International Studies Review* 13, no. 3 (2011): 411–31.

45. Decker and Pyrooz, "I'm Down for a Jihad."

46. Decker and Pyrooz, "I'm Down for a Jihad," 105.

47. Decker and Pyrooz, "I'm Down for a Jihad," 105.

48. Joshua D. Freilich, Steven M. Chermak, and Jeff Gruenewald, "The Future of Terrorism Research: A Review Essay," *International Journal of Comparative and Applied Criminal Justice* 39, no. 4 (2015): 353–69.

49. Freilich, Chermak and Gruenewald, "The Future of Terrorism Research," 359.

50. Madeleine Pownall, "A Rigorous Way of Dealing with Some Messy Real-World Data," *The Psychologist* 31 (2018): 38–41.

INDEX

INDEX

GPSR Authorized Representative: Easy Access System Europe, Mustamäe tee
50, 10621 Tallinn, Estonia, gpsr.requests@easproject.com

www.ingramcontent.com/pod-product-compliance
Lightning Source LLC
Chambersburg PA
CBHW032130020426
42334CB00016B/1105